Arsène Wenger

Arsène Wenger

The Biography

XAVIER RIVOIRE

First published in Great Britain in 2007 by
Aurum Press Limited
7 Greenland Street
London NW1 0ND
www.aurumpress.co.uk

A catalogue record for this book is available from the British Library.

ISBN-10: 1 84513 276 9
ISBN-13: 978 1 84513 276 7

10 9 8 7 6 5 4 3 2
2011 2010 2009 2008 2007

Designed and typeset in Minion and Helvetica Neue by
SX Composing DTP, Rayleigh, Essex

Printed and bound in Great Britain by
MPG Books, Bodmin, Cornwall

CONTENTS

FOREWORD

ARSÈNE WENGER SAT in the media suite at Arsenal's training complex at London Colney, paused for a second to gather his thoughts, then delivered his admission. 'It does feel strange not to be challenging at the top,' he said. 'We are so far behind the leaders, so I cannot say I did everything perfectly. I have to stand up first to say I am responsible for the fact that we didn't fight for the championship. I was more committed and worked harder than ever this year, but still I have to stand up for what I call a failure.'

It was mid-May in 2007, and Arsenal's season would peter out a few days later at Portsmouth's Fratton Park with a missed penalty from Julio Baptista and yet another opportunity spurned. The goalless draw left Wenger peering up at Manchester United, a red speck at the top of the Premiership 21 points away, with second-placed Chelsea also out of sight some 15 points clear. That pair still had the incentive of an FA Cup final ahead, while Liverpool, who had squeezed above Arsenal into third place on goal difference, would trot out in the European Cup final in Athens ten days later.

Of the Premier League's elite quartet, only Wenger had nothing left to compete for. The FA Cup had drifted out of reach at the fifth-round stage, and Europe in the first knockout phase, after Christmas. By then, the title was already long out of reach. Asked whether the 2006–07 campaign had been his worst at the club, the Frenchman's response was immediate. 'If you analyse the season globally, I would say yes. We want to finish as quickly as possible and start again. I would be happy if you said to me tomorrow we start again straight away, cut out the holidays and let's go for it again.'

More than ever before, Wenger must have felt as if he needed a break. His campaign had proved traumatic both on and off the pitch, another season of transition for his team further unsettled by the vice-chairman David Dein's shock departure in the spring and the emergence of the mysterious American businessman Stan Kroenke as a new investor and, ultimately, potential new owner. Wenger lost his closest ally when Dein was ousted, the man who had been instrumental in appointing the Alsatian in 1996 having grown deeply frustrated at the hierarchy's seeming unwillingness to grasp Kroenke's dollars. Arsenal are not accustomed to boardroom upheaval. The sudden instability was deeply unnerving.

But Wenger had other concerns. From the acrimonious departure of José Antonio Reyes on loan to Real Madrid early in the season, to his side's continued frailties both on the road and, occasionally, at their new Emirates Stadium, the Frenchman had seen his charges labour. He admitted that witnessing his young team stumble affected him more than at any other time in his career, the worry lines creasing his forehead as it became quickly apparent that this side was not ready to mount a sustained challenge at the top of the Premier League. In November, the frustration that had been welling up boiled over spectacularly on the touchline at Upton Park, as Wenger confronted his opposite number Alan Pardew following Marlon Harewood's last-minute winner for West Ham. The pair pushed and shoved each other, the visiting manager riled by Pardew's celebrations, with the fourth official Andy d'Urso desperately trying to usher Wenger away. This is a man who has rarely demonstrated any emotion on the touchline, let alone genuine fury. To see him so apoplectic took the breath.

That was a measure of the exasperation he has felt at being forced to play catch-up with the likes of United and Chelsea, his temper bubbling up again in December when he was sent to the stands against Portsmouth for using foul and abusive language towards the referee, Steve Bennett, and his assistants. His mood was not lightened by the injury complaints suffered by Thierry Henry, sciatic nerve, groin and stomach muscle problems wrecking his campaign, or the anaemic Champions League exit to a horribly weak PSV Eindhoven side in March. Not for the first time, Arsenal were profligate against the Dutch, their inability to convert even a fraction of their glut of chances proving fatal. To slip out of Europe to such limited opponents was ignominious at best.

Henry's £16 million departure for Barcelona a month into the closed season added to the sense of doom and gloom. Yet, amid the turmoil, it would be too easy to dismiss Wenger's Arsenal as an institution on the wane. Even in the muddle of the 2006–07 campaign, there should be a recognition of the progress made and the burgeoning promise for seasons to come. A decade earlier, Wenger had walked into a club struggling to compete with those at the top. Arsenal had not been in contention for the league title since winning the competition under George Graham in 1991, and the Scot's subsequent sacking for financial impropriety had tarnished the club's image. The celebrated defence, marshalled by Tony Adams who would soon announce publicly that he was an alcoholic, was ageing; the club's popularity – among the neutrals, at least – dwindling.

Back then, the team were synonymous with dour and stifling football, blanket defence suffocating to the mournful chants of 'boring, boring Arsenal' from the stands. Had the supporters been offered then the chance to see their favourites finish fourth, and reach the Carling Cup final and the knockout stages of the European Cup, playing some of the most scintillating football witnessed by the Premiership en route, they would have rejoiced regardless of the lack of silverware. Wenger's problem, perhaps, is that by winning three league titles, four FA Cups and reaching the finals of the Uefa Cup and Champions League so thrillingly, he has raised expectations. Any sense of 'failure' now is relative.

Furthermore, there remain indications that the latest dynasty of players nurtured calmly and quietly by Wenger at Arsenal can propel the club back to the summit playing the brand of exhilarating football which still sets this team apart from all comers. This, after all, was a youthful side who had subjected Liverpool's mixture of first-teamers and reserves to a 6–3 hammering at Anfield in January, a blistering performance which served to demonstrate this team's true potency. It was the Merseysiders' worst home defeat in 77 years, and a glimpse of what the Gunners youngsters could achieve.

There was the Brazilian prodigy Denilson on one flank, a player once courted by Liverpool but enticed by Wenger to London, and England's Theo Walcott on the other. It says much that the most expensive teenager in British football was rather eclipsed by his contemporaries that night. Alex Song and Cesc Fabregas – a phenomenon plucked from Barcelona – dominated central midfield; Jérémie Aliadière proved his pedigree as a slick forward runner; while Justin Hoyte, Johan Djourou and Armand Traoré were a sprightly presence at the back, with the excellent Kolo Touré directing play with the authority that, at 26, belied his years. It was a thrilling display even if, understandably, it could not be replicated in the final against an imposing Chelsea – the Gunners' midfield quartet boasted an average age of under 19 in the final at the Millennium Stadium – or every week in the Premiership.

Regardless, Wenger later admitted that developing this latest team represented one of his most satisfying achievements in management. 'This team has been five years in the making, a long project,' he said. 'They are the best group of young players I've ever worked with. It's a sensational feeling to work with them, go through it all with them and see them and know that they will never give up. They have the heart and resilience and it's fantastic to see people coping with the pressure at such a young age. They say life is too easy for young boys these days, but it's just a question of motivation: whether you want it enough. Quality players really want to win and are ready to fight.'

Arsenal's predicament following their move to Ashburton Grove has left the manager with very little option but to plough his efforts into harnessing the talent of the youth team. As a club, the Gunners simply cannot compete with Roman Abramovich's money-flushed Chelsea. The sight of Manchester United pledging to spend up to £50 million on three players – the youngsters Nani and Anderson from Sporting Lisbon and Porto respectively, and the England midfielder Owen Hargreaves – in the summer of 2007, just weeks after claiming the title, was a reminder that Arsenal must aim to progress by other means.

In that respect, Wenger had needed what older heads he could muster for the awkward 2006–07 campaign to steer his younger players through, so the loss of the likes of Henry and in particular William Gallas was devastating. Without the France international centre-back, Wenger had seen his plans seriously spoiled by defensive problems – he had lost confidence in Jens Lehmann in 2004–05, and used 26 different defensive combinations the following year – for a third successive season. In the end, his only option was to hope that, long-term, the testing induction could eventually prove to be the making of his young defence.

They will be better for the experience and their achievements. Certainly, with the more seasoned campaigners fit and even in Henry's absence, Arsenal remain impressive. 'If you look at the number of players who were not available at the end of the 2006–07 season and the quality of our performances over much of the campaign, we still have the right to be optimistic,' argued Wenger. 'I feel there can be focus still on developing the team we already have here. The team is growing well, and if we have everybody fit then we can challenge. After all, we have played some football of such quality that nobody else has matched. What I am more proud of than anything is that the club was very solid when we were hit very hard with our elimination from the Champions League at the beginning of March. Most of the other clubs in Europe would have exploded. But we will talk over the summer, work hard in pre-season and come back strong.'

That encapsulates the spirit of Wenger's Arsenal. The Frenchman remains a mystery to many, not least his rivals in opposing dugouts who consider him aloof. He does not conduct one-on-one interviews with the English press and remains an intensely private man, appearing to closet himself away in the Totteridge home which he shares with his long-time partner, former France basketball player Annie Brosterhous, and their young daughter, Léa. In truth, he is as likely to be poring over videos of up-and-coming opponents or scout reports of potential signings as he is playing the doting husband or father.

His is an obsession for football, something the onlooking English public found hard to conceive when he appeared – tall, alarmingly thin and bespectacled – at his unveiling press conference at Highbury back in the autumn of 1996. He smacked more of European politician than title-winning inspiration, his work as coach of Nagoya Grampus Eight in Japan having gone unnoticed in the Premiership. Sir Alex Ferguson pondered publicly, and rather contemptuously, the newcomer's credentials. The Manchester United manager would soon become well aware of what Wenger had to offer.

These days, the Frenchman is lauded in one pocket of north London for his successes, reviled in another for those same achievements, but respected up and down the country as the first foreigner truly to take the English game by storm.

He was a trailblazer. Having been greeted with damning headlines asking 'Arsène who?' he swiftly re-established Arsenal at the pinnacle of the domestic game and reinvented how the game was played, both on and off the pitch, in this country. There remain considerable challenges ahead. Wenger has yet to claim a European trophy, a failing that grates with him, and he must ensure that the Gunners disrupt the increasing duopoly enjoyed by Chelsea and United at the top of the Premier League. But few can doubt now that the man dubbed 'the Professor' has it in him to do just that.

Dominic Fifield, London, June 2007

THE MAKING OF THE
PROFESSOR

ARSÈNE WENGER, NOTEBOOK as ever in hand, opens the front door and welcomes his guest to his home. The summer of 2005 is drifting into autumn, the new football season having just kicked off, and Arsenal's manager still lives in the unassuming house that he chose upon his arrival in England some ten years previously. Snug in the leafy oasis that is Totteridge, a sleepy suburb in the sprawl of north London, from the outside there is nothing to suggest that this is the home of one of the most celebrated managerial talents in world football. Till a few years ago the only indication as to who lives here could be glimpsed through an upstairs window, flanked by white curtains, where a small Arsenal sticker could be spotted, betraying the occupant's attachment to the Gunners. Otherwise, in contrast to the less muted decor favoured by some of his players in their neighbouring houses, Wenger's home is tasteful, anything but pretentious, and exudes an air of peace and quiet.

In the lounge, the guest – a close friend – is treated like a king. There is a bottle of Saint-Emilion grand cru, uncorked and inviting. 'Arsène will drink a couple of glasses and leave his guest to finish the rest of the bottle,' says the friend with a smile, conscious that he is talking about the same Wenger who consistently declines the invitations of Sir Alex Ferguson, another wine enthusiast, to share a glass after every match between Manchester United and Arsenal. 'Back with his family at home, he's completely open. He laughs all the time and loves being surrounded by his friends. People think he's dour, scholarly perhaps, but his sense of humour is always there. But, at home, it's all low-key and never extravagant.'

The living room confirms as much. The decor and furniture are reassuringly understated and down to earth. There are no awards on show on the sideboards, no photographs hanging from the walls to commemorate the best moments of his remarkable and glittering managerial career. There are no winners' medals or cups on the cabinets. Wenger has won 20 trophies at clubs all around the world but in his home, where he lives with his partner Annie and their daughter Léa, there isn't a hint of those glories. Yet the fact that there are no reminders of that plunder does not mean all the stunning achievements masterminded by this man at football clubs all over the world are forgotten. It's just that the Wengers don't feel the need to be surrounded by the trappings of their celebrity.

There is a pull-down screen on which satellite channels broadcast games from all around the globe to tap into the home owner's obsession. 'But his house doesn't resemble that of a multi-millionaire,' says this privileged witness to the Wengers' inner sanctum, who wishes to remain anonymous. 'Arsène and Annie consider their family life out of the media glare to be precious. Léa can walk to school. There's nothing flashy about the way they live at home. Arsène leaves Annie to the finer details of household decoration, preferring to come home and put his feet up. He simply doesn't have the time – after all, he has matches to watch, transfers to finalise, even books to read.'

Not that the shelves are crammed with sports books. Instead, trace the spines and you will find a hotchpotch of weighty biographies, volumes on politics and history, even on religion, and written alternately in French and English. There is a book on Julius Caesar, signed by the historian Max Gallo, and another in English on Pius XII. Next to these books on well known figures from history are essays written by sociologists, the memoirs of the journalists Françoise Giroud and Jean Daniel, Jeremy Paxman's *The English*.

Then there is the background music which, just as in Wenger's Mercedes, adds to the sense of calm, whether it is classical or the mellow strains of Norah Jones. From the ornaments to the furniture, the books to the music collection, nothing indicates that this is the home of one of the best-paid and most respected football coaches in the world. It is as if the man from Alsace lives in a cocoon away from the outside world where all is tranquil and undisturbed, an oasis of calm.

Wenger in 2005 is a far cry from the little boy sitting on one of the pews of the church of St Louis in Duttlenheim in the late 1950s, bending over his missal and praying hard as he prepared for his first Holy Communion. And what were all his prayers and pleas for? They were for the village football team to select him. 'I've always told myself that there's nothing in life other than football,' explained Wenger the Catholic, for whom religion has always taken the form of a football.

The town signs welcoming you to Duttlenheim signify you are entering Wenger territory. The village is about 20 km south of Strasbourg and is home to 2,420 people; it is no coincidence that, just like Wenger's house in Totteridge, this pocket of north-eastern France is sleepy and unassuming. It was there, amid the sycamores and the cross-hatched timber-beamed houses, that the young Arsène laced his first boots and strode out in the basic municipal stadium, a pitch surrounded by rough fencing, hemmed in by the backs of houses at one end and flanked by the road at the other. For the record, Duttlenheim has provided one other notable historical figure: the watercolour painter Robert Dervillez, originally a gymnast, who had ended up opting for a career in the arts and who left the town a school of painting in his name.

The village where the young Wenger grew up, surrounded by the flat open country of Alsace, is a curious place. It rises up quite suddenly from the plain, a collection of ancient bijou houses amongst which are strewn barns and court-yards. The Wengers' house, with its steep sloping roof, sits comfortably among the bourgeois dwellings. A bit further up the road, on the right-hand side, looms the church before you hit the main road of this rural hamlet. In these unspectacular surroundings, Wenger cut his teeth and formulated his dreams.

'You wouldn't have ever imagined that a manager of such

standing in the English game would come from a place like this, a sleepy village full of rich landowners, but essentially with only one street,' said Jasper Rees, who visited Alsace whilst writing his book on Wenger, *The Making of a Legend.* 'In England, high-profile figures in the game traditionally tend to come from the lower classes, and certainly the less well-to-do families. That's about as far removed as it can get from Duttlenheim, this heavily Catholic and agriculturally prosperous corner of France. This is real farming stock. In the village on the crossroads there's a basic sort of "pub", La Croix d'Or, with a restaurant, all pine panelling and crammed with tables. Everything lacks any kind of pretension.'

The Wenger family ran that bistro and it was there that the future Arsenal manager grew up, along with his older sister and brother. Duttlenheim Football Club, a team that would win the Bas-Rhin regional Third Division title in the 1968–69 season with a side boasting the brothers Wenger, Guy and Arsène, would meet in that smoke-filled room. Duttlenheim FC owed much to Arsène that year, the youngster scoring in the pivotal match after only three minutes. 'After that, it was a case of holding on to what we had,' recalled a former team-mate with a smile. That year, Arsène finished with 13 goals in 18 matches. 'But his brother was actually a better player,' added another former stalwart at the club. The shirts worn by Duttlenheim back then were, appropriately enough, red. That colour would accompany Wenger throughout his professional coaching career, from Monaco to Arsenal.

That side was built around the brotherly partnership of

Arsène and Guy, though there was another Wenger in its ranks – Claude – who was not related to the pair. There are many Wenger families in Duttlenheim who were no doubt one and the same, but have been separated over the years. Guy played left-back while Claude, a right-back, was three years older than Arsène in the youth team at Duttlenheim FC back in 1963 – the latter was duly nicknamed 'Petit' ('Titch') by his team-mates. That stuck with him throughout his time in the youth set-up – he may now be 6 feet 3 inches, but his growth spurt didn't come until he was 14 – as he played in a number of different positions before settling for something akin to an old-fashioned inside right. As a child, he played in goal for the village; some of his team-mates even called him 'Yashin' after the Soviet Union's iconic goalkeeper Lev Yashin.

There is little to impress the visitor to La Croix d'Or. There are three small steps up to the plain door, the windows cheering up a rather grubby façade to the building with its heavy roof above. A sign outside indicates the road to Strasbourg. The pub remains old-fashioned, stuck in a time warp, and much as it was when the Wengers relinquished the business. 'It must have been difficult for a non-drinker to spend so much time in a place like this which revolves around beer,' said Rees. 'If your parents work in a bar every night, it's difficult to avoid the sight of *demis* being downed, and to avoid downing them yourself. It demands a strong personal discipline to resist.'

Arsène's parents, Louise and Alphonse, sold the bistro over 20 years ago, but the place remains almost unaltered. Just outside still stands a statue of Christ on the cross, flanked by two other religious icons. These three statues seem to keep watch over the two-storey building, around which are nailed signs for Fischer beer – billboards for Alsatian beer a matter of metres from the image of the crucifixion.

Even if the village is tiny, it still boasts a football team. The Wengers may have watched all of Arsène's games for the local side, but they were not keen for their son to stop his studies to pursue a future in football. 'It was alarming for his parents to see their son set his heart upon a career in which, in their eyes, all his academic diplomas and achievements would count for nothing,' said Rees. 'But he proved everyone wrong. He always had the courage of his convictions.' Strasbourg, where Alphonse ran a spare-parts dealership later taken on by Guy, would offer Arsène a taste of football at a higher level a few years later. Within a decade, he would be playing the odd game for Racing Club de Strasbourg in the top flight of French football, and even one in European competition.

Yet it was at Duttlenheim, where training would take place once a week, that the young Wenger made his mark. Back then, 'Max' Hild (his real name is Raymond) was a coach at AS Mutzig, neighbours and rivals. One Wednesday evening in 1969, Hild watched as the young Wenger, striding through midfield, dominated a game against his youth-team charges. Almost 40 years later, on a similar Wednesday evening at his home in Weyersheim, Max was preparing to reflect on that first meeting. He picked up the telephone, dialled his former protégé's number then, as realisation dawned, suddenly hung up with a smile. 'There's no point trying because his team's playing tonight.'

'I count a number of men far older than me in my circle of friends,' said Wenger when the name of Hild is mentioned. 'Max would always be the first in a long list of mentors, people from whom I have learnt so much.'

Ask Hild about the player he spotted that day and the memories pour out as if that local derby was yesterday. 'The first impression I had of Arsène? It wasn't really his performance that night which stood out, but it was the impact he had on the game and his influence on his team-mates. That was something extraordinary.' The young Wenger was not the captain of the Duttlenheim side, but he dictated their play, stamping his authority on the game. 'Yes, it was a bit like that. When he came to play for us at Mutzig afterwards, it was the same. He always tried to bring something different to the team, going that extra bit further. He was always eager to learn. He wanted to know everything, from tactics to team strategy, to how to improve.'

Hild recalls the youngster's desire to raise his game, and that of the team, and his constant quest for perfection. 'Arsène wanted to progress. Every single aspect of the game interested him, and he'd scrutinise the team's play and his own performances down to the finest details.' Meticulous even barely at the age of 20, Wenger – a young midfielder – was already showing signs of becoming the master strategist. He may have still been a player, but he was already a coach at heart.

Having joined Mutzig – a short drive from Duttlenheim and the equivalent of a Third Division side at the time which, despite being amateur, attracted gates of around 1,500 – and forced his way into their first team, Wenger once came face to face with Guy Roux, a legendary figure in French football having hoisted Auxerre from non-league obscurity to become an established force in the top flight. Roux's side took on Mutzig, and 35 years on he can still recall the impression made upon him by the tallest player in the opposition ranks.

'He was tall, even then,' said Roux. 'He actually played centre-half that day, and he was pretty effective. He had that ability to read the game, to predict what was going to happen. Looking back, he reminded me of a couple of players I've worked with since: of René Bolf, the Czech I had at Auxerre, and of my Polish player Pawel Janas [who played under Roux from 1982 to 1986 and went on to work with the Polish Football Federation].' Wenger would be proud to be compared to such players.

If Wenger had effectively emerged in the Mutzig team too late at 20 to forge himself a career as a player in professional football, his education in the tactics of the game was well under way. Alongside Hild, the young player would study the methods employed by rival teams, even venturing across the border into West Germany to witness first-hand how established managers approached the game. In this respect, he was years ahead of his time, opening his mind to new concepts and adapting his own ideas with everything he learnt. The stadia of Germany became his classrooms, the Bundesliga a laboratory where he experimented with formations, game plans and tactical nuances. Every Thursday night after training, Hild and his young protégé would indulge themselves in lengthy discussions about the game covering everything from strategy to organisation, tactics to technique. They would study the upcoming fixtures in the Bundesliga and cherry-pick where to visit: Munich and Stuttgart were not far away from Strasbourg, with Frankfurt just as accessible, even if the long-limbed Wenger would be forced to sit cramped in Hild's tiny run-around car, his chin almost resting on his knees as they zoomed across the border. This odd couple became regulars on the terraces.

'Back then, the Germans were streets ahead of us in France in terms of their football development,' recalled Hild. 'From 1960 through the 1970s, West Germany were at the top of the world game, winning the European Championships in 1972 and the World Cup on their own soil two years later, and had their own attacking style which swept all comers before them. Arsène would analyse the players on show, but he wasn't necessarily interested just in gawping at the best strutting their stuff out on the pitch. Instead, he wanted to know why some players played well, and why others struggled so badly in certain games. He was analysing things to that extent, scrutinising everything from the organisation of the defence to the make-up and formation of a side, and how that can benefit different personnel. Defence was the key, and back then, all the German defenders of the era could also attack – they knew their responsibilities, what they had to offer – but everyone in the team, from back to front, played some part in defence.'

That emphasis on defence at the root of his side has been evident in every side Wenger has put out since, offering a base upon which attacking play can be built. It was a philosophy groomed in the young Wenger during those trips with Hild; sometimes Max and Arsène would not return home from their expeditions into West Germany until three or four in the morning. 'We'd stop on the motorway for a sandwich and a coffee, never a beer,' added Hild. 'I've rarely ever seen Arsène drink . . .'

Another of Wenger's former team-mates, Jean-Noël Huck, who would later go on to represent France, recalled how the closest Arsène ever came to drinking alcohol was enjoying the odd shandy, even if he was always partial to chocolate and sweets. 'Ah yes, those slabs of chocolate,' said Hild with a smile. 'Instead of a pudding, he'd go for chocolate, always. He couldn't live without that.

'I remember us going to see Borussia Mönchengladbach play Real Madrid in the European Cup once and we made a bet en route as to who we thought would win, Arsène opting for the Germans and me the Spanish. He always liked the way Mönchengladbach played at the time – they had an attractive, free-flowing attacking style and were a potent force on the counter-attack, inspired by Günter Netzer in the centre of their midfield.' Netzer was the Dennis Bergkamp of his generation, a creative inspiration who would slice opponents apart with his passing. Bizarrely, and extraordinarily, Wenger would be compared to the great German midfielder after scoring four times for Mulhouse in 1975.

Arsène spent three seasons at Mulhouse, the second-oldest club in France, which turned semi-professional after decades in the amateur leagues in 1971, the year before Wenger joined. They had finished sixth the previous season but, following the departure of most of their professional players, theirs was a constant battle for survival to avoid relegation from the Second Division thereafter. In the last match of the

1974–75 season they came up against AS Nancy Lorraine, who included in their ranks a young Michel Platini. The Mulhousiens won through to maintain their place in the division by the skin of their teeth; Platini was destined for bigger things.

The spell at Mulhouse, for which Wenger earned around £50 a week as he combined playing with his studies of economics at Strasbourg University, represented a rare fracture in his relationship with Hild. The pair had worked together from Duttlenheim to Mutzig, and would again at Vauban and RC Strasbourg in the future, but now they separated for three years. 'I wouldn't go as far as to present myself as Arsène's second father,' said Max. 'It's just that our paths ran together for so long – his as a player, mine as a coach – and between us there was a great understanding. A mutual respect. We knew each other, loved our football and shared the same opinions about the way in which it should be played.'

Wenger's friends at the time were his club-mates from his early days, such as Jean-Noël Huck, and his team-mates from the Strasbourg and, later, the French university representative side. Jean-Luc Arribart has been Wenger's friend since their days together as students in Alsace. 'Back then, I really didn't think Arsène would become a coach,' he said some 30 years on, recalling their days together in the university team of which Arribart was captain. 'I remember he approached the university matches as a student would. There was a carefree air about that side, as you'd expect from students! There was always another prank just around the corner.'

What the French university side offered Wenger was an

opportunity to travel further afield. They visited Nigeria, Lebanon and, in 1976, Uruguay. Wenger spoke Spanish and had always been eager to explore South America, but for once the trip was not just a cultural or sporting adventure. The French finished third, but for Wenger, the trip was also a test. 'Arsène actually showed us another side of his character over there,' added Arribart. 'He ended up almost as the team's "pick me up". We'd both been injured just before the tournament but there was a chance we would be fit to take part at some stage. As it turned out, I recovered in time to feature and he never did, so he ended up just carrying the balls to and from training and games.

'But what he did do was keep us all amused with a never-ending string of jokes. Effectively, he'd come for nothing. He couldn't play, couldn't be part of the team as such, and it's difficult when you're the forgotten man of a squad, the one person not fit enough to play. Back then, it would have sounded ridiculous to consider what he would go on and achieve, but maybe we should have seen it coming. By the end of that trip, Arsène had almost taken on the role of assistant coach and team joker rolled into one. He's still got that sense of humour now. It must help him release the pressure of his job, but also win people over. In his role as manager of a major football club, he'll need to charm people at times, to laugh with them at others, and win them over. That job must be so stressful, so to have a release in humour must be a godsend.'

He needed a sense of humour at times with Mulhouse. Wenger struggled to command a regular first-team place in his first year at the club under the coaching of Robert Alonzo.

The manager was sacked in late 1974 as the club flirted with relegation, with Paul Frantz hired to perform a salvage operation. Frantz was something of a local celebrity, having coached at RC Strasbourg during the mid-1960s and established himself as one of the game's deep thinkers to the extent that he was once even offered a job on the coaching staff of AC Milan, only to turn it down because he didn't speak Italian. He had also earned himself a reputation not only for his almost scientific approach to coaching – he was the man who taught Aimé Jacquet (who led France to the World Cup in 1998), Guy Roux and Roger Lemerre in courses he ran for the Fédération Française de Football – but also for hoisting teams out of trouble. As he also lived in Strasbourg, he duly joined Wenger on the train, and the pair struck up a rapport from the start.

'We'd sit together on the train and we'd use that time to chat about football as well as to work,' said Frantz, then 78 and speaking at his home in Oberhausbergen in the summer of 2005. 'I remember those conversations we had as if they were yesterday because back then I was writing my book on coaching – *Football* – and I'd use those commutes on the train to work on it.' They would sit themselves down in an empty second-class carriage, the teacher and his young apprentice in their own little world. Occasionally, school-children or students would wander through the coach and recognise Frantz, the man who had steered RC Strasbourg to the French Cup in 1966 and had gone on to beat Milan in the Uefa Cup, and would be invited to take part in the chats. But Frantz was only interested in what Wenger, his young player, had to say.

'I saw in Arsène a young man who was going to be exceptional. I could sense he was a class apart. As a footballer, he was a type of person who was willing to seek advice and was happy to take it on board to change his game, to improve his game. Quite often, you come across players who don't ask why they're being told to do things. They only want to be given a training routine which they can understand and get on with. They don't want to know why that routine will help them. Arsène, on the other hand, would ask you questions all the time. We'd discuss problems with his game, but also we'd talk about football in general.

'We ended up saving Mulhouse that season, just about, but it wasn't just about that for Arsène. Those journeys on the train actually served as a motivation for us. I ended up using those chats we had to integrate Arsène into the team, where he effectively became my mouthpiece out on the pitch. He took the ideas we talked about in the carriage out on to the field of play, and he organised his team-mates along the lines we had talked about. I don't think I ever had to tell him expressly to do that. He just took it on board naturally.

'Of course, that didn't necessarily help him play better personally. He was very one-footed – he hardly ever used his left – and of average pace out on the pitch but, if he had a fast brain and was a fine tactician, he struggled to put his game plans into action sometimes because, essentially, he wasn't a good enough player. He'd huff and puff, but he'd come to football late. There are certain things in the game that you need to pick up when you're very young, when you're between eight and twelve years of age. After that, it's hard to pick up the basics. That's always the case.

'It's the same in other fields – swimming, football, music. If you come to these skills late, you can't reach the top. Natural ability is nurtured in those formative years. I don't think Arsène put on his first pair of boots until he was 13 or 14. Too late. He was missing something as a player, and he knew it. His passes weren't quite precise enough, and he didn't have that ability to spy a ball out of the corner of his eye to set a team-mate free. He was an excellent amateur player, but a poor professional. But, even then, he was still quite obviously someone of above-average intelligence. If, for some reason, the train wasn't running then one of us would drive and we'd have the same deep, often animated conversations in the car. He was never afraid to tell me he didn't agree with something I was saying. They were always pretty frank discussions, to be honest.'

The young Wenger's time at Mulhouse was spent balancing his semi-professional football career with his university economics degree in Strasbourg. 'It wasn't easy for him,' added Frantz. 'He'd be training with us, playing games and then going to university. Every second of his time was used up. In the end, it was almost as if he was studying by correspondence, sending his work in the post with football starting to dominate his life more and more. Remember, sometimes it felt as if we were spending all our lives on the train, either travelling to or from training or back from games as far away as Toulouse or Cannes. That ate into his time, just as it did with all of us in a semi-professional environment.'

Frantz left following the last-day escape against Platini and AS Nancy Lorraine, and Wenger also opted out that summer.

After spells at Duttlenheim, Mutzig and Mulhouse, all in the lower reaches of the French leagues, the young midfielder cum defender knew his level and, keen to cut back on the commute from Strasbourg, sought out a more local club. As it was, his decision was virtually made for him. In 1974, a recently formed club named AS Vauban – a residential suburb on the eastern edge of Strasbourg – had hired Max Hild as coach, luring Wenger's friend from Mutzig where he had put in 12 years' good service. The club had risen from the equivalent of the 10th division into the Fourth Division, at one stage going a remarkable 113 games without defeat. For Wenger, this was a chance to come home, even if it meant playing in front of gates of around 1,000 people.

Arsène understood Alsace, where he'd grown up and was amongst his people. His dialect was that of the locals. 'Language has a real influence on the spirit and culture of a people,' he once said. 'I also think that I owe much for what I've achieved in my life to the fact that I was brought up almost in a multilingual environment. Learning German or English has been so much easier for me as a result, and if I'd not learnt English, I'd never have been appointed manager of Arsenal.'

Alsace shaped the young Wenger, as a child growing up and as a young player plying his trade on the small amateur pitches of the region. He was Alsatian first, French second, and imbued with the local spirit shaped by years of conflict between France and Germany, the ramifications of which were inevitably felt most in this region sandwiched between warring countries. The locals talk of a 'them against us' mentality; Wenger bought into that.

Guy Roux once said that Wenger has the Alsatian's 'tenacity and ability to express himself'. Hild, who discovered and helped shape the young Wenger, recognises the Germanic traits – from perfectionism to professionalism – in his protégé which have served him in good stead: hard-working, strict, even controlled. 'The fact that we border Germany has rubbed off on us and given us a discipline and dedication which is, I suppose, inexorably Teutonic,' he said. 'You can see it in Arsène's desire to work feverishly. He's good at what he does, is talented, but also methodical. And there's never any pretentiousness to what he does. For all those reasons, he's clearly Alsatian through and through.'

Back then, the young footballer with the curly blond hair was well aware that his talent for the game was more physical than technical. 'What I was good at was man-marking,' he later acknowledged. 'I had a good engine, and endurance was my forte. I was often more athletic than the man I was marking. That was my game. If the man I was directly up against didn't attempt to run past me, I'd get horribly frustrated. It felt sometimes as if I hadn't even had a game.'

There was still success to be had under Hild at Vauban, whose rise through the divisions continued with Wenger a member of the side, until the coach was lured to the city's bigger club, Racing Club de Strasbourg. Hild was initially recruited by the manager, Gilbert Gress, to run the club's reserve team but, with the first team having qualified for the Uefa Cup, found his duties increasingly pushed towards scouting the senior side's next opponents. In his absence, as he travelled the continent scrutinising players, Strasbourg needed someone to take up the reins of the reserves. Step forward Arsène Wenger.

RC Strasbourg was the club of Wenger's heart, the side he had followed since his childhood and the biggest in the region. He was 28 with his playing career effectively stalling as he enjoyed life as a career student, but he came recommended by Frantz and Hild, which was enough to convince Gress that this was the man to take up the mantle of the reserve team. It was 1978 and this was a full-time job, Wenger's first. The onus was on him to guide and organise a group of youngsters and inspire those first-teamers either out of form or recovering from long-term injury who would find themselves thrust among the second string. He would plan training in his office at the team's Meinau stadium, then take it out on the practice pitches, yet the role would also offer him the occasional call-up into the senior side, usually at the last minute, and demand that he played regularly in the second string.

At first, he featured virtually every week in the reserves, which maintained his fitness levels and offered him the opportunity to step into the first team if required. Hild offered him the chance to move back from midfield into defence, a sweeper playing in the role enjoyed by Franz Beckenbauer, where his maturity and experience could better influence those around him. Gress watched the new recruit and recognised, just as Hild and Frantz had before him, that this was a player of limited ability but of huge intelligence. Someone who had a role to play if required. 'He had the positioning and game intelligence and, most of the time, Arsène did well for us,' said Gress of his leggy recruit. 'When

I needed someone, I had confidence in him to do a job. It was just a shame that he hadn't had a coach like me to play under ten years earlier – I would have turned him into an international.'

That was said with a chuckle. Wenger ignored the critics who doubted publicly whether he had the ability to play as a sweeper. He could point to the small part he played in steering RC Strasbourg to the title in 1978–79, and the fact that he had represented the club in Europe. Not that his one appearance in Continental competition was to be cherished. The first team's regular sweeper, the France international Jacques Novi, was injured, with players dropping like flies as resources became stretched, forcing Gress to turn to his reserve-team *libero* (play-making centre-half) to plug the gap for a critical Uefa Cup tie at Duisberg in November 1978. The first leg had been drawn 0–0 at Meinau, though any thoughts the French had of prevailing in the return leg quickly evaporated.

'That match was an absolute disaster,' admitted Gress, recalling the freezing conditions and miserable performance in Germany where his lightweight team were hammered 4–0, with Wenger labouring in their midst. 'I remember we played him as a *libero* in a league game at Nîmes, and he did quite well. But we had to play him in a critical game against the then champions, Monaco, in December that year, in front of a packed house, and nerves really got the better of him. I remember him looking completely giddy. It's safe to say he wasn't quite as comfortable that night . . .'

RC Strasbourg, with a squad of 15 professionals, remarkably ended that season having won the only top-flight championship in their history. Amongst their number was a certain Raymond Domenech, who would later go on to take France to the World Cup final in 2006, and from time to time Wenger would find himself thrust into the first team. According to Gress, Wenger did not take part in the celebrations which erupted when the team claimed the title, the reserve side's manager engrossed at the time with his job with the youth team.

Thereafter, the paths of Gress – a legend in Strasbourg – and Wenger went their separate ways, the pair not meeting again until some 15 years later. Gress left for FC Bruges after one more year at Racing Club, with Hild duly taking control of the first team and Wenger assuming added responsibilities with the *Centre de Formation* (the youth team set-up). The last time he and Gress spent an evening together, talking about football as they did back at Meinau, was at Monaco at the beginning of the 1990s. That night, after watching their respective teams go head to head out on the pitch, the two managers opted to waive dinner and instead enjoyed a game of cards. They played a game called écarté, allegedly invented by Napoleon Bonaparte and played across Alsace and Germany. It's a game that relies as much on skill as luck, and while no money exchanged hands that night, history does not tell who won the tête-à-tête between the coaches. 'But I haven't seen him since,' added Gress through a grin.

It was at Racing Club that, in 1979, Wenger played his last game of first-team football. He turned 30 in October and had come to accept that his future lay in the dugout, not out on the pitch. He went on to run the reserve and youth-team set-up at the club between 1981 and 1983 and, with his name gradually slipping off the squad sheets for reserve-team fixtures, it began appearing instead at the foot of the page next to his new job description: head coach. Indeed, he had taken control of his own team for the first time just before his 32nd birthday and flung himself fully into the role of coach, taking the training sessions in the morning, organising travel to away games and meeting the parents of his players, and forever preparing the sessions ahead. 'His strength was to know his limits,' said Frantz. 'Anyone who is intelligent recognises where his strengths lie. You can only go as far as your ability will take you.'

Wenger realised that he had initially shocked and even disappointed his parents with the emphasis he had placed on breaking into football, but he also recognised where his talents might be better placed. Whilst at Racing Club, he had started to study at the Regional Centre for Popular Sports Education (CREPS) for his coaching badges, beginning with a course to coach children and then an intensive six-day course to allow him to progress to the national coaching badge. He put into practice some of the methods he had heard outlined by Paul Frantz earlier in his career, and was fascinated by isometrics – the system of strengthening muscles and tuning up the body, whilst not necessarily changing a player's bulk.

Frantz had studied American swimmers in the 1950s when coming up with his theories, adapting what he learnt for footballers to strengthen the adductors and abdominal muscles. At Strasbourg, Frantz was well known for making his players undertake specific eight-minute exercises which would be conducted with their manager standing amongst them, stopwatch in hand. Wenger would later instigate such short but intensive programmes with his own players. The Arsenal manager's insistence that those players not in possession are always on the move could also be traced back to Frantz's teachings, such was the influence on Wenger of those journeys spent travelling to Mulhouse.

But it was not just physical and tactical exercises that intrigued Wenger. Diet became critical to his thinking. Arsène enjoys the pleasures of life, but only in moderation. It is as if he limits himself so as to enjoy the moment even more. One long-standing friend summed him up: 'He loves going to top-class restaurants but, when he's there, he doesn't eat very much at all. What he likes most of all is quality. And, when he's had enough, he passes his plate over to me to finish off.'

The need to have balance in one's approach – in mind, body and sport – was cultivated by Wenger whilst at Strasbourg. He took the concept on board and it dictated his approach, and he was always intrigued by the intellectual aspect of football. Just like his house in Totteridge, Arsène Wenger is fiercely protective of his home in Alsace, to which he returns each summer. Occasionally he allows the odd peek into his private world. Once, confronted by a battalion of journalists, Wenger was asked: 'Were you a good footballer?' With a smile, as if he was addressing his friends or family, he replied: 'I was the best . . . well, the best in my village.'

Before he had an opportunity to manage his own team – a chance eventually offered to him by AS Nancy – Arsène Wenger's career took him briefly to la Croisette and the French Riviera. The summer of 1983 was a period of transition. The challenge which lured the Alsatian to the Côte d'Azur was as simple as it was ambitious – he was charged with taking AS Cannes to promotion into the French top flight, working alongside the club's first-team coach Jean-Marc Guillou. The pair had first met when Guillou, a former captain of the full French team, had visited Alsace playing for the Variété Football Club, effectively a travelling celebrity XI. They had struck if off straight away to the extent that when Guillou was appointed player-coach at Mulhouse in 1982, he had attempted to broker a deal to bring Wenger in as his No. 2 only for his chairman ultimately to block the move. Partly as a result of his dismay at that decision, Guillou eventually resigned, but when he was named as Cannes's new first-team coach, his thoughts returned to recruiting the young Wenger. The Alsatian grabbed the opportunity to move south with both hands, leaving behind him Max Hild after ten years and a world he knew like the back of his hand, and stepping into the unknown. 'Arsène was at the right place at the right time,' recalled Guillou.

'I learned values in Alsace which allowed me to be appreciated anywhere,' explained Wenger in 2000. 'Discipline, a way with words, a willingness to work hard, and a respect and confidence in others – it may come across as a bit naive, but it has paid dividends over time!' Back then, the reward was a place on the bench alongside Guillou at AS Cannes and, consequently, a chance to work with a man who had been to the very top of the professional game as a player.

Richard Conte, now director of public relations at AS Monaco but then general manager of AS Cannes, recalled the summer when his first-team coach Jean-Marc Guillou informed him of his intention to recruit an unknown called Arsène Wenger as his assistant. 'Arsène landed at Nice airport on a flight from Strasbourg one evening and the pair of them came round to my house to discuss the possible move,' said Conte. 'That was the first time I'd met him. We spoke about the contractual arrangements that night. He had in mind certain sums, but at the time we were scraping the barrel a bit financially. Our budget was tiny and we couldn't match his demands.'

The negotiations went on all night, the talks veering from the script Conte had envisaged. Just as the general manager and Guillou thought they had reached an agreement with Wenger, Arsène would reconsider and point to other fees or clauses that weren't necessarily quite to his liking. 'Despite the fact that we were coming at the talks from different directions, I remember that meeting as being quite cordial and constructive,' added Conte, who would become president of AS Cannes in 1987. 'Even so, it wasn't until the small hours of the morning, when Arsène appeared to be tiring and on the point of walking away, that we finally struck a deal. In fact, it was the desire to work together shared by all three of us that eventually paved the way to reaching a compromise. Of course, inevitably, no one left entirely satisfied. Arsène accepted less than he had hoped for, and we ended up paying more than we'd envisaged. They were still modest terms. We just couldn't make him a bigger offer. It was worth 12,000 francs per month [about £300 per week] and 3,000 francs for his rent over three years.'

It was a paltry salary for an extremely promising young coach, but it was the first step Wenger took towards earning the huge £2.5 million annual salary he enjoyed from the mid-2000s at Arsenal. (That sum puts him fourth in the list of the world's highest-paid managers, behind the leader José Mourinho, Sir Alex Ferguson at Manchester United and the then England coach Sven-Göran Eriksson, but appreciably ahead of the France coach, Raymond Domenech.) Yet that meeting with Conte and Guillou was a pivotal moment in the young Wenger's career. It was a first step on the ladder. Conte later put that night of negotiations which ultimately led to the signing of a contract into perspective, recalling a visit to Arsène at his home in London in 2005. 'I arrived the day on which Arsène had received a new contract offer from Arsenal. The proposed deal was still unopened in its envelope, and Arsène's daughter Léa was playing idly with the letter. Arsène turned to her and said: "You see this offer. Well, it's the same offer that I received once at Cannes . . . but with a few more zeroes on the end." '

Wenger had holidayed on the Côte d'Azur as a child, but even in the blistering heat of the south coast he retained a distinctly Alsatian approach to his job. Headstrong and forthright, he soon forged himself a reputation. 'He was a winner,' said Conte. 'Competitive nature is deeply rooted in him.' Taking training on pitches baked and bleached by the Mediterranean sun, Arsène Wenger flung himself into life at AS Cannes. He, Jean-Marc Guillou and Richard Conte would indulge in fiercely competitive games of two-a-side football, joined by Boro Primorac – a Bosnian footballer who would later work with Wenger at Grampus Eight and Arsenal. 'We'd play them with small goals, and they were properly competitive, real battles,' said Conte. 'We'd stumble from the pitches at the end with cuts and bruises as if we'd just played in the match of the century. You fared better in the games if you were up for the physical challenge! It wasn't quite rugby out there but, at times, it came pretty close . . .'

Wenger soon made his mark at the club. 'Aside from his strengths teaching technique and his knowledge of the game, Arsène is someone who boasts exceptional concentration,' said Conte. 'He would cut himself off entirely from the outside world to prepare, plunging himself into his thoughts ahead of a game. He would read specialist books on isometrics, would spend hours in preparation for matches and discussing the smallest points with the club's fitness staff, not only about football but also about other sports such as athletics or swimming.' Down on the south coast, Wenger would dip into these other fields to find out what methods were practised and whether any of the disciplines might be used in football, adding an extra dimension to everything he'd learnt from Hild and Frantz in Alsace.

The newly appointed assistant ended up lodging in an apartment in Villefranche-sur-Mer, which he rented from a painter. 'He didn't have any furniture,' recalled Guillou. 'He had only strictly what he needed. He didn't care about comfort. He was totally disconnected from those realities. The only important item of furniture was a good bed. He was very pragmatic. If you have to spend an amount of time looking for nice furniture, that's time you're using up when you could be studying videos of games.'

Each night he would sift through the pile of video tapes, choose one and then plunge himself into the match. Which player amongst the 22 on show would be worth trying to sign? This obsessional study of videos was a key part of Arsène's preparation and scouting throughout his career.

'His light was always on, no matter what time of night it was, when I got back home so I'd pop in and say hello,' remembered Richard Conte, who was later Wenger's neighbour in his second stint in the south of France, at Monaco. Most nights, Wenger was too engrossed in the game to offer Conte anything more than a brief, nodded 'hello'. 'He was lost in his own little world. He'd watch those videos all the time. Video after video after video. He was completely oblivious to the outside world. I could turn up out of the blue at any time of night, and stay with him until whatever time in the morning, sitting in the chair next to him, but he'd stay fixed and obsessed with what was going on on the screen. He'd only really realise that I'd been there when I'd announce: "Right, good night then. See you later." That's usually when he'd snap out of his trance and actually try and start a conversation!'

The young coach also stamped his insistence on feverish hard work on the squad, approaching the job almost with monastic zeal. Guillou described his assistant's approach as 'Stakhanovism', with excessive time and effort put in when it came to preparation and the hours spent out on the training pitch. 'We ended up making mistakes even if our intentions were good,' he admitted. 'The squad we had were all eager to learn, but we asked too much of them. It was hard to get them to play as a team. Results improved in the last four or five months of that season, but we made them work like idiots to achieve that much.' Cannes missed out on promotion but did reach the quarter-finals of the French Cup, their relative upturn in form during the spring of 1984 coinciding with a period Guillou spent away on business in Africa attempting to sign the young Ivory Coast player Youssouf Fofana. During that time, Wenger took control of first-team affairs at AS Cannes, combining his work with the seniors with his hours at the club's *Centre de Formation*. It was his first taste of life in charge of a senior side.

'Arsène wasn't a revolutionary,' said Guillou. 'Efficiency was his key quality. I see at Arsenal now similar things to those he instigated at Cannes back then: training is varied but aimed at improving specific areas, and he's instilled in his players a collective focus to achieve a set objective. When it comes to games, he has the ability to analyse calmly and succinctly when everyone around him is panicking. He always had that. That ability in itself helps calm people down.'

Added to those qualities was loyalty. When Primorac later became inadvertently embroiled in the controversy surrounding Olympique de Marseille – he was coaching Valenciennes when Bernard Tapie, then owner of l'OM, sought to bribe his opponents to throw a vital league match – Wenger offered his old friend a job. They have been inseparable ever since. The same applies to Guillou. Years later, in his role as owner of the Belgian club Beveren, Guillou would forward names of talented young African players to Wenger at Arsenal, including the likes of Emmanuel Eboué, and would often visit Arsène in London. (The Gunners' relationship with the Belgian 'feeder' club prompted a Fifa investigation in early 2006 over allegations of money-laundering, but the governing body eventually cleared the

Premiership club of any wrongdoing.) The pair would argue, albeit only playfully, whenever they were reunited. 'Arsène plays devil's advocate, adopting an argument with which he isn't totally in agreement and then taking me on,' he added. 'But no matter. Talking with Arsène is always interesting.'

After only one season at Cannes, in the summer of 1984 and at the age of 34, Arsène Wenger enjoyed his first big break. People knew of the up-and-coming young coach back in his village in Alsace, and his reputation had already stretched from Strasbourg to Cannes, but already talk of his methods and his rigour had started to spread around France. People were starting to take notice. Jean-Claude Cloet, who played under Wenger at Cannes and counted Nancy amongst his former clubs, ended up acting as the middleman in a deal which secured Arsène his first managerial position. 'I remember we were sitting having a fruit juice on the terrace at one of the cafés in Cannes in December 1983,' he recalled. 'I told Arsène that the president of AS Nancy, Gérard Rousselot, who I knew from my time in Lorraine, was on the lookout for a new first-team coach. I asked him if he'd be interested. Arsène replied that I could mention his name . . .'

At the time, the director of football Aldo Platini, Michel's father, was rather more doubtful of the youngster's credentials but Rousselot stubbornly followed the advice offered to him by Cloet. 'I assured him that Arsène could do the job with his eyes closed. At Cannes, after only five weeks working under Wenger, I remember thinking to myself: "What the hell is he doing wasting his time here? He's far too good for us."'

Rousselot, with Platini won over, dispatched his director of football to strike a deal with Wenger, with agreement reached in Cannes on a three-year contract worth around 25,000 francs per month (around £2,500). Arsène was back closer to his family in Alsace, but not necessarily back home – in Lorraine, they pronounced his name with a soft G (as in 'avenger') – though he was as enthusiastic as ever. Nancy had made their name in the 1970s when Michel Platini had been a leading light in their midfield, but by the early 1980s their star had moved on to St Etienne and beyond and the club was on the wane. Gates had slipped to below 6,000, half as many as had flocked into the stadium in the club's heyday, with money tight as a result. Having flirted with relegation from the First Division the previous year, they turned to the young coach in part because he was cheap – they were desperate.

With limited funds to buy players, Wenger took to scouring the transfer market looking for bargains. He unearthed some gems, but also some players Nancy might prefer to forget. Samuel Lobé, a striker recruited on a free transfer, managed only 12 matches in four long seasons at the club before sinking without trace in the lower leagues. 'Arsène picked up and played players who never featured again in Division One, like Denis Hindelang [plucked from the lower leagues, but a player who was forced to wait a year before he played his first game after suffering a debilitating disease of the blood only then to be called up for national service],' added Cloet. 'But he always had an excellent relationship with his players. He loved them all.'

Wenger attempted to strengthen his side where he could and surrounded himself with people he knew and trusted. He plucked Jean-Luc Arribart, his old friend from the French university side, from Stade de Reims with the 29-year-old – a journeyman through the lower leagues throughout his career – duly becoming his eyes out on the pitch. It was an approach Arsène had taken on board from Hild and Frantz, using a player who was on his wavelength to orchestrate the side on the turf and ensure the machine ran smoothly. Between 1984 and 1986, Arribart witnessed at first hand how the young Wenger coped with his first managerial position, and the horror with which his friend railed at a defeat. 'We lost one game at Lens, conceding three or four goals, and back then it really got to him,' said Arribart. 'He'd get so worked up by disappointments like that. On the way back from that match, he actually had to stop the team bus to vomit a few hundred metres away from the stadium. He threw up in a ditch. The defeat had literally turned his stomach and made him physically ill. He's learned to control himself more since, but back then there was real anger when things did not go well.'

Damien Comolli, who was in charge of player recruitment for seven years at Arsenal under Wenger, can corroborate the change in his friend's physical, and psychological, approach over the years. 'He'd often make himself physically ill after a defeat,' he recalled. 'In his third season at Nancy [1986–87], when the team were eventually relegated, he lost the last match before the mid-winter break. Arsène's reaction was to tell me not to come round to his house for the next two weeks. He shut himself away on his own for that fortnight, and didn't even have his family around for Christmas. He hated losing that much.' He would blame himself, and no one else.

At Nancy, like everywhere else he had worked, Wenger was always the first in to the club's Forêt-de-Haye training ground in the morning and the last to leave in the evening. 'Nancy was the first professional club Arsène had taken on as first-team coach,' said Arribart. 'He embraced the job passionately. I suppose when he arrived at AS Nancy Lorraine, he really couldn't lose. He threw himself into the role 3,000 per cent. He lived for the job, existed for football. He only had football in his life.' (His girlfriend would come and visit from time to time, but football was his existence.) The club duly became his laboratory, a place where he experimented, trying out ideas he'd concocted and developed over his years waiting for this chance.

He varied training sessions, keeping written assessments of how his players had fared, and even took the team away on a pre-season intensive training camp in Val Thorens, an Alpine ski resort boasting the highest-altitude football pitch in France. 'He wasn't entirely sure in what direction he wanted to take the team, so he tried out a few,' said one of his former players. He scoured the information he'd collated over his first season in an effort to refine techniques for his second year in the job.

'He'd introduce lots of different exercises and new approaches, whether in training or tactics, and then he'd sit back and see how we coped with them,' said Arribart. 'It was a kind of apprenticeship for him because he was putting into practice what he'd been toying with in his "laboratory" for years. He saw how we did and either pursued that technique or ditched it. But he always kept things interesting. He made us understand why we were doing things, stressing what our responsibilities were out on the pitch. He had a real ability to get his message across and convince everyone that what he wanted us to do was right.'

He brought in a dietitian and a doctor who came into the training ground and instructed the players, and even their wives, as to what they should and should not be eating. Recuperation, diet and treatment became his Holy Trinity. 'He was very proactive in his approach, but he trusted us to take on board what he was telling us,' added Arribart. 'It wasn't as if he'd spy on us and see if any of us went out in the evening or not. There was a trust there. He'd talk to us, and we felt involved in what he wanted the club to be like. He asked a lot of his players, but, at the same time, he'd speak with us and see how we felt about the things he was making us do. He listened to what the squad were saying. But he was still learning. There were still areas where he was less com- fortable, as his reaction to defeat showed. He became more mature when he went on to AS Monaco.'

Tactically, Wenger was forced to juggle his playing resources with his options severely limited by the club's lack of financial clout. In 1986 a left winger called Eric de Meco arrived on loan from Olympique de Marseille and, having failed to impress on the flank, was transformed into a wing-back, a position in which he later represented his country. Eric Bertrand went from striker to full-back and flourished. But, despite the manager's skills at improvisation and a respectable 12th-place finish in his first season, Nancy were always a club punching well above their weight.

The best players upped and left each summer despite Wenger's attempts to keep them, the Uruguayan playmaker

Ruben Umpierrez joining the Parisian lower-division club Matra Racing, Bruno Martini – a goalkeeper who went on to play 31 times for France – moving to Auxerre. Arsène was holding back the tide. The team stayed up by the skin of their teeth in his second season, beating his former club Mulhouse in a play-off to avoid relegation despite contriving to lose the second leg 2–0 to progress 3–2 on aggregate, but there was an inevitability about their demotion a year later.

That relegation remains the only demotion of Wenger's 30-year football career. 'When Nancy went down after struggling for the entire season, Arsène congratulated his players who were, at his own admission, at best only mediocre,' added Jean-Claude Cloet. 'He said they had done all that they could, that they had given their maximum. He even said he was proud of them. Who else would have reacted like that?' Within a matter of weeks after this failure, one of the biggest clubs in Europe was knocking on Wenger's door to offer him a more promising future than life in the Second Division. AS Monaco awaited.

La Turbie. Altitude: 480 metres. Number of inhabitants: 3,043. The road bends up into the hills, high above the Principality some 10 km away, with the prefabs in staggered rows tracing the road to the entrance to AS Monaco's training ground. One of the most powerful clubs in French football plots its progress here, at this giddy altitude on the hillside overlooking the Mediterranean. Inside the first of the training blocks, a red tracksuit top hangs from the rack. Emblazoned on its breast, in striking white letters, is the number 25. It belongs to Arsène Wenger. 'At Turbie, Arsène didn't have his own office,' recalled one of the players who worked under Wenger at Monaco. 'Instead, he shared a workspace with all the other coaches and technical staff. Our training complex was pretty basic. You'd go in the entrance and on the left-hand side was the treatment area where the club doctors worked. At the far end was the first-team changing room. There was a waiting room to the right, and in the next room the coaches worked. That's where Wenger spent his time.' Arsène would make this journey up into the hills to Monaco's training pitches daily between 1987 and 1994. The facilities may not have been plush, but it was there that he planned and plotted some of the greatest victories in the club's history, a league title in 1988, and a French Cup success in 1991. It was there, too, that he also picked over the bones of high-profile and costly defeats, from the titles that slipped away to Olympique de Marseille in 1989 and 1993, to the Cup Winners' Cup final surrendered to Werder Bremen in 1992.

Arsène Wenger, when managing Arsenal, once said: 'I always honour my contract.' That statement needs qualifying. Twice in his career, at Nancy and later at Grampus Eight, Wenger infuriated his then employers by listening to offers and then allowing himself to be seduced by other clubs. In his defence, the guilty suitors who came calling, AS Monaco and Arsenal, offered the ambitious young manager appreciable steps up.

In fact, the man who should have ended up coaching Monaco in the mid- to late 1980s was none other than Gilbert Gress, the manager who had brought Wenger to Strasbourg in the late 1970s and had played him in that ill-fated Uefa

Cup tie on a freezing night against Duisberg. In 1986 the l'ASM president Jean-Louis Campora had approached his first-choice candidate with a view to bringing him to Stade Louis II only for Gress, who had left FC Bruges for the Swiss club Neuchâtel Xamax, to decline the chance to move to the south of France. Disappointed at that rejection, Campora took advice from Richard Conte and duly turned his attentions instead to Gress's protégé, a man of far less standing and experience than the coach of Xamax: Arsène Wenger. Conte would end up negotiating Wenger's move to Monaco in secret over the ensuing 15 months. Monaco's initial approach was made over a year before Arsène eventually took up the reins, while he was still attempting to keep Nancy in the French top flight. The Nancy president Rousselot refused to release Wenger from the final year of his contract, despite his coach's clear desire to take up the challenge in the south, and, with Monaco unwilling to pay a compensation package to their rival club for his services, Arsène – as disappointed as he was – was forced to honour his deal.

Yet his dialogue with Conte and, indirectly, Campora was maintained throughout that final year at Nancy while Stefan Kovacs, the 65-year-old former Steaua Bucharest and Ajax coach, was used as a stopgap at Stade Louis II. Wenger knew where he would be working next over a year before his deal at Nancy expired, a rare advantage in a world where jobs are accepted and lost at a frightening pace. He never spoke a word of this at the time, aware that he was under contract, but the knowledge that he had a job to go to must have offered some consolation when Nancy slipped out of the First Division in May 1987. Regardless of that failure, Monaco's interest was maintained and the free agent was immediately snapped up.

That summer, Wenger packed his bags and headed south, naturally turning to his old friend from AS Cannes, Conte, for help finding lodgings just as he had done a few years previously. The pair duly became neighbours in the same apartment block in Villefranche-sur-Mer, some 250 m from the seafront. It was an elegant little flat, comprising three rooms and enough space in which to live comfortably, even if it was only supposed to be a temporary arrangement before he found somewhere bigger and more permanent to live. As it was, he ended up staying there throughout his seven years at the club with his friendship with Conte developing in that time.

Conte found the Wenger who had returned from Nancy even more determined to succeed than he had been with Cannes. The pair would sit up for hours, Wenger talking football and, steadily, Conte getting to understand his friend better. 'Those sessions would go on for ever,' he said. 'Gradually, we got to know each other better, though I think it was always up to me to steer the conversation occasionally away from football and on to other things. Arsène was always obsessing over the training session he was going to implement the next day. I remember he used to go jogging when he could – he found that a source of relaxation.' Those jogs took him along the seafront, or up into the hills around Villefranche, with his long legs pounding either the sand or the tarmac. Conte would join him on the cross-country treks. 'With his character and his tenacity, he had set ideas as to what he wanted to do. I remember one evening, down on the beach, he didn't really fancy the route I'd planned out. I don't think I'd told him beforehand exactly where I wanted us to go that night, and when he saw where I was taking him, he just shot off in the other direction. He'd thought the route was going to be shorter. I remember thinking he was right behind me and, at one point, I glanced back to see him 200 metres away and running in the opposite direction. He just knew what he wanted to do and would make sure he did it, that's all.'

Even before he took up the reins officially at Monaco that summer, Wenger had been working behind the scenes to put together a team at Stade Louis II which was both elegant to watch and also strong, sturdy and efficient. A team built in his mould. Glenn Hoddle, granted a free transfer by Tottenham Hotspur, had been plucked from under the nose of Gérard Houllier at Paris St Germain and headed for the Principality. Patrick Battiston, out of contract at Bordeaux, was intrigued by what Wenger was proposing at Monaco and moved south. Mark Hateley, the England striker whose career was stalling at AC Milan having fallen foul of the Italian clubs' three-foreigner rule, came across the border into France. As well as bringing in high-quality players and reviving confidence amongst the established squad, whose results had suffered over the previous few years (their last league title had been claimed in 1982, with their last silverware the French Cup of 1985), the new coach had to strike up a rapport with the players.

Once the squad had returned from their pre-season training camp in Switzerland, the manager made a point of speaking to each of them individually, whether they were key members of the first team or back-up players from the reserves. 'I remember, above all, that he wanted to give me a message: that I was part of his plans for the forthcoming season and I had a part to play at the club under his management,' recalled Manuel Amoros, one of the side's stalwarts and, for a while, the most capped France international. 'But he also wanted to get an idea of my state of mind, and a picture of what the mood at the club was like. I got the impression he wanted to establish a rapport with us, myself and my team-mates, so he could go on to relay to us what he wanted us to do out on the pitch.'

Amoros, now coaching Kuwait's under-18s, appreciates that he owes much to the tutelage he underwent with Wenger. The new manager's ability to inspire his players would become evident with others in that team, such as Luc Sonor whose game he improved to the extent that he ended up in the France side.

Jean-Luc Ettori, a veteran goalkeeper who had arrived at Monaco aged 20 back in 1975 and would go on to play 602 games for the club in an 18-year spell, had just endured something of a torrid season when Wenger arrived. He remembers even now the first words uttered to him by the new coach: 'I want to see the Ettori that I used to see playing all the time.' 'I learnt so much from him,' said Ettori. 'I took on his passion for the game, his patience, his desire to work so hard, and his intelligence rubbed off on me. One day, he told me: "What's important is that your team-mates have complete faith in you, even if you don't have complete faith in yourself." At half-time he'd restore your confidence even if you'd had a nightmare in the first half.'

The Wenger who took charge at La Turbie was very different from the more carefree Wenger who had made so many friends back at Mutzig, years previously. He was approachable and almost fatherly in his outlook with his players, but he was completely obsessed with football and engrossed in the game. 'He virtually lived at the training ground, with his apartment back in Villefranche-sur-Mer anything but homely,' recalled a club-mate from the late 1980s. 'All he had in his flat was a bed, a settee and his television. It was always in a right state, with clothes flung everywhere, and he'd never attempt to keep it tidy.' His office back at the Louis II stadium was just as Spartan. There was a chair, a desk and a television, video cassettes as ever strewn around the place. Hours and hours of footage of games from all around the world. He'd spend his hours flitting between La Turbie and his office at the ground, in the middle of the Principality, occasionally breaking up his work with the first team to visit the youth team's coaching staff to discuss the youngsters' development. His work stretched around the clock, his enthusiasm never dampened.

The players gradually became accustomed to his style. Claude Puel, a defensive midfielder and one of the most experienced players at the club when the new coach arrived, noted that the new manager boasted three essential attributes: tactical nous, an ability to analyse on the spot, and a willingness to keep things simple. 'His training sessions were always interesting, though he didn't put too much emphasis on physical or endurance work. On the other hand, he was the first coach I'd played under who would give us specific tactical training. He set that trend at Monaco.'

'There weren't many First Division teams at the time who played zonal marking in defence,' added Fabrice Dubois, a reserve-team player with Monaco back then who recognised early on that the new senior side's coach was something of a groundbreaker. 'You'd see that style with a few national teams, but rarely at club level in France. Arsène put that in place at Monaco. I remember the tips he'd give us and little tactical nuances to help us mark our opponents, almost allowing us to get inside the forward's head to predict where he would make his run. That's invaluable when you're doing zonal marking.'

Yet, while the manager may have appeared innovative, Puel rejects the idea that Wenger was a revolutionary. What struck him rather more back then was Arsène's desire to get his idea across quickly and simply to his team, remaining calm and almost detached even when games were threatening to boil over. 'His management style was well considered, well thought out, and even though he did occasionally get very angry, the pressure very rarely seemed to get on top of him,' said Puel. 'What struck me was his ability to analyse on the spur of the moment. His pre-match talks lasted no longer than ten or fifteen minutes. He only made a few points at half-time, too, keeping things brief and to the point.'

'He may have been a great technician, but above all he understood people,' added Dubois. 'He saw his role as to transmit the confidence he had in his team to the players, and give them self-belief. He may have been charismatic and a great thinker, but he kept things extremely simple. He knew his subject inside out, and the players admired him for that. I think he actually respected footballers, and people in general, and that helped him.'

Even if Wenger retained a certain distance from the squad, never allowing his charges to get too close, what surprised many of the staff at AS Monaco and the players in particular was his desire to ask them questions and throw the floor open for their opinions. 'He was curious about things,' said Amoros. 'Curious because he was keen still to learn. He was a young coach who wanted to understand the game better and open his mind to new ideas. He acknowledged, I think, that he was still learning. Even when he wasn't out on the training pitch, he spent lots of time in his office scrutinising the role played by everybody at the club, from players to his back-room team. That allowed him to analyse in what direction the team and club were going. I think it was that openness to new ideas and willingness to see the club evolve that made you realise even back then that this was a man destined for great things.'

Inevitably, certain aspects did change immediately under the new manager. He brought in specialists – physios, sprint coaches, weight experts, and a team doctor – to hone the players physically, and kept notes on the squad's progress in terms of their fitness. Likewise, the dietitians were soon in place. 'Suddenly, out of the blue, we'd find the canteen crammed with Kellogg's cereals, white cheeses, white meat rather than red, pasta and purées,' said Amoros. 'We all bought into his ideas. Of course, we'd eaten things like pasta before he'd arrived but never really thought about why we were eating them. Under Wenger, the meals and their benefits were outlined to us in a very clear and easy way to understand.' But it wasn't just in diet that the coach was so meticulous. It stretched to tactical preparation as well, with the team sitting through a 45-minute lecture (with the help of a video) ahead of each game, detailing which opponent each player should pick up and how the other side liked to play. 'He had a drawing board and he'd scribble diagrams on it, telling us what to expect and what to do,' added Amoros. 'We'd sit through it before we left for the ground before a game and he'd tell us the team line-up we'd be putting out. I can still see that paper board now . . .'

Wenger's tactical planning was at the forefront of new techniques in his profession. At Monaco, Wenger used a data-collection program called Top Score, put in place by his friend Jean-Marc Guillou. The system worked by analysing and interpreting each player's individual performance, giving a mark for everything he did during a game, whether attacking or defending. It was a precursor to the modern-day ProZone, the analysis program used extensively in the Premiership which tracks players' movement and performance in minute detail.

'The majority of the players who scored highly in Top Score went on to enjoy very successful careers,' said Arsène, with two of the best examples being George Weah and Lilian Thuram. 'George often walked away from games with the best score. The results accumulated by Top Score used to reassure me of my judgement when other people at the club were doubting players' performances. At one stage, everyone was saying my faith in Thuram was completely misplaced, and that he didn't warrant his place in the team. I actually started asking myself whether I'd called it correctly by playing him every week. But, when I consulted Top Score, there it was in black and white . . . I was right.'

In private, Wenger would speak with Hoddle and Hateley in English. He'd ask his African players such as the Ivorian Youssouf Fofana (who had arrived at the club in 1985) or those from the French overseas colonies such as Thuram (the defender, originally from Guadeloupe, graduated into the first team in 1990) about their experiences back home. The manager would ask them whether they were happy, ask how their families were, but he would always remain enigmatic and slightly distant. There was a natural authority to him that was maintained throughout. Ettori, looking back, likened him to a shepherd looking after his flock. 'That's not a bad analogy,' said Amoros. 'He certainly was an important figure in the development of AS Monaco because he knew how to take the team on, introducing new ideas en route, whilst keeping the established members of the club happy.'

During 1987–88, his first season in charge, the team got behind him and swept all before them in the league. 'He'd surrounded himself with people who he trusted,' said the defender Manu. 'From his first day at the club, we'd been won over and things went well.' AS Monaco were crowned champions in May, their first league title in six years having been secured largely as a result of the meticulous, almost scientific work undertaken by their manager. All those hours spent in preparation had paid off, though the success was also due to Wenger's conciliatory style with the players. 'If he'd spoken to us in a different way, and hadn't maybe kept us onside, it might not have gone as well as it did,' admitted Amoros, who would leave for Olympique de Marseille a year later, enticed by the prospect of playing for a better-supported club. 'As it was, everyone bought into his ideas and hung on his every word. At no stage was there a problem between any of the players and the manager, and that was obvious when we went out on the pitch for him.'

The success achieved in the Principality was rooted in the work Wenger undertook on the training pitch, but it also benefited from his labours that often went unnoticed behind the scenes. For Arsène, the ability to act astutely in the transfer market, scouring the globe for fresh talent, was paramount. Ultimately, to uncover a gem was, for him, almost as satisfying as claiming silverware – a precursor, perhaps, to his days at Arsenal. The Alsatian sniffed out some bargains: there were youngsters or players who had been shunted to one side in France, but whose careers he sought to resuscitate; or others who had been forgotten and yet found the Monaco manager keen to take them under his wing. He looked further afield to previously untapped markets, in particular Africa. At one stage Henri Biancheri, the sporting director at ASM, was dispatched to Cameroon with his mission clear: to sign a player of huge potential called George Weah. Within a few weeks, the Liberian had left his club, Tonnerre Yaoundé, for a life in Monte Carlo. He'd never see a single casino during his time in the money-flushed Principality.

'At first, I thought Arsène interfered too much in my private life when I arrived,' said Weah, who was Wenger's first signing from Africa. 'It was almost as if he was running my life against my will but, in the end, all the sacrifices he made me make paid off. He was always there to encourage me, not always just in his role of coach, but also as a father figure. I appreciated his support even more because he was white and I was black. I've often suffered racism from white footballers over my years in the game. But Arsène, a white man, always took care of me, always gave me good advice and would repeat, over and over again: "If you work hard with me as I ask you to do, you will become one of the best players in the world." During the five years I spent at Monaco, Arsène inspired so much confidence in me. He taught me how to live, how to respect others, how to respect the game, and the sacrifices you have to make to do well.'

Yet the successes enjoyed by Wenger at La Turbie and Stade Louis II, with his side clad in red and white roaring their way to the title, began to prompt jealousy elsewhere in France. Pascal Olmeta, the Marseille goalkeeper at the time, voiced the opinion shared by many within French football when he said: 'It would make me furious to see Monaco become the first *French* club to win the European Cup.' Back then, Luc Sonor had retorted: 'Personally, when it comes to European competition, I'd always be right behind any French club competing, even l'OM.' But for some, the tax haven and Principality of Monaco will never be accepted into the family of French football. For Wenger, the spirit of 'us and them' must have conjured up memories of his time back at home in Alsace, a heavily Germanic area of France which has changed hands often in the course of history.

Yet within the club there was a sense of solidarity which united the players, the coaching staff and even the juniors in the youth-team set-up. Everybody was working towards the same end and, in this gilded environment, one rule was paramount: absolute fairness. There was to be equal treatment between players, equal treatment between players and the management, with everyone fighting for the same cause, and even eating (and drinking) the same thing. Wenger surrounded himself with dietitians to guide him in his choice of food. When his cook at Monaco tried to tempt the Alsatian with calorie-laden local specialities, Wenger retorted: 'It is out of the question for me to eat different food than the players. I will have exactly the same as them.'

The club's dietitian at that time, Yann Rougier, confirmed the coach's rigid attitude. 'Before he had arrived in Monaco, it had been customary for there to be two tables – one set for the players, the other for the management,' he said. 'Each effectively ate what he wanted, ordering their favourite food from the chef, and the managers even demanded the best wines, especially vintage. When Arsène saw that, he asked me exactly what the players needed to eat in order to perform better. I gave him a list of food and drinks and, from then on, pre-match meals – including for away games – were made up of exactly what I had recommended.'

The Monaco coach did not tolerate any rule-breaking, even on diet, and insisted that his back-room staff were subjected to the same rules as his players. Rougier was impressed by this hard-line approach. 'At first, when they saw low-fat butter on the table, still water served at room temperature, and crudités accompanied by oil and lemon, some wanted to go and eat in the next room.' On one occasion, when the entire team and staff were staying at a hotel on an away trip, certain members of the coaching set-up tried to sneak food more to their taste – and not exactly food which complied with the imposed diet – into the dining room. Wenger spotted them and was furious. 'I forbid you from bringing food into the dining room that the players cannot have,' he declared. 'If you cannot do without it, I insist you leave the room immediately!'

'Before our European Cup match against Manchester United at Old Trafford, I saw Wenger go down to the hotel dining room some four hours before the meal,' said Dr Rougier. 'He asked for the bottles of mineral water that had been put aside for the pre-match meal to be brought out by the hotel staff, which confused them as there were still hours to go before the team were due to take their seats at the dinner table. But Arsène knew that if the bottles were removed from the fridge at the last minute they would be too cold when the players drank them, and with cold drinks hindering digestion he wanted water to be served at room temperature. When the bottles arrived, he touched them to feel their temperature and even ran his finger over some of them to see if there was any condensation. When the players arrived, the water was at the perfect temperature. Oh, and in the end . . . we won the match.'

Didier Roustan, whose Foot Citoyen association boasts Arsène Wenger as its honorary president, was no less surprised by this rigour, some would say severity, in respect of the club's cooks and coaching staff. He was, after all, equally demanding with other employees. 'Arsène is generally a peaceful man and I have only seen him get angry once, in Monaco, when he confronted a stadium groundsman who had done a bad job,' said Roustan. 'The groundsman was insolent and patronising in response to Wenger's criticism, and that prompted Arsène to fly into one of his rages. I had never seen anything like it. It wasn't cruel as such, but the "strict" way he spoke to the groundsman really surprised me, and the man soon backed down. Wenger has this strict, hard side, but also a very dry, deadpan sense of humour, and he can be very witty. He makes me laugh, but it is his real class, both in terms of his appearance and morality, that I remember most. It is a false calm which is not at all detached. He likes to go to the heart of the matter.'

In 1995 George Weah, who had scored 59 goals in four seasons for Monaco, won European football's major individual accolade whilst playing for AC Milan. France Football's *Ballon d'Or* (Golden Ball) was to be presented to the forward in the Italian city, and when Weah learnt that Wenger too was to be in Milan on business, he got hold of a ticket for his mentor and invited him to the evening event, albeit without explaining precisely why.

Arsène, none the wiser, accepted the invitation and duly sat down to dine surrounded by the guests in tuxedos and the numerous bottles of champagne. Wenger still didn't know the name of the winner of the main award and Weah, now a politician and head of the opposition in his home country after a stab at the presidential elections in Liberia, to this day chuckles at the memory of that ceremony. 'When my name was announced for the *Ballon d'Or*, I told the hall that we had a very special guest present,' he said. 'Of course, it was my former coach, Arsène. I said that he, not I, deserved the award.' 'Big George' then asked his former coach to leave his seat and join him on the stage. Amidst a flood of emotions,

Wenger went pale and seemed to shrink in the spotlight. Perhaps his mind had gone back over his own career: time spent on the pitch and on the bench, the leather and rubber balls he practised with so diligently back in Alsace, his apprenticeship on the terraces of the *Bundesliga*, the hours of training, black and white pictures and video cassettes; decades lived only for football.

Hesitantly, he joined his ex-protégé on the podium. This former amateur from Duttlenheim, who had worn the kit of small clubs from Mutzig to AS Vauban, stood there brandishing the *Ballon d'Or*. He could barely even hold it . . . 'He was really very nervous,' grinned Weah. 'I thought he would die that evening – I really thought he might have a heart attack! I will always be grateful for him and I always tell people that it is thanks to him that I am the player and man I am today. This is why he deserved the prize more than me.' The connection between the pair almost prompted a reunion in the mid-1990s when the protégé was ready to rejoin his mentor at Arsenal, only for Wenger to pursue another striker who had made his name at Monaco: a certain Thierry Henry.

Figures both within and outside the club soon noted Wenger's ability to integrate and assimilate. Those in the youth and reserve set-up were also charmed by his altruism. Fabrice Dubois, a second-team player who was suffering from osteoarthritis of the knee which restricted him to the sidelines, recalled the manager's approach. 'Whenever he had the chance, he'd take me with him to professional training sessions,' he said. 'That was a great comfort to me. It meant he hadn't forgotten me.'

The club's doctors could not come up with a precise diagnosis for Dubois's injury. They investigated whether his pain was the result of a cartilage problem, but it persisted. Dubois, sitting in his office as manager of the Châteauroux youth team, remembered mentioning these problems to Wenger. The coach of the first team listened to the semi-pro intently. 'Right away, he told me: "Go to the administrative department – tell them I sent you there – and ask them for a ticket from Nice to Strasbourg to go and see Professor Jaeger."'

The young injured player did as he was instructed and went to Colmar, where he saw one of the world's foremost knee specialists. 'To get the appointment, I knew Arsène had gone over the heads of the doctor and my own team coach at the time. He didn't have to, but he did it.' Dubois found out, after tests, that he did indeed have cartilage problems. A few years later, on the eve of the 2002 World Cup, Arsène Wenger did exactly the same thing when he sent Robert Pires to see the surgeon. 'His kindness touched me,' said the former France midfielder, 'but Arsène would keep continuing to surprise me.'

Generosity, for Arsène Wenger, goes hand in hand with the most demanding standards. But, occasionally, he could be intransigent. Dubois can recall an incident in the prefab dressing rooms at La Turbie which makes him shiver anxiously to this day. 'Arsène was having a right go at a player,' he said. 'It was Luiz Henrique, the Brazilian international. He was a player of real standing, a midfielder who had even scored against France at Parc des Princes and had captained a great Brazil team, yet Arsène was willing to shame him in front of everyone. All because he had apparently arrived five minutes late for training. I don't think Luiz understood French very well, but Arsène was gesticulating and pointing at his watch, so he soon understood his mistake!'

In fact, the Brazilian had broken one of Wenger's golden rules. All players, without exception, must be in the changing room half an hour before the beginning of a training session. Punctuality, which ensured the players were in optimum condition before training, was one of the lessons that Fabrice Dubois took from the Wenger era at Le Rocher. 'This is a trick that has stayed with me,' he said. 'I ask my youngsters to be in the changing room 20 minutes before training starts. This means they have a bit of time to talk amongst themselves, exchange pleasantries, but above all prepare calmly so they can start the session in good condition.'

There was no time for Wenger's players to sunbathe or enjoy the view from the top of La Turbie. The sessions instigated in training, as well as their duration, varied from day to day but were mainly limited to two or three tactical exercises aimed at ensuring good team cohesion. 'In terms of relationships, Wenger saw everyone every day, but only intervened to speak to individuals when he had to,' noted Claude Puel, now managing Lille but a former player-manager at Monaco. Alongside Hoddle and Puel, two other Monaco players of that era – Dominique Bijotat and Franck Dumas at Sochaux and Caen respectively – would go on to enjoy careers in the dugout, and all will have taken inspiration from what they learnt from Wenger.

'At one point I felt Arsène was leaving me on the bench too often,' said Puel with a smile. 'He had organised a small match between us during training and he decided to take part. I tackled him in the game, he went flying and landed on his back. He couldn't move. He wasn't happy, but that didn't stop him putting me in the starting line-up for the next game.' This tolerance – a word commonly used in relation to Wenger – could be explained by his dedication to and empathy for his players, according to Puel. 'He respects players and they realise as much. His slender and tall build also give him a natural authority, and he doesn't need to shout or raise his voice.' Gilles Grimandi, another Monaco stalwart who would later join Wenger at Arsenal along with Manu Petit, puts it another way. 'Arsène made his players afraid,' he said. 'Few dared to stand up to him or talk back to him.'

The young and immensely talented Youri Djorkaeff was also regularly left on the sidelines by Wenger. The coach felt his younger players could learn a bit of humility during their apprenticeship from regular stints on the substitutes' bench. Hard work and strict discipline were two mantras preached at La Turbie and were subsequently taken by Claude Puel to Lille. During Wenger's sessions, three distinct qualities complemented each other: looking out for one another, paying attention to detail, and the work ethic.

'At Monaco, Wenger was a young leader,' recalled Puel. 'He was only 38, but he sweated blood for his team. His technical, physiological and tactical skills never stopped improving.' However, that first championship in 1988 aside, the time and care spent in preparing for matches never really prompted tangible rewards. Monaco may have claimed the Coupe de France, the French equivalent of the FA Cup, in 1991, but they had lost the 1989 cup final 4–3 to Marseille and lost the final of the Cup Winners' Cup in 1990. Invariably, they were the nearly men of the French league: they finished third in 1989, and were frustrated runners-up in 1991 and 1992. The following summer would see a restructuring of the team and set-up. The end of an era beckoned.

In the summer of 1992, AS Monaco was a side in limbo between two eras. Wenger was intent upon revenge, as the club's rivalry with Olympique de Marseille reached its peak. L'OM had just walked away with the championship for the fourth year in a row. The pretenders from the Côte d'Azur had fought hard, against the odds in Arsène's opinion, but for the second season in a row, they had ended as also-rans. Although 1991–92 had technically been one of their most successful seasons, Monaco had failed to win any trophies, and the time had come to restructure and plan a fresh future.

With the summer transfer market in full swing, and with training due to resume at La Turbie, Arsène Wenger took some time out to visit the plushest restaurant on the seafront in Nice. As he descended the steps leading to the *Beau Rivage* beach, the Monaco trainer entered this haunt of the stars. The reservation was not in Wenger's name, but in that of the restaurateur, Robert Zaigue. The proprietor was used to celebrities, regularly hosting the likes of David Niven and the French comedian Jacques Weber, yet he was still impressed by the Alsatian's charisma.

'He had an immensely seductive quality, the type of quality only men who are completely oblivious to it can possess,' he said. 'He reminded me a little of a romantic hero from a bygone age. But you can't compare Arsène with an actor or artist, because stars of stage or screen work for themselves, while Arsène works for a team. He has a unique personality, and cannot be compared with anyone else.'

A table for two had been set facing the sea in a corner of the *Beau Rivage*, with Wenger ordering a litre of Badoit mineral water to quench his thirst. There were no aperitifs, no wine and no digestifs. 'Wenger exudes kindness and simplicity, but he has the discipline and rigour of the sporting greats,' noted the restaurateur, who these days is also an expatriate based in London and the owner of the biggest French library in the United Kingdom. Wenger ate and left the restaurant as quietly as he had arrived, Robert Zaigue thanking him as he departed and saying he hoped the manager 'would continue his great work with AS Monaco'. 'He responded with extraordinary simplicity: *One does one's best.* I noted he used *one* rather than *I*. And he told me this while looking me in the eye, in that upright stance of his.' But, etched on Wenger's face, there were already signs of concern. The innocence and insouciance had already started to fade. Since the spring of 1992, suspicion and questions had started to surface.

Jean Petit, Wenger's right-hand man at ASM for seven years, reflected on that period of uncertainty. The names in that team of 1992 trip off the former assistant's tongue: Djorkaeff, Fofana, Passi, Rui Barros, Thuram, Weah. 'We had the best players in France,' he said. 'With such a squad, with such players, we wanted to keep the structure in place for subsequent years. It was so frustrating that we didn't manage to do that . . .' There were hints of a lump in his throat as his voice trailed off. When he talks about this era his words are tinged with sadness. Petit recalled how the spring had started so well: reaching the final of the Coupe de France, as well as the Cup Winners' Cup final. The team's domestic and Continental campaigns had both been a success up to then; now the only thing missing was the trophies.

Monaco travelled to Lisbon for the European final against Werder Bremen, one of the best sides at the time in the Bundesliga. The eve of this Continental clash had seen the other semi-final of the Coupe de France in Corsica, pitching Bastia against Marseille at the Furiani stadium. But tragedy had struck. Two temporary stands collapsed, leaving 18 dead and 2,300 injured. 'It was bizarre,' said Petit. 'We were watching the television and these incidents were being shown in a loop, 24 hours a day. We wondered how such a thing could have happened. When we heard the news we decided amongst ourselves that we couldn't play the final. The authorities also wanted to cancel the match at first as a mark of respect for those who had died, but then they changed their minds. Apparently, life went on and we had to play, which wasn't what we wanted to hear.'

For Wenger, those 48 hours passed in something of a daze. The manager was wallowing almost in a depression. 'Arsène was inconsolable,' explained Petit. 'He asked what we were doing over there. We were about to play a match in Portugal, when football had been, well, killed by this tragedy.' On Wenger's orders, players were instructed to remain closeted in their hotel and were forbidden from going into town, reflecting the manager's concerns about press intrusion. In the corridors of the hotel the team, lead by the Corsican Ettori, prepared sombrely for the match, attempting to block out their sense of pain. It hardly helped that a party of French journalists, who had been present at Bastia as the tragedy had unfurled, duly arrived in Lisbon to cover the game. Deeply affected, Wenger opted to leave his side and travelled to Corsica to pay his respects to the victims. 'You can't play when other people have lost their lives,' said Petit, sharing his manager's sentiments at the time. On his return, Arsène Wenger spoke to the assembled press before the Cup Winners' Cup final, merely indicating that those who had died would be on the minds of those sent out to play.

'On the night of the game, we arrived at this massive stadium in Lisbon which can house 120,000 people to find only 15,000 spectators sitting there,' said Puel. 'There was absolutely no atmosphere. The banks of empty seats made it feel like a non-league game. It was unnerving, and we were all affected. Even Wenger, whose job it was to overcome such situations and motivate us, ensuring we were concentrating on the job at hand, was subdued. It was a non-match, a flat occasion.'

Monaco lost meekly, succumbing 2–0. Wenger's post-match assessment was significant: 'When you have lost the final of the European cup, you have hit rock bottom.' Ettori reiterated the coach's sense of despair. 'For him, the best homage we could pay the Corsicans was to win, and in some way make up for their loss,' he said. 'But what happened instead was horrible.'

If the game was anticlimactic, the subsequent break-up of

the team was another source of intense regret. 'For me, the disintegration of that squad took place in May 1992,' said Puel. 'We had just finished a great season. Some 15 days from the end of the championship, we were still tied with Olympique de Marseille with hopes of claiming the title, and we had reached the finals of the Coupe de France and the Cup Winners' Cup, but we ended up fading horribly. As a group, we had a great team – not technically brilliant but with real character. George Weah, Rui Barros, all players with flair. We were causing trouble to all the great sides of that era, beating the likes of AS Roma and Feyenoord. Then the team broke up. That is a shame because we had so much more to achieve.'

There is a familiar photograph dating from the Wenger era at AS Monaco. In it, Arsène, spectacled and grinning manically, hugs his assistant Jean Petit with their temples pressed together and both smiling from ear to ear. Their expressions may be slightly different, but pure joy radiates from each. Both are wearing dark blue overcoats with the crest of the club, and are celebrating winning the 1988 title. The pair would only be united in the joy of success once more – at Parc des Princes for the 1991 Coupe de France. Petit often reflects on this period at the end of the 1980s and the beginning of the 1990s, when their main rival was Olympique de Marseille. This was an unequal battle in more ways than one.

'We finished as champions the first year that Arsène held the reigns, then we were second five times in a row [in fact ASM was third in 1989],' said Petit. 'We should have been able to share Marseille's five victories more or less equally –

I'm not saying we were better than l'OM, but I think we should have been able to win two or three of the five titles.' In actual fact, that Monaco were unable to prevail against their rivals was not because they lacked the skill to compete, but because Marseille were playing an underhand game.

Paul Frantz was a confidant of Wenger's during his period with Monaco and is even more forthcoming. 'One day, Arsène admitted to me that this was one of the worst times in his life, the worst thing he had had to deal with,' he said. 'His greatest disappointment was certainly the setback he suffered with Monaco. And the perpetrator – well, it was none other than Bernard Tapie. He bribed players on the Monaco team, which is the worst thing you can do. When you buy players from a rival team, you automatically kill the opposition dead.'

The rivalry between Wenger and Tapie, the controversial president of the biggest club in France, would even verge on the physical at times. 'The battle between Tapie's l'OM and AS Monaco was raging at the top of the table one year,' recalled Didier Roustan. 'In the tunnel at Marseille's Vélodrome stadium after a heated match between the two clubs, Arsène had to be physically restrained after flying into a rage following a distant shouting match with Tapie in the corridors. The match had been particularly physical, especially on the part of Marseille, and Arsène wasn't happy. Tapie, with his usual delicacy, was condescending and shouted at his rival manager: "I've fucked you over, you and your shitty Monaco!"'

All Wenger's long-standing doubts were confirmed when Jean-Jacques Eydelie's autobiography was published in

January 2006. Eydelie, a former Marseille midfielder, revealed that he had been asked to contact three players at Valenciennes by the l'OM board ahead of a critical league game in 1993 to offer them bribes. 'All l'OM's players knew about it, and most of them had even participated in the arrangements,' stated Eydelie. He also described in detail the illegal approaches made to opponents. 'When I was still with Nantes, a really important player with l'OM called me. He asked me to do what I myself asked the Valenciennes team to do a few months later. He told me: "I know you're going to be at Marseille next year, so it would be good if you could help us with this match."'

Eydelie was subsequently banned for 12 months by Fifa for the part he played in the scandal which cost Marseille their 1993 French league title, and their chance to defend the European Cup, and saw them relegated to the Second Division for two years. Tapie was later jailed for six months. Wenger has always maintained it must have been easy for l'OM's opponents to fake their intent. 'You barely have to lift your feet [to cheat],' he said. 'All you have to do is take a corner a bit too far to the left or right, or be in marginally the wrong position either defensively or offensively. And you can even give the impression of having played well.'

After the statements made by the repenting Eydelie in his book, the Arsenal boss's judgement on l'OM's president was clear. 'We are talking here about the worst period in French footballing history, a time that was rotten to the core thanks to the influence and methods of Tapie in Marseille,' he said. 'What Eydelie said just confirmed what everyone was thinking.'

A full year before the Valenciennes controversy surfaced, at the end of the 1991–92 season, Wenger had suspected foul play, and that bribes had been passed between Marseille and some of his own players. That season, Monaco finished second in the championship after failing to catch up with l'OM. Previously excellent Monaco players had suddenly become clumsy in front of goal, or even in their own half. Needless fouls conceded penalties at crucial moments. Wenger said at that time that it was impossible for Monaco to become French champions. Later, he stressed that l'OM were 'a magnificent team, with exceptional players'. His implication was clear: the great Marseille didn't need to resort to cheating. One match, in particular, alerted Monaco's coaching staff. It was a 3–0 home defeat in April 1992 against the league leaders, with the performances of three of the AS players called into doubt. The trio were considered by the coach and his deputies as rotten eggs within the team, but Wenger refused to comment publicly on what he suspected had happened. He never made accusations or named names. He waited, saw how things developed, before eventually choosing his moment to act.

In that spring of 1992, with Monaco's pursuit of Marseille in full flow, Wenger called a meeting with one of the players on whom his suspicions centred. In the dressing room at La Turbie, the manager, accompanied by Petit, spoke with the accused. 'We asked him questions, we said that the whole situation was strange and that we had some doubts etc.,' said Petit. 'And then, at a given moment as Arsène had instructed, we laid a trap for the player. There were only three of us and he fell for it, telling us everything.'

Wenger's deputy was willing to testify in court as to what the pair had been told – 'I said to him, if you need me as a witness I'll be there' – but Wenger also suspected other team members of 'treason'. They opted instead to refer the case to the club's president, Jean-Louis Campora. So, why did the Monaco team not make a complaint? 'Because these things are always difficult,' added Petit. 'It was our word against that of the player. Unless it had been recorded, there would always have been some doubt. Arsène and I knew what was going on, we told our president, and there you have it.'

In 2006, some twelve years later, Wenger spoke of the stench of corruption which had tainted that troubled period. 'I wanted to warn people, make it public, but I couldn't prove anything,' he said. 'It was very hard. At that time, corruption and doping were big things, and there was nothing worse than knowing that the cards were stacked against us from the beginning.'

A Monaco source gives another reason for the club's reluctance to act in 1992. 'Wenger and Campora were both discreet people,' he said. 'In my opinion, this is what made them act as they did.' Evidence remained in short supply. Should the confession of the entrapped player have been made public? 'It would have just been claims and denials,' said Petit. 'When you claim something or deny something, there are always those who say: "We must have had something to do with it." Others think the claims are motivated by jealousy.' In the end, Wenger would resolve the problem in his own way, in private.

The Valenciennes affair would erupt a year later, in May 1993, the long-standing doubts about Tapie's honesty confirmed when a suitcase containing 25,000 francs was found buried in the garden of the in-laws of the Valenciennes player Christophe Robert. With confessions made and the corruption proven, Uefa banned Tapie's team from playing in the European Cup the following season. Ironically, it was Monaco who, after Paris St Germain had declined, took the place of l'OM in the competition. Jean-Luc Ettori and his team would go as far as the semi-final, where they were beaten by AC Milan. The former goalkeeper admitted that the confirmation of the corruption had been a huge shock. 'The story knocked us all for six,' he said. 'Arsène didn't want victory at any price – he had a great sense of morality, and that's why he's still in the game. Staying in such an environment is even harder for people like him – it takes more hard work, but this is precisely why he is still around.'

Another sad irony is that it was an Alsatian, the Valenciennes player Jacques Glassmen, who finally spoke out and brought Tapie down. L'OM would be stripped of their title as French champions, but would keep their European Cup which had been claimed against Milan at the end of the 1992–93 season. Yet, well before the law or the media, Wenger had long been aware that something had been going on behind the scenes. Claude Puel has never forgotten the bitterness felt by the Monaco manager at the unfair domination enjoyed by l'OM. 'Wenger's frustration was totally normal,' he said. 'Something was up, and the Monaco team knew it. The Valenciennes case just confirmed what we already knew. It was hard to take that we hadn't been competing on a level playing field with Marseille.'

Jean Petit confirmed the simmering antipathy between

Wenger, moral and modest, and Tapie, so publicly immoral. But the Monaco coach was to suffer an even worse blow as he felt he had lost the confidence of some of the board of directors, and that some even perhaps doubted his innocence. 'But Monaco hadn't been involved in the scam,' said Petit. 'The divorce between Wenger and the club really began because, after seven years at the club, Arsène suddenly felt that he no longer had the full support of the board. All the support he had received at the beginning started to ebb away towards the end.'

Wenger, hurt by the methods used by Marseille, said of the setback: 'We are living in an environment where only winning counts. Anyone who loves sport knows that when two boxers enter the ring, there can only be one winner. Yet, for all that, for a good fight you need two heroes. Unfortunately, today, too much attention is paid to the winner. I find that sad. Cheats are forgiven, as long as they win.' Wenger has often been criticised in England for 'not seeing anything' when his players are involved in dives or fights. That is because he puts loyalty to his players above all . . . as long as they remain within his 'ethical framework'. However, this loyalty is perhaps not always reciprocated. In the summer of 2006, Wenger would feel frustrated when Ashley Cole, a player he had nurtured through the academy at Arsenal and into the senior and full England teams, completed a transfer to Chelsea some 12 months after the Premier League had investigated claims that the full-back had been 'tapped up' by their west London rivals.

For the next two seasons, Monaco lost their sparkle despite the presence of jewels within their ranks. Players were still unearthed by Wenger and his team of scouts, and others lured to the Principality to delight the locals, such as Jürgen Klinsmann, who left in 1994 to join Arsenal's bitter rivals, Tottenham Hotspur. That year, the team had finished a lowly ninth and Wenger, on the verge of his eighth season, seemed to be losing his mystique. After two defeats against Nice and Le Havre, he was dismissed at the beginning of the autumn, after seven years of brilliance but missed opportunities. Arsène had been fired for the first time in his career, and he felt the time had come to leave: to get away from France and Monaco, where he was no longer wanted, and even far away from Europe, where he had already been forced to reject an approach from Bayern Munich by his ASM president Campora.

Now, all he wanted to do was escape. 'Whether you like it or not,' explained Wenger at the time, 'European culture is slightly one-dimensional. When you go from one country to another in Europe, you don't really have the impression of changing cultures.'

In Cannes in January 1999, with the annual film festival in its final stages, Wenger reflected on his sacking in Monaco and explained the sense of injustice he had felt at the time. 'Unfortunately, in France, the responsibilities of coaches are limited,' he said. 'However, often they pay for decisions which they themselves did not take. There is, therefore, a certain ambiguity [to the role].'

He felt compelled to defend his record, having felt so constrained at the end of his time at the club. 'There is increasing instability in the modern game, and this unfortunately puts the quality of the game and the spectacle it provides at risk,' he added. 'Everyone recognises that the perfect situation is to win every match. However, nobody can achieve this, even the best among us. It follows on from this that you need a certain stability, a certain confidence within the club which helps coaches to deal with difficult periods without becoming a scapegoat when results don't go the right way.' However, this confidence that Wenger needed was no longer on offer from the ASM board of directors. With that in mind, he started to listen to distant calls for his services.

In October 1994, Wenger flew to the United Arab Emirates, where Fifa had convened a series of tactical conferences. During the presentation he delivered to coaches from emerging football nations, Wenger offered a technical report on the World Cup finals, which had just been held for the first time in the United States. Listening keenly among the audience was a delegation from Japan, a country in the process of ploughing huge resources into developing its own national championship, the J League having been founded in 1993.

In Japan, major companies such as Mazda traditionally support a club to promote its success and ensure its financial viability. During his stay in the Emirates, the Alsatian was approached by Toyota, the owners of Nagoya Grampus Eight. The offer placed on the table was tempting. Wenger saw a chance to come up for air, and step back from life in France. 'I had worked for ten seasons in the French First Division, non-stop,' he conceded. 'I had reached an age where I knew that if I didn't seize this chance to try something different, to discover a totally different culture, I probably never would.'

Wenger was following his instinct, but also sought advice from others. While giving his conferences in the Emirates he met with an English journalist called Jeremy Walker, a specialist in Japanese football. With roles reversed, he rattled off dozens of questions on the game in the Far East, as well as on cultural customs. Walker responded to what was almost a sociological examination of Japan. He was surprised, years later, when Wenger called him by his first name during a press conference. Very rarely does Wenger name-check a member of the media, so it amounted to a compliment from Arsène.

Intrigued and interested in what Walker had said, as well as by the enthusiasm expressed by friends like Richard Conte, Wenger went to Nagoya in mid-November where he visited the Mizuho Stadium and attended a match between Grampus Eight and Hiroshima Sanfrecce. There he watched Gary Lineker, one of England's most prolific strikers and a former Tottenham player, make his last appearance for Nagoya. Japan at that time was the Qatar of today. Zico and Toto Schillaci were playing out their days in the J league as if it was a retirement home, but wasn't this financial paradise too fake for a down-to-earth person like Wenger?

'When I was contacted by Nagoya, I had never been to Japan before,' he recalled. 'I visited the club and I was enticed by its board of directors. The team was languishing at the bottom of the league, and I told myself: "Imagine starting with a team in last place."' Grampus had indeed just finished in last place in the 'autumn season' (known as the Nico

Series). Twelfth out of twelve, Nagoya couldn't be demoted only because, at that time, there was no Division Two into which to slip.

The attraction to work in the land of the rising sun was real, but negotiations would drag on for a whole month, with doubts appearing to hamper matters on both sides. Wenger returned to Villefranche-sur-Mer, close to his neighbour and friend Richard Conte. 'At that time he had a lot of questions about his future, and particular about families,' said Conte. 'He saw my children growing up and, although he was happy in his relationship, he kept on saying: "I don't have any children . . ."'

When Arsène finally departed for Nagoya, it was certainly not on a whim. He had reflected on the offer from Toyota throughout November and December before committing himself. 'In Japan I was faced with a different culture, different values, and at a moment in my life when perhaps I needed a fresh start,' said Wenger. 'When you are involved in football to this extent, where the sole priority is to win all the time, you end up neglecting other aspects of your life.'

The Japanese negotiators had their own unique style, but the whole process was frustrated by their indecision. Jean Petit recalled those weeks of waiting. 'Things dragged on until Arsène asked outright: "OK, do you want me or not? If so, here are my demands, so let's not discuss the matter any more."' Irritated by their failure to decide, and also frustrated, undoubtedly, by the lack of offers from elsewhere, Wenger gave the Japanese a 48-hour deadline. This was a challenge thrown down to end the procrastination. The Japanese yielded and offered their terms, and Wenger duly committed himself to Grampus Eight, signing a two-year contract in return for an annual salary of 75 million yen, or about £450,000 (£325,000 in today's rates).

Conte insists to this day that the manager's willingness to take such a roundabout route to the top ultimately attracted major clubs back in Europe. 'When, some 20 months later, he received offers from Bayern Munich, Arsenal and RC Strasbourg, he said to me: "You see? Who would have thought that going to Nagoya would have brought in offers from such great clubs?"'

'Maybe he wanted to get away from it all,' added Petit. 'For seven years he had done an exceptional job with AS Monaco, bringing the club up to European standards. That wasn't easy. He said he left because he couldn't live without football, but Arsène wanted to discover something else.'

Even during the painstaking negotiations with Toyota, Wenger never lost faith in his calling. Signing with Grampus only made him more human, as his old colleague Jean-Luc Arribart remarked. 'The time he spent in Nagoya was important to him spiritually and philosophically,' he said. 'It helped Arsène find himself, but it was only when he went to Arsenal, with greater resources at his disposal, that he really came into his own.' However, before the Gunners came Grampus.

Wenger stepped into the lobby of the international airport through which some 10 million passengers pass each year. This was a man who had come to Japan to get away from it all, only to find himself swept along in the mayhem of the airport foyer. He left the terminal, still lost in thought, and entered the chaos and smoke of the fourth-biggest town in Japan, Nagoya, the Pacific lapping at its port side. A city of two million inhabitants. At the beginning of 1995, there was not much tranquillity to the scene into which he stepped. The port of Nagoya, in fierce competition with Yokohama, Kobe and Osaka, swarms with cargo ships and docks. This industrial city, located 366 km south-west of Tokyo, is linked to the capital by the Shinkansen, the bullet train, which travels between the two towns in an hour and forty minutes. Nagoya, in Aichi prefecture, is a major megalopolis on Honshu, Japan's main island, and Aichi, host of the 2005 Expo, is a key Japanese economic centre. Agriculture and urbanisation cohabit alongside traditional crafts and high technology, with everything a chaos of Chinese products and aeronautical parts, artistic figures and ceramics. Aichi is also famous for its wooden cabinets, its calligraphy and Buddhist altars but, as curious as he was, Wenger wasn't here to discover such treasures. He had a mission to carry out: rebuilding a failing team.

In truth, he never doubted that his time in the Far East would be nothing more than a stopover to greater things. Yet the Frenchman still wanted to immerse himself in the place. This was an environment diametrically opposed to the plains of Alsace, its constant hubbub so alien from the main street in Duttlenheim. Wenger passed billboards and passers-by, long avenues and flamboyant new buildings. Nagoya isn't the ideal city for window shopping – the small stores in the centre are clinging on in the face of massive competition from large stores and giant malls. A network of restaurants and cafés (the *chikagai*) extends from the exits of metros and the basement of Meieki station. From his chauffeur-driven car, Arsène hadn't yet experienced the humidity (the average temperature is 15 degrees Celsius, climbing to 35 in summer). But, just as he had when arriving in Nancy, Cannes or Monaco, he immersed himself in his thoughts, pondering tactics or recruitment plans. He hardly noticed the suburbs, which were home to the Mitsubishi plants, or the town centre. Some 10,000 km from London, Wenger was driven almost oblivious through Nagoya, a city reconstructed after the bombardments of the Second World War with its planning influenced by the proximity of the town of Toyota, the site of factories of the same name. Toyota, his new employer.

The day after Wenger's arrival at Grampus, the 4.5 million readers of the *Chûnichi Shinbun*, the major regional daily newspaper, turned to the front page to read the reports detailing the Kobe earthquake. Some 6,400 people had lost their lives, with a further 40,000 injured. The disaster of 17 January 1995 dominated the headlines, but football fans, whether of Grampus Eight or their rivals, flicked to the sports page to discover that a foreign *gaijin* was about to take his first coaching session of the Nagoya team.

Arsène Wenger was ready and eager to lead his new troops, yet would immediately be faced by an almost insurmountable obstacle: the language and the alphabet. To get to the training centre and avoid getting lost on the way, the coach soon learnt to use his instinct, being guided by sight, usually by using the immense billboards as markers. A decade later, Wenger found it amusing to recall such a crude method of navigation. How many times did his internal GPS system fail? 'Whenever the adverts changed.'

But little by little, and left to his own devices, Arsène learned. 'I needed three or four months to understand how people would react,' Wenger later said. Once, he admitted, he had committed the faux pas of saying 'Hello, Mr Suzuki' to one of his physiotherapists when in fact he had been talking to Mr Kawasaki. 'Addressing a Japanese person wrongly is the greatest insult,' said the Frenchman, who continued the tradition he had started in France by surrounding himself with faithful aides de camp. Although there was no Aldo Platini or Jean Petit, as there had been at Nancy and Monaco, he unearthed another deputy. 'My deputies have always been necessary to help me adjust to a new culture. On the other hand, to manage egos, there needs to be a single decision maker in the team.'

The deputy to whom he turned was Boro Primorac, the ex-coach at Cannes and Valenciennes, whom he headhunted from France after the Olympique de Marseille match-fixing controversy. Caught up in the corruption and threats from Tapie's followers – the French courts later confirmed that the Marseille president had received Primorac in his Paris office to try and force him to cheat – the outcast was supported by one man. Arsène Wenger. The former Monaco coach advised his friend to give evidence in court, perhaps attacking his enemy, Tapie, through his protégé Primorac. The Valenciennes coach revealed the extent of the corruption . . . while Wenger remained mute.

Jean Petit, advisedly, stayed behind despite attempts by Wenger to persuade him to pack his bags and travel to Japan. 'Arsène asked me to come with him,' he admitted. 'He said: "Listen, I'll take you with me if you want. But I warn you –

I'm going over there, and I have no idea whether I'll like it or not. Who knows if I will be off again in six months? And you have a family . . ." He let me weigh up the pros and cons. I was tempted. But by the time the job in Japan was confirmed, I was already committed to a club and could no longer leave.'

The Swiss manager Daniel Jeandupeux freely admits to having taken a number of his coaching principles and methods from Wenger. From the headquarters of Le Mans, he traced his friend's development. 'When he spoke to me about Grampus, he said things which were completely surprising,' he said. 'For example, over there, footballers plunge into relaxing hot baths when they feel like it. In France, it would be considered unthinkable for footballers to have a bath 30 minutes before a match. But apparently they find it calms the nerves . . . They aren't bothered by it. That confused us at first, but Arsène accepted it, as he took a general, almost global view as to what he was experiencing. His analysis of situations is very clear. He is always learning, taking things in.'

Upon his arrival in mid-January 1995, Wenger opted against exploring the public parks, the imposing castle with its lawns, plum and cherry trees, that Nagoya has to offer. Instead, he flung himself into his work, day and night, sometimes even going to bed after dawn. Yet the communication problem remained. 'When you get up in the morning you can't speak the language, but you know that 20 or 30 players are expecting great things of you,' he conceded. He took the time to meet with both his small army of players and his trusting directors and administrative staff, the decision makers of Grampus and Toyota. He studied a brief history of the club, which had been founded in 1950. He also learnt that its name and new crest were made up of two strong symbols of Nagoya: the two golden whales (grampuses) which adorn the castle, and the 'Maru-Hachi', a figure eight surrounded by a circle. Wenger's crash course over, he prepared for his baptism of fire before the fans.

In the Mizuho stadium, a giant rectangular screen displayed the face of their new trainer to Grampus's expectant fans. The image projected up on the giant low-definition screen wasn't exactly flattering, what with the coach's long brown hair, somewhat severe face and academic glasses. Creases extended from the nostrils of his Roman nose and, with his thin lips and strong brow, he had no physical resemblance to any of the supporters gazing up from the stands. But the spectators understood that his frank, courteous face and civil smile belonged to a potential saviour. Alongside the portrait, six characters revealed his unusual name: Arsène Wenger. The fans, so regimented with their red and white banners (coincidentally, also the colours of AS Monaco and later Arsenal), were yet to discover that their beloved players, so badly managed before the arrival of Wenger, would initially continue to struggle under the new coach. Indeed, they would lose eight times in a row, the worst losing sequence in the coach's career. At the beginning, the fans were left to bide their time and come to terms with the team's new European recruits, unaware of the often unorthodox recruitment methods which had lured those players east.

One evening, in his hotel room as usual, Arsène sat in front of the television watching a Brazilian domestic match and analysing the performance of the players. One caught his eye, but he could not decipher his name. He went down to reception to get the help of a Japanese translator and, with his help, identified Carlos Alexandre Torres – son of Carlos Alberto. The Brazilian would become one of the first acquisitions of the Wenger era at Nagoya. Two others unknowns who had nevertheless impressed Wenger back on the fields of Navarre would also boost the new manager's ranks. Franck Durix, a real foot soldier, all ruddy-cheeked and agile, had captained AS Cannes in the French leagues, while Gérald Passi had scored the goal which had won AS Monaco the Coupe de France back in 1991. He had since been transferred to St Etienne, but Wenger knew the player. Both would buy into the team spirit he hoped to establish at Grampus.

While Wenger was happy to recruit players from France and bring them to Japan, he would later pluck a player from Grampus and lure him to Arsenal. Junichi Inamoto joined him in London from Gamba Osaka, though his transfer was never a success, the player subsequently enjoying spells at Fulham, West Bromwich Albion and Cardiff but never proving his quality in the English league. The Japanese player recalled the first time he saw Wenger in a rage a few weeks after the Frenchman's arrival in Nagoya. After the eighth defeat, Wenger, usually so calm and poised, exploded. No more soft treatment, no more kind words, but a question asked of all his players: 'What are you afraid of?' He challenged them, wondering whether they considered them-selves to be real professionals or not.

During the mid-season break, he took them to Versailles

where he attempted to restore battered confidence. 'Don't look at me to ask me what to do with the ball,' he would shout from the touchline. 'Make the decision yourself.' The students eventually applied what they had learnt and the victories started to mount. They would end that season propelled up the table, finishing runners-up after beginning life under their new manager bottom of the lot.

Masaru Hirayama, a defender who joined Grampus Eight in the same year as Wenger, developed under the Frenchman's stewardship and played 16 matches for the first team before succumbing to injury and, eventually, leaving for pastures new. He remembers Wenger's rages. 'If we were losing at half-time, he could be furious when we got back into the dressing room,' he recalled. 'You could hear his shouting echoing through the changing rooms and the corridors outside. However, even if he was furious, he remained a true gentleman.

'For example, he never swore, but he would pounce on any sign of psychological weakness: missed passes, sliding tackles or losses of concentration. And he'd remind us of those mistakes that we'd made in the first half. He would also say things like: "You're a load of wimps." We didn't like that. We respected him enormously and didn't want him to think we weren't giving our all. But his methods worked.'

Wenger would leave a lasting impression on the young Masaru. 'I watched the team start to win under his leadership. He is unbelievably thoughtful, a great analyser of a game, and so charismatic. He gives personal advice to each player, including reserves.' Hirayama, who enjoyed a lengthy spell writing on Wenger for the *Observer* magazine, was posing proudly in the gym of the school where he teaches and trains the junior football team. From beneath his mop of black hair, he spoke with passion. 'With Wenger, I never really knew what to expect when he arrived. I didn't know much about him, except that he was French and he wanted us to play like Europeans.'

He has kept press cuttings and photographs from his time at Grampus Eight, the manager clad in his Nagoya kit, a Coq Sportif design with a strange mix of colours: yellow, red and white. On the long sleeves the T, for Toyota, stands out with the number 13 printed across his back. In Japan, that is the number of joy and prosperity. The defender, nicknamed 'Mr Grampus', is certainly happy to have worked under such a coach, who proved himself strict but fair. 'At the beginning, Wenger seemed very pernickety, paying attention to each individual. However, he never lost his group perspective: for him, the team was an entity, one and indivisible. He never just played his favourites and, instead, took the time to watch each of us – not only the key players and the first team, but also the regular substitutes and the reserve squad.'

Hirayama soon understood the importance of time-keeping, as Luiz Henrique eventually had in Monaco. 'If you arrived late to a meeting he could get very angry,' he said. 'Punctuality was very important to him – he was strict and that made us want to follow him and live up to his expectations. At that time, there were a lot of foreign managers in the J League [the Englishman Stewart Baxter, for example, had taken charge of Mazda's flagship team, Hiroshima Sanfrecce] and, at other clubs, the players were very suspicious of

imported tactics and training methods. At Grampus, however, players followed Wenger completely. We had total
respect for what he was doing.'

Not only did the Grampus players listen to their tactician-
in-chief, they allowed themselves to be guided utterly by him.
To manage his troops, Wenger relied on certain key
elements. Just as he had used Ettori or Amoros when he
arrived at Louis II, he asked Durix and Passi to mentor the
young Japanese players and guide them out on the pitch
under his tutorship. Arsène also relied on Dragan Stojkovic,
the ex-Marseille midfielder who had fallen out of favour with
the previous regime. Reinventing the Yugoslav was key to his
success. 'When I arrived, Stojkovic was languishing on the
sidelines and wasn't getting a game,' said Wenger. 'But I
discovered a player with an extraordinary pride and desire to
win. He worked like mad to get back into the team, to
recapture some of his old form and fitness. We made him
work very, very hard, but we wanted him in the side. He was
an exceptional player, real class.'

The Alsatian liked class. He has nurtured it throughout his
career, and he would place Passi in the same bracket as
Stojkovic. 'I had the opportunity to work with great players
like Passi, but I also benefited from the renaissance of
Stojkovic,' he added. Under the Frenchman, the Yugoslav
went on to win the player of the championship award for two
successive seasons in Japan. 'Finding a guy like him in Japan
was almost a miracle,' added the manager. 'Imagine the
courage he needed to go there, alone. That was a stroke of
luck for us. He had been forced out at Marseille apparently
due to a knee problem, but he recovered sufficiently to make

his mark. In Nagoya I found an exceptional player who gave us the best years of his career.'

Bizarrely, Stojkovic – even having been abandoned on the sidelines – had been consulted by the Grampus board when they were considering appointing Wenger. As a player who had featured in the French league, and had confronted Arsène's AS Monaco, they wanted to know what impression the manager had made. 'I told them: "If you have even the slightest chance of signing him, then do all you can to make sure it happens,"' said Stojkovic. 'They asked me why I was so enthusiastic and I answered: "Get him here and see for yourselves." I was right.'

That enthusiasm was shared by Masaru Hirayama. 'Arsène was very effective, and there was no time wasted in any of his training sessions,' he said. 'Everything was completely focused. In Japan, coaches make their players sweat for three or four hours in a row, but Wenger explained that humans could not concentrate for more than 90 minutes at any one time. Our sessions, therefore, never went on longer than that. He would also take great care to explain himself, so we knew exactly what we were doing and why we were doing it. Firstly he encouraged us to work as a team, then as a defensive block, and finally as individuals.'

'It was as if I had been sent back to France in the 1940s and 1950s, when professional football was in its infancy,' said Wenger, offering his own slant on that first season in Japan. 'The players were discovering how to be professionals. For the first time in my career I had to hide the ball from players so they would stop training. This was something amazing – something I wasn't used to at home.'

Faced with naive if hugely enthusiastic footballers, the former economic science student opted for simplicity as the best approach. The guidance given was brief, the instructions clear. 'It was very simple, very logical and very effective,' said Hirayama. 'It was all a matter of psychology with Arsène. On his instruction, during matches and even in training I never tried to do things that were too complicated. Our overall strategy didn't change depending on the opponent. He always said if we played to our own strengths, we could win. Before each game, he was very direct and consistent in terms of his tactics. Most of his efforts went into preparing us psychologically. He'd merely repeat: "Get hold of the ball. Be confident of winning." Of course, he expressed himself through a translator, but he always seemed very excited, passionate. As he was ordinarily such a gentleman, those rare flashes of emotion really stood out.'

Japanese football at the time was a strange mix of the archaic and the modern. If the tactics had been dated before Wenger arrived, there were also state-of-the-art training facilities on offer – the Frenchman supervised the construction of those at Grampus. The ideology of the game in the Far East, however, was more problematic. Almost in desperation, aware as he was of his squad's technical deficiencies and of their rather aged approach to the game, Wenger asked his players to go back to basics. One concept was easily understood: their body is a temple. 'We were a very fit team with a lot fewer injuries than other teams I had worked in,' said Hirayama, himself abruptly struck down by injury. 'That peak level of fitness was down to the two body-building sessions we'd undertake before and after each ordinary training session. Wenger himself didn't lead these sessions, but made sure they were carried out correctly.

'At other clubs, or under the orders of other managers, players only worked on general all-over body-building, but Wenger always made sure our work was focused on muscles we, as footballers, needed specifically in our game. This made us more mobile as well as stronger.' All those mental notes taken by Arsène in discussion with Paul Frantz, back in Alsace, had clearly been applied on the Pacific coast of Japan.

Dietary aspects were clearly a necessary supplement to physical exercises, just as they had been at Monaco. 'He didn't tell us what we had to eat or drink,' explained Hirayama, 'but he discreetly kept us on our guard. Before each session, we were weighed and our fat was measured. We received a warning if this ratio grew to 11 or 12 per cent. And if our fat ratio exceeded that limit, we were excluded from the squad until we had worked off the excess weight. This threat was strong enough for us to ask the trainer for dietary advice to keep us under 10 per cent.'

If Wenger's managerial techniques had developed at Strasbourg and Cannes, then his time in Nagoya allowed him to mature fully. 'He kept us at a respectful distance and never tried to be one of the lads,' added Hirayama. 'When training was over, some managers would join their players for a beer and something to eat, but Wenger never did. He separated his work and his private life completely.' Hirayama, now a teacher at the Fukui Keishin school, still applies Wenger's methods in his teaching daily. 'My main problem was psychological. I would lose my confidence very easily, and after the slightest error I'd feel like quitting the sport,' he said.

'But Arsène took me to one side and encouraged me to carry on, to continue making mistakes as, in his opinion, that was the only way to learn. That really changed things for me. I had never met a manager before who gave me so much self-confidence.'

The memory of Hirayama's biggest mistake haunts him still. In the crucial match against the league leaders Verdy Kawasaki, he missed a penalty – an 'easy' chance to claim the title and complete a remarkable turnaround. 'In the changing rooms after the game I was devastated – devastated to have let my team-mates and the fans down. They were furious with me, the supporters. But Wenger supported me, saying it wasn't as easy as it looked. I started to feel a lot better. After talking to him, negatives became positives, which is typical of him. He was always considerate about people's feelings, never dressing them down in front of the team, always taking them to one side and discussing things calmly, face to face.'

Although the team finished their first season as runners-up, a position to which Wenger had grown accustomed during his time at Monaco, the second campaign would yield a trophy. On 1 January 1996, Grampus Eight claimed the Emperor's Cup (the equivalent of the FA Cup) by beating Hiroshima Sanfrecce 3–0. Tokyo's national stadium was basked in sunshine that Monday afternoon, with the 47,021 fans present witnessing the first silverware claimed by Grampus in their history. Durix and Torres, both French recruits, played their part in the triumph and, although the J League was claimed by Kashima Antlers, Grampus gained some measure of revenge by winning the Japanese

Super Cup, which pits league and cup winners against each other.

The drip feed of trophies, combined with the respect earned by Wenger off the pitch, saw his reputation swell. 'People over there are incredibly kind and pay attention to the smallest detail,' said Richard Conte. 'The Japanese of Nagoya, for example, had observed which water he drank, and they gave him a bottle of his favourite water as a gift. They also knew that he loved chocolate, so they would give him a bar, always accompanied by a few words: "Thanks for everything you are doing." He received a great deal of recognition, and endless messages of thanks. Each letter was accompanied by a small gesture. They had noted his habits and wanted to please him.' A few months after Wenger's departure, Conte returned to Nagoya and observed the impact left by the man from Duttlenheim. 'I saw the reputation he had left behind him. I contacted Arsène's interpreter in Grampus and members of the club and saw the positive image he had left behind him in Japan.'

Wenger accepted such plaudits and gifts with good grace, but kept his distance and was uncomfortable at the thought that he was idolised. 'We all regarded him with great respect,' added Hirayama. 'He was amazing. Of course, the praise he received was partly thanks to our good results, but mainly it was due to his way of managing the club. On the pitch, thanks to him, we developed a reputation for coming from behind. How many times were we losing at half-time only to win in the end?'

For Wenger himself, the success was starting to heal the wounds inflicted by Olympique de Marseille's underhand tactics back in France, and his hurt at his divorce from AS Monaco. And he was growing used to life in Japan. The billboards leading him to the training centre were no longer his only guidance, with his routine long since established. 'He surprised the media and the public with his ability almost to wave a magic wand and establish Grampus Eight among the best clubs in the country,' said Takashi Kawahara, editor of *Weekly Soccer Digest* in Tokyo.

The language, however, remained an obstacle. He may have spoken German and English, and was able to communicate in Spanish or Portuguese, but Japanese remained something of a mystery. His translator was his shadow, and Kawahara was quick to reject the suggestion that the Alsatian is a perfect linguist and a cultural chameleon. 'I never heard Wenger speak Japanese,' he said. 'Of course, he could say *Arigato* (Thank you) and other common greetings, but he was totally incapable of expressing his thoughts in Japanese.'

Hirayama confirms as much from the manager's team talks. 'He would always use an interpreter to give instructions or explain something in particular to a player. We knew that he was intelligent and could speak several languages, but his Japanese was limited to congratulations and encouragements: *Genki desu ka* (How are you?), *Daijobou desu ka* (Are you OK?) and *Gambarimashou* (Give it all you've got!). But it was enough to relax us and motivate us.'

During that second season, however, the Nagoya manager started feeling a certain sense of isolation and distance. His speaking skills may have been limited, but his desire to feel more at home prompted him to accept an offer from the television channel Fuji to act as an expert analyser whenever the Japanese national team were playing in Europe at competitions such as the Confederations Cup in 2003. That year, Japan would face Les Bleus, with the Arsenal midfielder Robert Pires captaining the French line-up. Wenger was offering his analysis on that game, won by the hosts 2–1. 'We were pleasantly surprised by the Japanese,' said Pires post-match in an interview conducted live on air with his club manager. 'They are clearly improving. It is a pleasure to see such talented players – they caused us a lot of problems.'

'Since I first went there, Japanese football has made great strides,' admitted Wenger, who has continued to chart the progress of the Japan national team and domestic league from afar. 'They have learnt how to structure themselves, and their tactical appreciation has developed. The Japanese are not the kind of people to do things by half. They set up a good youth policy and copied what worked best in Europe, with an added element: the respect for their own culture. They also called on quality personnel, good trainers who did their job well. All this explains why Japan have made such rapid progress.'

He may barely speak the language, but Wenger has become as much a media figure in the Far East as a foot-balling legend. His players, for their part, came to love his occasional eccentricities as well. There was the scatty academic to Wenger, the manager occasionally disappearing with his 'head in the clouds', though that just made the Japanese love him all the more. The Frenchman took his squad to Australia on a training break during his reign and arranged for the players to meet at 6.30 p.m. precisely in their hotel reception to undertake a 'group walk' before dinner.

'We knew he insisted all the time on punctuality, so we were all down there in the lobby, but the only one to arrive late was him,' said Hirayama. 'When he arrived he was totally embarrassed and he apologised with this humble smile. We fell about laughing! To see this man we respected so much apologising meant a lot. It only confirmed what a great man he was. Without this strange distraction, he might have otherwise seemed too focused. But his occasional awkwardness just proved that even he wasn't perfect, and that reassured us.'

'Living in Japan was a decisive experience for me, in personal but also footballing terms, because I rediscovered the pleasure of training,' said Wenger when reflecting on his time in the Far East. 'I was totally unaware of Japanese football, and my knowledge of the country's culture was basic, as my experience would later show. Those years spent in Japan were a turning point in my life. In Europe, although there are cultural differences, you don't really notice them. In Japan I was forced to open my eyes, to re-examine values I had held since childhood and the life I had led up to then.'

The Catholic Alsatian, who had held his prayer book in his hands to plead for FC Duttlenheim to win, had been immersed in a society which, while not pious, was at least spiritual. The traditional Japanese religion is Shintoism, whose ceremonies are held in sanctuaries. Buddhism is similarly popular: Buddhist ceremonies are held in temples with the Astuta sanctuary, in one of Nagoya's large parks, one of the three main places of worship in Japan. It houses one of the three treasures of the imperial family: the Kusanagi sword. Noh plays and religious ceremonies are held there almost every weekend.

Despite the many interesting aspects of the local culture in which he could have immersed himself, Wenger's time away from the first team was taken up with the construction of Grampus's training centre. His approach was similar to that he would adopt when overseeing the building of Arsenal's complex, with a desire to create a serene atmosphere in which his players could work. For example, the weights room at the Gunners' centre in London Colney looks out upon streams, ponds and countryside, an attempt to ensure that physical effort is softened by the beauty of the surroundings. There is an element of spirituality in architecture. In Japan, he took on ancient Japanese values in his design of the centre. His Grampus players saw him as a type of 'Samurai Arsène', shouting and raging in the changing rooms, while the public saw him as *kamunushi*, capable of invoking the gods of nature. This ambivalence – warrior and priest – was part of the technician's character.

'The Zen side is part of Arsène's detachment from an event, a game or an argument,' said Damien Comolli, who would become the coach of the under-18s at Nagasaki between 1996 and 1997 on Wenger's recommendation and go on to work with him at Arsenal. 'This Zen attitude would allow him to make the right decisions in the most pressurised of situations. Or at least not to make a hasty, and most likely wrong, decision. The other aspect is what you don't see: he is seething inside, passionate, committed. He hates to lose. This is why he is difficult to define. But this ambivalence is what makes him who he is.'

It is as if Wenger is a Dr Jekyll and Mr Hyde character, though his Zen persona seemed to prevail most often. 'Managing to detach himself from an event as exciting as a football match is unique,' added Comolli. 'I have never met anyone other than him capable of not panicking, for example when his team are losing. I don't know if that is his main driving force, but it is certainly one of his qualities. This is clearly one of the reasons for his success.'

In Nagoya, immersed in a country still developing its football, Wenger managed to reconcile his two sides. 'My biological and cultural origins made me think that truth is a relative value,' Arsène once stated in *L'Équipe* magazine. 'My experience in Japan with Nagoya strengthened this view point. There I developed my tolerance for other people, for difference. Often too much, undoubtedly.'

Wenger confirmed as much later. 'On a footballing level, I learnt things of course, but I learnt more on a personal level,' he said. 'I became more tolerant, more understanding than I had been. Before, I was too obtuse, too stubborn, too bad-tempered. Over there I rediscovered my main motivation as a manager, without the bad sides. I learnt to rediscover my joy for training, for guiding players and giving them what they need. I rediscovered the love of the pitch, for training routines. But what I really took away with me from Japan was respect for the country itself and the Japanese people. I can say unreservedly that I spent a great couple of years over there. We all have places where we have lived which arc unique, and Japan is that for me.'

Gilles Grimandi, who would go on to scout the south of Europe for new talent for Wenger's Arsenal, noticed the difference between the often irascible Monaco manager and the Zen coach he found in north London. 'Japan taught him to stand back from events and avoid stress,' said the former midfielder. 'His formula, which he tells me all the time, is: "You need to go back to basics." The older I get, the more I see he's right. Of course, all the minor details are important, but at any given time you mustn't lose yourself in these details and you need to concentrate on the basics, whether good or bad.'

Wenger had been in Japan for 20 months when, towards the end of the summer of 1996, the first rumblings were heard that he was to be summoned back to Europe. The newspapers in England began speculating about 'Wenger, the Japanese' who would soon, apparently, be on his way to Arsenal. Few knew that David Dein, vice-chairman at the London club but effectively the mover and shaker at Highbury, was a friend of the Alsatian, and Dein had decided the time had come for Arsenal to restructure, rebuild and reinvent itself. The pair's relationship dated from 1988, during Arsène's time at Monaco, when Dein was introduced to him by a mutual friend. Their respect for each other was instant, but Dein's liking for the AS Monaco manager would deepen throughout the evening; a game of charades was organised among the guests, and Wenger's sense of fun and intuition won the Englishman over.

There was competition in the closed season of 1996, with RC Strasbourg – Wenger's first love – also keen to lure the Frenchman home. Indeed, the board in Alsace believed they had secured their man, only to be knocked back at the last. 'I had already given my written agreement to Arsenal, who then decided to hire me,' said Wenger, who would not renege on his commitment. Arsenal it was. Videos of the team's stuttering performances were sent to Nagoya, with the hours spent scouring the screen not aimed at seeking out new recruits for the Toyota team to which he was still contracted, but instead to spot which areas of the Arsenal line-up needed strengthening.

As it was, there was no acrimony this time around. The board of directors at Grampus Eight agreed to release Wenger four months early from his contract, allowing him to move to London, at the beginning of September 1996. Their willingness reflected how grateful the Japanese club was for the success the Frenchman had earned it, though there was sadness when Arsène announced his imminent departure to the team.

'I have had other good managers, but he was exceptional and had a really big influence on my life,' said Hirayama. 'When I stopped playing, I was motivated to become a schoolteacher so I could pass on to my students all the great things he had taught me, not only about football, but a real philosophy of life. Being a good man is more important than being a good player. I often told my students that they should do everything possible to improve themselves, but that they shouldn't be afraid of making mistakes. I try to be logical and effective, concentrating on the humanity of individuals. I try to imitate Wenger.'

'Will I ever come back to Japan?' pondered Wenger. 'The answer is yes – definitely. I will go back out of curiosity, nostalgia, whether on a private basis or for football, which I can't rule out.' To say that Wenger rejected Western materialism after his stay in Nagoya is an exaggeration, but he certainly developed a type of 'behavioural minimalism' which is reflected in the decor of his home in London. The circle is thus closed. If the Alsatian's foundations had been laid down by life in the French league and Japan, the fortifications were to be flung up as a Gunner. In the autumn of 2005, almost ten years after leaving Nagoya, Wenger opened the door to welcome his guest to his home in Totteridge. That notebook in his hand as ever was actually a pamphlet of sudokus. The Japanese influence remains.

• 2 •

GUNNER

ARSÈNE WENGER CLIMBED the steps leading up to the wrought iron door, standing open to welcome him. Two Art Deco lamps gave the entrance to the stadium almost a feel of the roaring 20s, though the Frenchman hardly glanced up as his long legs crossed the threshold of the institution where he would work for the ensuing decade. The new manager hurried under the crest adorning the classic façade. Large capital letters spelt out 'Arsenal Stadium' above him, and the north flank of the building was bathed in the mellow September sunlight.

The Frenchman's appointment as manager of the north London club had been announced on 28 September 1996, almost two weeks previously, but this was the first time he had entered the arena as manager. Highbury. In the entrance hall he could not have missed the huge red cannon set into the marble floor, the gun a symbol of the old armament factories next to the club's previous home when it was based south of the Thames and known as Woolwich Arsenal. The emblem had greeted visitors since 1936, the date the East Stand had been constructed. The Alsatian would have noted the bust of Herbert Chapman defiantly presiding over the scene. Chapman (1878–1934) was the managerial legend to whom Wenger, and all his predecessors, had to measure up. His benchmark. This, after all, was the coach who had led the Gunners to their first championship title in 1931, thereby ensuring that the trophy was claimed for the first time by a side from the south of England.

There were two other successes, in 1933 and 1934, as well as an FA Cup triumph during Chapman's nine-year stewardship. The Gunners, inspired by their visionary manager who had been one of the first instigators of modern physiotherapy and preparation techniques, would win five league titles in the 1930s. Following in the footsteps of this founder figure, Wenger, 62 years after Chapman's death, would state that his role was to 'reinvent' this club. Arsenal, after all, had not won the league title since 1991 under George Graham and, having had to settle merely for the odd cup success in the interim, were in clear need of revitalisation.

A few days before he had officially taken up the reins at Highbury, the Alsatian had sent his Grampus Eight side out one last time, on 28 August 1996, for a J League fixture. 'I have a confidentiality agreement with Grampus and I can't break it, so questions only about the game, please,' the manager announced to the media post-match in Nagoya, aware of the presence of a number of English journalists seeking to quiz him over his imminent arrival at Arsenal, and attempting to find out just how long his move to England had been on the cards. In fact, just as discussions had been carried out in private with Monaco when he was the manager for Nancy, Wenger had courted offers of a move to London on numerous occasions in the past.

Contact had first been made some 18 months before when the Frenchman had been invited by the Arsenal chairman, Peter Hill-Wood, to dine at an exclusive restaurant in Chelsea, a stone's throw from the chairman's home. On the menu that night was the possibility of Wenger coming to Highbury, with Hill-Wood initially encouraged to make contact by David Dein, his vice-chairman. In the end, the instinctively more conservative Arsenal board opted to appoint the disciplinarian Bruce Rioch as George Graham's successor, yet, while Arsène had been rejected, he was nevertheless flattered to have been considered.

The idea of moving to England would remain in his thoughts throughout his time in Japan with Grampus Eight, and in the summer of 1996, Hill-Wood and Dein revived their interest. Rioch had just endured a season of 'what might have been' – Arsenal had finished fifth but a distant 19 points from Manchester United at the summit – but was to be sacked five days before his second year in charge. Now the Arsenal hierarchy found the Frenchman even keener to be considered, with Wenger anxious not to be forgotten by the West and fearful that a route back into the European game might pass him by. With that in mind, he agreed readily to their proposals. Just one hour was needed for the three of them to close the deal, in stark contrast with the protracted spell of negotiations which had seen Wenger leave for Japan in the first place. 'Firstly, I had the impression that I would be forgotten if I stayed three or four years in Nagoya, and wouldn't have the option of returning,' admitted Wenger. 'Then there was the question of whether I really wanted to spend the rest of my life in Japan, for all that I had fallen for the Japanese way of life. At some point I knew I would have to make a decision about where my future lay. But, above all, it was the lack of contact with top-level football that persuaded me to return.'

Hill-Wood later maintained that Arsenal had long 'felt he was the right man for the job'. 'We wanted a radical change, and told ourselves that Arsène was what we needed,' added Dein. 'No one here had heard of him, so appointing him was a bit like a game of poker. But our board of directors had never been afraid to take risks.' Well before August, Arsène, from his base on the Japanese archipelago, had been focusing on Arsenal.

The Frenchman already knew Highbury, having been Dein's guest at a game a few years previously. 'I had known David Dein for a long time,' said Wenger. 'We grew close after the first time I visited Highbury.' The Alsatian had immediately fallen under the charm of this old-fashioned, 38,000-seater stadium squeezed in amongst the hubbub of north London. Returning there seemed natural to him, like coming home after a long journey abroad. 'Moving to England from Japan felt like going home, as if I was going back to France, such is the culture shock when you've been living in the Far East,' conceded Wenger. He would not be the first foreign manager to make his mark in the Premiership, with Ruud Gullit having effectively set the tone after taking charge of Chelsea (in contrast, Dr Josef Venglos's time at Aston Villa in the early 1990s had not been considered a success), but his arrival would open the door to other French coaches to the English game. Gérard Houllier, Jean Tigana and Alain Perrin would follow, bringing their French staff with them, taking their lead from Wenger.

Wenger's adventure began in that great marbled hall at Highbury. Leaving the bust of Chapman behind, Arsène turned right and started to climb the long staircase up, breathing in the history of the place, its majestic past unfurling before his eyes: the heavy wooden doors of the changing rooms, the portraits, paintings and photographs decorating the walls, the engraved trophies. He reached the first floor, his hosts guiding him down the long corridor leading to the manager's office. Only once he had entered that room did Arsène Wenger feel the full weight of tradition weighing on this club.

Opposite the antique desk was a huge bookcase, the shelves lined with row upon row of red books, a collection of leather-bound editions charting the history of the club back as far as 1886, when the owners of the munitions factory in Woolwich first permitted their workers to kick a small leather ball around after forging iron all day. This was the Gunners' Bible, reflecting over 100 years of a footballing institution. It would be Wenger who would light the touchpaper to make them an explosive force again.

The vice-chairman and chairman, Dein and Hill-Wood, stood in the doorway as Wenger sat at his desk for the first time, as if trying it out for size, and were confident they had just pulled off a coup by appointing him. Through the tall windows, the last traces of the summer of 1996 shone on to the new manager as if this was the place he belonged. Further along, in one of the neighbouring rooms, the 20 major trophies won between April 1930 and September 1996 glimmered in their cabinet. 'I had promised myself that I would only return to Europe to manage a great club,' said Wenger. 'As soon as Arsenal became a possibility, they became my focus. I never hesitated about going there for a second.' Thus began his reign across the Channel.

Arsène had arrived in a country whose love for football had just been rekindled. England had hosted the European Championships that summer and, in June, Terry Venables's side had reached the semi-finals before Germany prevailed – inevitably – on penalties. A trio of Arsenal players, Tony Adams, David Platt and David Seaman, had participated in the Euro 96 campaign and, while these three would soon have their chance to meet the new manager at Highbury, the English press were still coming to terms with the fact that a Frenchman had been plucked from Japan to manage Arsenal, long considered to be the club of the establishment and a very 'British' institution.

In one of those moments of destiny invariably thrown up by football, one character was key to his appointment. The former Monaco midfielder Glenn Hoddle had acted as the link between Arsenal and Wenger. 'I had just been appointed as England's manager [in 1996] when I was asked for my opinion of Arsène by David Dein, as no one in this country, to be honest, had heard of him,' said Hoddle, ironically enough a former Tottenham midfielder. 'I just said to David: "Do it. Bring him here." I could understand why people had reservations, but he had been a success everywhere he had been as a manager. Having worked with him, I knew what he could bring to an English side.'

Wenger was to be entrusted with all aspects of the football side of the club by the Arsenal board, from training to selection of the first team, the recruitment of players to the renegotiations of contracts for squad and staff alike. 'A "coach" in England is the figure who chooses his deputies, his team and targets possible transfers,' explained Wenger. 'Generally, the best trainer, for me, is not the one who wins all the time, but the one who gets the most from a team, even in village-level football clubs. Being an English-style manager is the profile I like best – I like it when the manager has some choice. On the Continent, the "general manager" can take charge of recruitment, for example, and contract nego-tiations, so those matters are out of your control. Of course, on the other hand, having to deal with everything demands a lot of work, a lot of energy. You can exhaust yourself. But you need to remember that for 90 per cent of players, their career is played at the club in which they developed, graduating up through the ranks: only 10 per cent have the mental capacity to play anywhere.'

Acceptance of that fact places yet more emphasis on creating an environment, from top to bottom, at a club which makes players feel as if they belong, a feeling Wenger has cultivated since. The Gunners manager neatly sum-marised his many functions: 'I am a manager of time, emotions and decisions.' Platt's initial impression when experiencing Wenger's management technique for the first time was to ask whether the Frenchman was 'always so calm and peaceful'. Where the Arsenal players had been used to the ranting and raving of Bruce Rioch during his 14-month reign, Arsène was thoughtful and measured in communicating with his team. This was, in many ways, a refreshing change.

Yet the reaction among the English press to the Alsatian's appointment was distinctly lukewarm. Even frosty. The *Evening Standard* summed up the sense of perplexed pessimism, its headline blaring: 'Arsène who?' 'I was greeted with great scepticism,' admitted Wenger. 'I wasn't very well known, I was a bit, well . . . different. Here, foreign trainers were extremely rare – there was Gullit, who was a bit of a special case given his status as a well known former player, not to mention his successful spell at Chelsea. I didn't have that. They didn't know me in England. It was a real gamble for the Arsenal board, as it was for me, too.'

Euro 96 and the Champions League may have caught the imagination of the English fans, but their idea of football remained distinctly insular. 'I felt like I was opening the door to the outside world,' explained Wenger some ten years later. 'I proved that you could be successful in England even if you weren't born in England.'

Yet the journalist Jasper Rees, who was in London in September 1996, denied that analysis. 'It is wrong to say that Arsène was seen as an exotic character back then,' he insisted. 'He was distant, and almost unemotional, and that's why he stood out as being different from the other managers in the Premiership. He became known as "the Professor". When Wenger came here, his aim was to topple Manchester United from their pedestal at the top of the domestic game. With that in mind, he assembled a strange team: an odd blend of experienced English players and young athletic French players.'

Wenger was presented to the media one morning at Highbury in September. He entered the room dressed in a white shirt and Arsenal tie and stood on a podium, behind him a purple wall bearing the club crest and the motto *Victoria concordia crescit*: 'Victory grows out of harmony'. Wenger discussed the team he hoped to construct and ignored the most pressing problems he would face, chiefly those of two of his key players, Tony Adams and Paul Merson, who were suffering from alcoholism, and the lack of adequate training facilities at the club. He also touched upon the need to add to his squad, as well as his back-room staff. Arsène made it clear that he would maintain the spine of the group: the goalkeeper David Seaman, the centre-half Adams and the prolific centre-forward Ian Wright, who had found himself thrust on to the left wing during Rioch's last days at the club. 'I want to expand the group,' he said. 'In terms of numbers, the squad is a bit tight. I have seven or eight players available, but the best are also the oldest.'

For all Wenger's impressive performance at his unveiling, the English press remained dubious, especially with a European campaign fast approaching. On 25 September 1996 he flew back from Japan to watch his new team play Borussia Mönchengladbach at the Mungersdorfer Stadion in Cologne for the second leg of the Uefa Cup first-round tie. This was the Alsatian returning to his roots, back to the country he had visited all those years previously with Max Hild. On this occasion, he was accompanied not by his mentor but by David Dein, his friend turned boss, and, about to take up the reins at the club, the intention was to take a back seat and watch the team from the stands.

Arsenal had travelled to Germany having already lost the first leg 3–2, leaving them an awkward deficit to claw back. The programme listed the Arsenal manager as Stewart Houston, the caretaker manager who had filled in after Rioch's sacking only to resign at the end of August. By the time the team arrived in Germany, Pat Rice, a former Arsenal captain and youth-team coach, had taken over as caretaker manager, with his team duly put under considerable pressure throughout the first half, holding on grimly to retire at the interval with the scoreline 1–1 and their chances of progress intact, if only just. Yet, awaiting the visiting players in the dressing room at the interval were Dein, the vice-chairman, flanked by the new man in charge. Most of the players had yet to meet Wenger, recognising him only from the press conference he had given a few days earlier, but there he was, rolling his sleeves up and addressing the tactical changes he wanted implemented in the second half. Principal among them were his orders for the defence to switch from a three to a back four. The captain Tony Adams, taken aback by the sudden overhaul, and his team-mates carried out the new man's orders, yet there was to be no fairy-tale revival. Arsenal lost 3–2 that day, and 6–4 on aggregate. Ironically enough, Mönchengladbach would be beaten by Monaco in the next round, though that was scant consolation for Wenger.

'The decision he took at half-time surprised me, and the way he did it annoyed me as well,' admitted Adams some years later. 'When I saw him go into the changing rooms and take control of the team, I couldn't believe it. I suppose the board of directors wanted him to get stuck in as soon as possible because they knew Arsène and what he was capable of doing. But I wanted to win this Uefa Cup tie the way we had planned in the build-up, and suddenly this guy who hadn't been at the club two minutes arrives, this French guy, at half-time and switches us to 4-4-2? I said to myself: "What the hell is all this? We're more than capable of playing with three at the back!" He changed the system and we ended up losing. What was even more irritating was that at the end of the match, Arsène didn't say anything to us. Not one word. He left with David Dein, and there we all were waiting for some kind of explanation. I was really angry, but who could I take it out on? I turned to Pat Rice and yelled at him. To be honest, I was spitting feathers and gave him both barrels, even though it wasn't his fault!'

Adams, an Arsenal legend, a loyal servant for 18 seasons and captain for 15, with eight trophies won en route, would later recognise evidence of the impatience of David Dein surfacing in the changing rooms at Mönchengladbach. 'He wanted Arsène to manage the team right away, but we hadn't even been officially introduced,' he added. 'Let's just say that Dein and Wenger could have handled it differently at the time. I thought that introducing Wenger with the season a month under way was inappropriate. Without him we were in fourth place and not doing badly at all.' The mistrust and reticence would continue for a while yet, though Adams recognised that his own knee-jerk reaction at the time might have been down to his own personal problems. 'I had been sober for only three weeks, and I was quite irritable at the time. I think it was a good idea Arsène left the changing room when he did. He had nothing to do with my moods, and it was easy to blame everything on him.'

*

On 30 September 1996, a few days after the failure in Germany, Wenger arrived at Arsenal's training ground at London Colney at around 9 a.m. The sign announcing 'University College Hospital' just beyond the wooden barrier at the complex's entrance was a reminder of who owned the property at which the club had made its home. Arsène was one of the first to arrive that day, his imminent first session as manager looming large. As he drove up the driveway, he passed half a dozen pitches on his right side – all visible from the road – as he approached the low, white buildings ahead. Inside, they housed antiquated changing rooms and a cafeteria whose glass windows looked out on to the main training pitch. There was no room for an office for the manager. The whole set-up was dated, even amateur.

It was a couple of hours before Wenger met his new team, drifting into training in dribs and drabs. Tony Adams, Mr Arsenal, was particularly anxious to meet the new man in charge. The centre-half was a bastion of George Graham's successful team and would play 673 games for the club, scoring 49 goals, over the course of his career – but, after Mönchengladbach, he already had concerns about Rioch's successor. The pair, manager and captain, sat on a bench outside in the sunlight and assessed each other. Both knew the club was entrenched in a transitional period, and that a huge challenge lay ahead. This was no time for an argument between the two senior figures at the club.

Adams was sceptical, intrigued as to what the Frenchman was like. Was this man an impostor? A genius? A fraud? 'The players didn't like change, yet at the same time they were impatient,' he said. 'We were all worried about change, and whether it threatened our own future at the club, but we wanted to see what it would bring. I was still unsettled after the disappointment of Mönchengladbach, and that conversation was really the first time we had spoken. I brought up the decision to suddenly change the formation when we'd spent so much time preparing with three defenders. I told him what I really thought. I understood that he loved the defensive solidity possible by a 4-4-2 formation – after all, we'd played it for years at Arsenal, and had become synonymous with that line-up. I myself appreciated the benefits it offered, but I told him to his face that he had made the choice at the wrong time. You don't do things like that in the middle of such a key match. I said to him that he had put our entire season in jeopardy by doing what he had done.'

The centre-half was just as forthright in his assessment that, nestled in fourth place in the Premiership, Arsenal had been doing quite nicely without Wenger. Arsène listened. Firstly he appreciated the frank words of the captain, and liked his honesty. Rather than defend his tactical choices, Arsène asked Adams to talk about the club, about what they had achieved in recent seasons, and to describe the players with whom the new manager would be working. 'We sat there on that bench and I got the impression he wanted to find out as much as he could about the club, to know the place inside out,' said Adams. 'He wanted to know everything that had gone on before his arrival. I tried to give him all the information I had available, trying to be as honest as possible.'

The Alsatian accepted the criticism that had been levelled against him and liked the captain's intensity. This, after all, was the kind of passion and enthusiasm which had attracted him to the English game in the first place. 'Great Britain is a paradise for footballers,' he said. 'Here there is an intense, almost intimidating passion. But it is much easier to live with than without.' Wenger embraced that passion. He spoke at length with Adams, and the pair were reconciled.

Not far from them, the first-team players were drifting in and out of the cafeteria, some having ordered their customary full English breakfast – sausages, beans, toast, eggs with dollops of ketchup, which Adams had also indulged in after drinking sessions (he claimed he drank, on average, some 30 pints every weekend). Back in 1996, Adams was in the process of maturing into a sober captain reaching veteran status in his career. He spoke to Wenger about his problems in that initial meeting, with the new manager sympathetic and supportive. 'Arsène told me he had grown up in a pub and said how he had seen alcohol change people, trans-forming their personality,' he said. 'I didn't so much feel empathy, as he had never drunk himself, but sympathy. Yes, he was compassionate, he understood.' As it was, Wenger would not only provide support for 'his centre-half, but would end up extending his career.

The Arsenal cafeteria was a social place, the players gathering to eat their meals before and after morning training. It was a place full of raucous laughter, where friendships were forged and nicknames appointed. Where Wenger would steadily become known as 'the Professor' among the Arsenal fans, the English players in his first team christened the new manager 'Windows', a reference to his spectacles, and also 'Inspector Clouseau', likening him to Peter Sellers's clumsy character from the *Pink Panther* films. The similarities stretched further than their shared and hugely pronounced French accents. 'Arsène is terribly clumsy,' offered Adams with a smile. 'I remember one day, in the canteen, we were all sitting down eating our meal. The gaffer went to serve himself some cake, which fell off his plate when he turned round to speak to someone. He was so distracted that he returned to the table with an empty plate. It was only when he sat down and stabbed his fork into nothing that he realised what had happened. We all burst out laughing.'

The players were always ready to wind their manager up, albeit playfully. Once, before a game at Crystal Palace, the Frenchman went to the toilet and, whilst he was in the cubicle, there was a bomb alert at the ground. Initially it appeared as if the team would have to be evacuated from the stadium, though the scare was quickly recognised as a false alarm. Not that anyone told Wenger. The manager sprinted out of the toilets, buttoning up his trousers, in a blind panic demanding to know what was going on. This was a chance for a wind-up. 'What, a bomb?' gasped Arsène in his broad Alsatian accent, inadvertently quoting one of Sellers's most infamous lines. Tony Adams, Ray Parlour and company fell about giggling. 'Raymond,' said Wenger to Parlour, with realisation slowly dawning, 'are you taking the mickey out of me or what?'

Yet the pranks and wind-ups were a small challenge given the other problems confronting Wenger upon his arrival, not least his players' willingness to hit the tiles after a game on a Saturday afternoon. Wenger fell back on his tried and trusted methods: tolerance, listening, laughter. 'He has a very dry sense of humour,' said Damien Comolli, who would work with Wenger at Arsenal for seven years. 'It's almost distant, like him. He makes me laugh when he is really relaxed, when his team aren't playing. Then he is constantly joking. He seems cold on the outside, but in fact he is always mucking about.' At the restaurant, at home, during international competitions he is watching for pleasure, Wenger likes nothing more than having fun.

'There were so many hilarious incidents,' said Adams. 'It is public knowledge, at least within the Arsenal changing room, that Gary Lewin, the physiotherapist, would have to hold down Wenger's chair on the bench at Highbury. It would flip up whenever he stood up, and if Lewin hadn't done that, Arsène would have fallen flat on his backside after celebrating every goal. I remember one day, during training, he wanted to join in our five-a-side game. He slipped, crashed to the ground and a ball, wellied by someone, ended up smacking him right on his nut. Slap bang on the side of his head! But he took it well – he is a total clown.

'I often ask myself how such a clumsy guy can have so much class in public. But laughter is key to everything he does. Those around him can identify with him. Not only does Wenger love a good laugh, but he can laugh at himself. He is this gangly wise man. He might seem slow when he is relaxed, to the point where it becomes annoying, but it is the innocence of Arsène that I love. Because he is a clown, this Clouseauesque character, he kept his human aspect. His clumsiness is really endearing, but doesn't stop him from being highly intelligent and humble. It just works.'

The Gunners quickly realised that their new manager was intent upon fostering excellent team spirit at the club. 'Above all he loved camaraderie,' said Adams. 'I know that he appreciated Ray Parlour, who was a bit of a roughneck but a nice guy if you knew how to take him. Arsène liked to discuss things and respected everyone's point of view.'

David Dein (who left in April 2007) watched his manager winning over his battle-hardened troops from a distance, transforming those wild horses into disciplined soldiers. Some time later, when travelling with Wenger, the vice-chairman would playfully enter 'Arsène Wenger: maker of miracles' into the hotel register, though that reflected just how appreciated the Frenchman had become at the club.

Dein may appear elegant now in his tailor-made suit and red scarf, a successful businessman who spends his holidays on the Côte d'Azur and berths his yacht at Antibes, but his roots are in the dusty London suburbs. He started building his fortune in working-class Shepherd's Bush, initially importing tropical produce. The nest egg he built up was eventually invested in the club closest to his heart, Arsenal.

In the early 1980s he paid almost £300,000 to buy 1,161 shares in the club and his empire-building had begun. He has since expanded his holding to more than 9,000 shares, worth an estimated £60 million, and was appointed vice-chairman of the club in 1985. Dein was to prove the lynchpin upon whom Wenger would rely when he arrived at Highbury. 'He is the best manager in Europe, as well as the most reliable,' said Dein. 'He transformed our club from top to bottom, even with training techniques and diet, which allowed our players to play for longer. He made average players good, good players very good, and very good players great. Arsène also has this authenticity with players.'

As well as mutual respect, humour plays a role in their friendship. At the end of Wenger's first season, Dein turned to the manager and asked him what had changed most radically at the club since his arrival some 12 months previously. The Alsatian, deadpan, retorted: 'Your French.' The manager and his vice-chairman were often to be found at the same table in San Daniele, the Italian restaurant near Highbury, where the intelligentsia of Arsenal used to dine after matches. Alex Fynn, a football consultant and one of the creators of the Premier League alongside David Dein at the beginning of the 1990s, knew the two men well. 'They operate as a mutually beneficial duo,' he said.

Fynn recalls a charity evening organised by the Variety Club in the luxury Savoy hotel on the bank of the Thames, to pay tribute to Wenger's contribution to English football. Wenger was the guest of honour. The guests, totalling around 400, forked out for their tickets largely to have the chance to listen and chat to Wenger at the end of the formal dinner. However, any questions that they wanted to ask had to be submitted in writing beforehand, so they could be vetted. Inevitably, there was the odd crank among their number. 'My name is Allan, but everyone calls me Al,' read one. 'Your name is Arsène – do your friends also shorten your name?' Fynn sat next to Dein that night. 'Of course, Arsène would have answered if he had understood the question,' he recalled. 'He would have found the right words and would definitely have seen the funny side. But generally, and though they shared the same sense of humour, David Dein was too protective to let Wenger deal with it on his own.'

When it came to matters on the pitch, Dein acted

differently with his head coach, allowing him great latitude and following his advice on recruitment. Wenger was happy to accept Dein's protection, but above all appreciated his trust. A member of Arsenal's board of directors declared: 'In ten years, I never saw Dein disagree with Arsène.'

'Nowhere else would Arsène have the latitude that David Dein gave him in Arsenal,' said the former Monégasque Jean Petit. 'They have a real understanding. One day I said to David Dein: "Everybody is talking about your team and Arsène, saying he is the best manager in the world. That's true, but in my eyes, the strongest thing about it is you. You were the first to think about inviting him to London." He responded in impeccable French that the tabloids had criticised him for his choice, portraying him as a fool: "Why did he go looking for this guy?"' Dein, already a French speaker, would become more and more of a Francophile once in daily contact with Wenger, to the point of seeking to work with AS Cannes as Arsenal's feeder club, and even signing a partnership agreement with AS St Etienne at the end of the 1990s. The use of feeder clubs was something of an innovation in the English game when compared with the practice on the Continent, but Wenger, with his deep knowledge of French football, recognised it as a means of adding to Arsenal's firepower. Any extra edge that could be gleaned would be beneficial.

Yet Arsenal were not only to benefit from French connections. Back in the summer of 1995, Dein had recruited Dennis Bergkamp from Inter Milan, the Dutchman costing a then record fee of £7.5 million and becoming the first major foreign star to switch to Highbury. Wenger, at Grampus

Eight at the time, had been consulted over his recruitment. Dein and Hill-Wood had sought his advice and the Alsatian had agreed the striker would be a good signing. Having worked with Hoddle at Monaco and Stoijkovic in Nagoya, Wenger had learned not to be intimidated by top-quality footballers. His was not blind admiration for their talents or achievements. Rather, he expected them to bring with them all that they had learnt from their careers, but then continue their education under him.

Yet when Bergkamp witnessed the sacking of Rioch – who had nominally brought him to the club – and the appointment of Wenger in his stead, he was initially doubtful. 'At the beginning I was a bit confused,' said Bergkamp. 'I wondered what this meant for me. Arsenal, and Rioch, had bought me the previous summer, and I wondered whether I would fall out of favour with the new boss just as I had done at Inter previously.' Yet Bergkamp respected the reputation of the man who took up the reins, having taken note of the career path enjoyed by the Alsatian from the south of France to distant Japan. 'When I was playing with Ajax [prior to signing for Inter], we often compared ourselves to Monaco, in particular the way both teams deployed two attackers. I was up to date with his match philosophy.'

Bergkamp had real pedigree. When he and Wenger met for the first time, they found common ground on which to base their future relationship. 'I had wanted to come to England, I had always wanted it,' he said. 'For me, for a long time, the English supporters – from all clubs – have been the best in the world. They sing, each player has his own song, it's unique.'

'Here in England, we get the feeling that the fans suffer in

silence with their team, but support them vocally,' added
Wenger. 'That's the dream, anyway. In other countries, in
general, they support in silence and destroy with passion.'
This understanding and empathy with the British fans was
one of the keys to explaining why Bergkamp and Wenger hit
it off from the outset. They had common goals. The other
link between them was born of how they liked the game to be
played.

'As soon as he arrived, I knew that his approach suited me,'
said Bergkamp. 'The teams of Arsène Wenger play offensive
football, aiming as a priority to exploit their strengths. This is
perfect for me. I was asked why I had signed for Arsenal
during my first season with the club. This, after all, was a
team with a certain reputation and at whom opposing
supporters would chant "boring, boring Arsenal." They had
a reputation for defensive football, for squeezing out 1–0
wins, but I knew that a new Arsenal was being born. At the
end of a few weeks, a few months, I realised that it was a
unique club. And after that, everything went well, thanks to
the arrival of Wenger, of course, who was exactly the
manager we needed at that time. Everything changed, and
look where it took us in the end.'

The pair went into battle side by side – one on the pitch,
the other in the dressing room. Indeed, they seemed to feed
off each other. 'I was always like this, even at Ajax,' said the
Dutchman. 'It is important to show that you can fight, for the
supporters and the team. And here, in England, it is vital.'

'You watch matches between Premier League teams,
mainly made up of foreign players, who play real English
football in terms of the rhythm of the game,' said Wenger.

'That is to say that it is the public and the relationship on the pitch that motivates you.'

In keeping with that, Bergkamp was never afraid of using an elbow or going in with studs showing to play his part for the team, and was sent off numerous times as a result. 'In my heart, I know what is really important for our sport: winning matches, claiming trophies,' he said. 'But it is normal for the public to support players with style and flair rather than those who only have to work at it.'

'There is always a balance to be found between basic principles,' added Wenger. 'For me, football is above all a game with principles of organisation but, at the same time, a certain freedom of expression. What attracted me to the game was the fact that players can express themselves.'

In his first few training sessions with Bergkamp, Wenger insisted the striker work on his strong points – his artistic side – rather than spending time trying to improve areas of his game that were not really in his nature, such as tackling. 'Working on technique is very important to me,' said Bergkamp. 'Arsène would tell me that his idea was to give me a certain liberty, almost a free role, rather than make me play within a rigid system.' Wenger would later use the same theory to coax the best out of Thierry Henry after he was signed in 1999, asking the forward to refine his sprint, his dribbles and shooting, and transform a player who had lost all confidence at Juventus into a world-class striker.

Not that Bergkamp and Wenger always saw eye to eye. Some four years after Wenger's arrival, just after Euro 2000, Bergkamp announced his retirement from international football to concentrate his time solely on the Gunners. 'Yet, when I took this decision, Arsène warned me that he might not be playing me as often in the future,' recalled Bergkamp. 'I said to him: "Hang on a minute. I've just ended my international career to dedicate myself exclusively to my club, and you're telling me I can't play every match?" It was strange to say the least.'

Resentful, Bergkamp, already considered a veteran and with more than 30 goals under his belt for the club, was vocal in questioning his role as luxury substitute. Wenger dodged the complaint by merely doffing his cap to the Dutchman. 'People say we have more than 27 million fans throughout the world,' he said at the time. 'If this is true, it is to a great extent thanks to Dennis, and if anyone symbolises true team spirit in our game, it is him.' Placated by this public show of support, Bergkamp remained a bastion of the club during its most successful spell in the modern era.

Wenger's first Premiership game in charge had come back on 12 October 1996 at Ewood Park, nestled in among the terraced houses of Blackburn. The Lancashire side had won the title in 1995 for the first time in 81 years under the management of Kenny Dalglish, following huge investment from local businessman and chairman Jack Walker, inspired by the goals of Alan Shearer and Chris Sutton. Arsène Wenger took his place on the bench, his side an awkward blend of experience and bright young things. There was Nigel Winterburn, a veteran of the George Graham defence that had sucked the spirit from opponents in the early 1990s, alongside Patrick Vieira, originally developed at Cannes but recently recruited from Milan, an unknown quantity in the Premier League.

'The atmosphere was strange because this was my first match, away from home,' recalled Wenger. 'We won, but only just. It was a real eye-opener. I said to myself at the end: "If this is what English football is like, then this isn't going to be easy."' This was a tough baptism. John Hartson and Martin Keown were booked for ugly fouls, while Blackburn pummelled the visitors with long balls. As far as Wenger was concerned, the 'kick and rush' style was from a bygone age. Arsenal prevailed thanks to two goals scored by Ian Wright. 'I wasn't sure how the older players would react to my instructions, as they hadn't really said a lot in the build-up to the game, but on the pitch they showed great technique and organisation,' said Wenger in the aftermath. 'The aim is always to win, while pushing your limits.'

It was the start Wenger had wanted, and his side were winners from the outset, even if they had not really shone at Ewood Park. The new manager sat at the front of the coach on the journey back to London filled with satisfaction while, behind him, the victorious players started chanting: 'We want our chocolate back.' Their playful singing was a cry for the old customs to return, for chocolate bars to be distributed among the players post-match. Arsène, a lover of chocolate as he is, merely smiled: chocolate and other sweets would not reappear in the Gunners' dressing room.

Back at the start of the 1996–97 campaign, Rémi Garde, Wenger's first recruit and signed on the new manager's insistence while still in Japan, had arrived to find Arsenal a club that paid little attention to diet. 'There was a little sweet jar on the table in the dressing room,' he recalled. 'Now I organise birthday parties for my children and they get the same stuff – all these coloured jelly babies. At Arsenal, we used to think these liquorice sweets were effectively Band-Aids [to make the players feel better]!'

A France international, handed his place in the national team by Michel Platini, Garde would be the first-ever foreigner to wear the captain's armband at Arsenal. He had observed, intrigued, the lax approach to dietary health upon his arrival. 'I saw all these boiled sweets and jelly babies in the dressing room,' he said. 'It was like an orgy of sweets. They were there instead of the cereal bars and energy drinks you'd be used to seeing in the French First Division. These sugary foods would be considered completely out of the question for professional sportsmen in France. But, to be honest, it was quite funny to see how things were done.'

Garde, recruited from RC Strasbourg, knew exactly what would happen once Wenger had found his feet at the club. 'Little by little, he made our regime more Continental, a bit more French. He didn't take the sweets away the next day, he didn't kick up a fuss, but he invited a dietitian to speak to the players and explain that sugar was not good for energy levels. Through a whole range of explanations, Arsène was able to modify these habits.' Slowly but surely, the Mars bars, jelly babies and bottles of Coca-Cola began to disappear and Wenger's influence took hold.

Gilles Grimandi, recruited from Monaco a year after Garde, heard many stories about the infamous sweet jar. 'It was no longer there by the time I arrived,' he said. 'Arsène had already got rid of it by then, but I knew from talking to some of the older players that in the first year some treats had still been permitted. It took a while before they were phased out completely. I could see the difference between the Arsène I knew of from Monaco and the one who had arrived in London. He was cooler in Arsenal, in any event at first. I think it was Japan which completely changed him.'

While discreetly ridding the changing room of the sweet jar, Arsène also began to introduce the eating habits and dietary supplements he had studied in Japan. Wenger had been impressed by how little obesity there was in Japanese society. As a result, all the cooked vegetables, fish and rice he had witnessed was meticulously imported into the Arsenal canteen. Proteins were combined with carbohydrates, with chicken breast and broccoli replacing fried chicken and chips. 'Suddenly, diet became a big issue with him, and he unfroze the budget so we could eat healthily,' said Tony Adams.

The dietitian who talked to the team about sweets was employed to explain to the players the benefits and principles behind the radical change in their diet. The same food would be ordered for away trips, even on flights to European games. Once, after a game in Greece, a guest among the travelling party recalled eating a 'horrible' meal on the plane back to England. In fact, it was food 'Gunners style', with no trace of flavour. 'It was the famous Wenger regime,' the passenger on the Athens–London flight recalled with a smile. Even here, though, the manager persuaded rather than imposed. For example, Nigel Winterburn was allowed to tuck into his favourite eggs on toast pre-match as long as he didn't add baked beans.

Whether on the pitch or in the canteen, one footballer among the Arsenal squad inherited by Wenger treated life as one big laugh. The chief clown in the Frenchman's squad was Ian Wright, the man whose brace against Blackburn had gifted the new manager's reign with a winning start to usher in the new era. Grimandi, who now works as a scout for the club, recalled his first encounters with the former Crystal Palace marksman. 'He was mad,' admitted Grimandi. 'Ian is someone you come across only once in your career. Even a guy like Sylvain Wiltord, who is a Premier League joker, is light years from Wright.

'In the minibus which took us to the training ground, he'd be the one who kicked things off. He loved music and he used to regale us with his dances. But the highlight was always the fly on the windscreen gag. Wrighty would get off the back of the minibus, then run like crazy around the front and throw himself against the windscreen. It used to crack us all up. Arsène wasn't often with us in the minibus, but he saw Wrighty's joke from outside. He didn't say anything.'

The manager never joined in, but he did appreciate the camaraderie on the bus. Garde, who would go on to become assistant manager at Olympique Lyonnais, was another who recognised Wright's importance off the pitch. 'For a long time, he was one of the only English players to strike up a relationship with the French lads at the club,' he said. 'Thanks to his humour, he could make fun of us – he was pretending to mock us, taking the mickey, but this was above all a means of communication. It wasn't so obvious as there were only a few of us from the manager's country, but Wright's humour helped to unite the two groups. He played a phenomenal role.

'He'd plunge his hands into that sweet jar whenever he could, but the stereo he carried around with him all over the place left a big impression on me. I wasn't the only one to be influenced by the sounds coming out of its speakers. One day, in the changing rooms right after a match, I was coming back with Arsène behind me and we heard the noise booming out of the dressing room. Wrighty was in charge of the CD player again. We looked at each other and he must have guessed my thoughts. But, if there was no music, I think we would have missed it.'

It had its benefits. There would be no motivational chanting in the home dressing room at Highbury ahead of games. Instead, with Wenger standing there in blazer and tie and half-naked players dancing away to the thumping music, Wright would lead the way. This was a throwback to the way Wimbledon would prepare for games with their infamous Crazy Gang in the late 1980s and early 1990s, when Vinnie Jones would take charge of the ghetto blaster. 'All this was totally new for Arsène,' said Grimandi. 'I don't think he would have accepted it in France because it wasn't part of our culture, but of course in England it wasn't something you could stop. Music causes many reactions, including dance, and some players, like Ian Wright, really relaxed. It doesn't mean they were indifferent to the match or not focused, and Arsène accepted this.'

With that in mind, Wenger allowed Wright to lug his stereo wherever he wanted, whether for home or away matches, and even to training. 'The atmosphere in the changing rooms before a match was more like a party than silent concentration,' said Wenger. 'Dancing, music blaring, short preparation, they had been playing and succeeding like that before my arrival, and I had to respect habits like his while changing what was necessary, like, for example, training. The English weren't mad about that. Some of the older players had a great life and didn't do much training at all, but were always on top form come Saturday with a very positive mental attitude. This is what you need – a top-level player can't succeed if he isn't intelligent.'

Bergkamp, one of the more reserved members of Wenger's squad, watched Wright joking and jiving in disbelief. 'Coming from such a professional footballing culture like Italy, I was surprised by what I saw when I arrived in England, sure,' he said. 'Music before a game would have been unthinkable at Inter Milan.'

Yet for Wright, who had come to the game late after joining Palace from the non-league club Greenwich Borough at the age of 24, the absence of music blaring away in the dressing rooms prior to kick-off would have been unthinkable. The England striker would score 185 goals for the Gunners, a club record which was eventually surrendered to Thierry Henry in October 2005 – both players key members of different sides sent out by Wenger at Highbury.

Wenger's indulgence for Wright and his pranks was one of the hallmarks of his management skills. Another of his strengths has shone through during his time in north London: loyalty. Max Hild, at 80, has remained in close contact with his ex-apprentice and has always been welcome at Arsenal. 'When I came to London, especially at the beginning, Arsène always greeted me very warmly,' he recalled. 'After the match he'd invite me to his office and ask me for my thoughts on the match. I'd just say: "Well, I saw such and such a good player." He'd listen intently to everything I said. But he doesn't need my advice any more. Arsène has become his own boss.'

The autumn of 1996 had proceeded smoothly on and off the pitch until, as winter approached, the players arrived at their University College Hospital training ground to find the changing rooms had burnt down during the night. With few options open to them, the management staff opted to use a neighbouring hotel as a base for the players to change. Arsenal's first team duly descended upon Sopwell House, a five-star hotel, to prepare for their daily sessions. This was a throwback to an England of bygone days, and the sight of tracksuited players trudging through reception en route to training sat rather awkwardly in these environs. Guests would mingle with Marc Overmars, Dennis Bergkamp, David Seaman and Tony Adams. Back then, Fabrice Dubois spent a few days observing Wenger at work, and was intrigued as to how the Arsenal manager kept so many high-profile figures content within his squad.

'I went to Sopwell to see Arsène and we chatted for hours in the hotel's rather grand surroundings,' said Dubois. 'I told him he was lucky to have so many great players upon which to call. He responded: "That's actually the most difficult thing, keeping them all happy. But in general I don't have too many problems with the great players really because of their status. I don't need to motivate them because they know they have to be good and perform well to stay in their national team." Even so, the fact remains that, even if Arsène only added a couple of new players in his first few months at the club, there was an impressive roll-call at training and not all of them could play every week.'

The Gunners squad would take a minibus from the hotel to their training pitches, with Wenger driven to the ground by his assistant, Pat Rice. The pair would oversee training from start to finish, the Frenchman's blue tracksuit flapping against his long pins in the breeze. He would often deliver short, sharp pep talks before each session, then start the players off with a 30-minute game limiting the number of touches each man could take in possession. 'To get the English training during the league season, you have to be strong,' said Wenger. With that in mind, he stuck to a timetable from which he rarely deviated: Sunday, rest; Monday, training in the morning; Tuesday, a session in the morning then another in the afternoon; Wednesday, Thursday and Friday, training in the morning. This schedule would change according to midweek domestic or European games, but other than that it was rigid.

When a match took place on a Saturday afternoon, the morning of the game was reserved for a warm-up session. 'I remember these short sessions,' said Rémi Garde. 'It wasn't just stretching the muscles, it was holistic, including a short stroll before matches, with sessions taking no more than 15 or 20 minutes. I think this sprang from his experience in Japan. It was almost a stretching of the spirit, a psychological warm-up based on small movements.'

This gentle physical warm-up, this soothing of the soul 'to counteract lethargy', was mainly carried out in a room of the hotel, and Garde remembered how intimate they were. 'These small confined rooms gave the exercise a rallying feel, with Arsène urging his troops on. He didn't really speak, but he made us undertake a range of movements which became a ritual. It wasn't yoga or t'ai chi, but it was very Zen. Some players approached these sessions as a purely physical exercise, while others got more from it. I wouldn't go so far as to say it was spiritual, but Arsène's approach wasn't far from it.'

The sessions were not compulsory: each player was allowed to decide whether or not to attend. 'But Arsène considered these sessions as vital to a player's preparation,' said Garde. 'He just has a way of not having to impose his will. You just needed to understand that it is the right thing to do. And, in general, when you are around him, you follow him.'

Yet tactical planning was key to the group as a whole. There, in St Albans, the manager found the perfect atmosphere to apply the methods he had learnt at Milanello, AC Milan's training centre, when the young Wenger had visited Arrigo Sacchi whilst coaching at Monaco. Sacchi, like Wenger, had had a mediocre playing career but had qualified as a manager through the celebrated academy of Coverciano. He had subsequently worked from Rimini to Milan, via Fiorentina and Parma, collecting trophies en route – one Serie A, two Champions Leagues, two Inter-Continental Cups and two European Super Cups with Milan. He was considered 'the modern prophet of football' with his zonal marking techniques and free-flowing attacking style inspiring, among others, Rafael Benitez before the Spaniard progressed to success at Valencia and Liverpool. Wenger, like the Spaniard, counted Sacchi as a mentor.

Christian Damiano, who won the European Championships as coach of the French under-18s with a side which
included Thierry Henry, had also studied with Milan and
Real Madrid, but was surprised just how open Wenger was to
such outside influences. 'In the beginning, he was very much
tactically inspired by German football, but bit by bit he
evolved,' said Damiano of his compatriot. 'He always
questioned himself and wanted to see the very best that was
out there. He was very close to Sacchi at Milan, and that had
a huge influence on the way he approached the game. He
went to Milan all the time, accompanied by Jean Fernandez.
He is still inspired by current trends and performances. I
would even say that he has always been influenced by them.
At the same time, at Arsenal he implemented everything he
had learnt in France.'

Fabrice Dubois would argue that Wenger constructed the
'made in Arsenal' style of play by scrutinising individuals
rather than general systems. 'You just have to look at how he
managed Overmars and all these great stars in training
during his career,' he said. 'The minutiae that he worked on
were incredible. He got them all to stand in position, then
move just a few metres to the left then the right. Basic stuff,
but all geared towards improving their awareness, movement
and mobility.'

Christian Damiano, who would become Gérard Houllier's
assistant at Liverpool, has followed Wenger's methods since
his years as an apprentice. 'Easy technical exercises have a
tendency to put the player in a certain comfort zone and
cause a certain lack of vigilance,' he said. 'It is therefore
necessary to introduce targets into easy exercises, and make

them more demanding by introducing one or two hurdles to motivate them and keep them concentrated. It is mainly an issue of permanent adjustment in relation to the players. The great footballers like this challenge in any event, but they always need to be placed in an attractive situation.'

With less talented players, Wenger adopted a specific approach: exploiting their strengths and relying on the talents of others to haul them through. If Ray Parlour's ball control left something to be desired, Wenger would ask his team-mates to pass the ball to his feet at a precise angle. Arsenal would lean on Parlour's energy and industry, and the flair players – like Overmars – around him would complement that style. One of that number, Patrick Vieira, would take such exercises on board and, gradually, come into his own.

The Frenchman always boasted the promise to develop into a great player. Whilst in Japan, Wenger had sanctioned two purchases for the Arsenal squad, with his compatriots Rémi Garde and Vieira plucked from Strasbourg and Milan. Wenger followed a similar course of action to that he had employed in France, luring a blend of talented youngsters and older, experienced campaigners to his ranks. Garde fell into the second category. Vieira, brought up at AS Cannes where he was spotted by Wenger before opting to join Milan, was definitely a bright young thing.

The Senegal-born midfielder claimed an Italian Cup with the Milanese, in May 1996, and featured in a handful of league games, but the Frenchman spent most of his time shivering on the bench. Wenger, though, had continued to monitor his situation. Conscious that Vieira was in limbo at the San Siro, and well aware of the potential he could offer, Arsène made his move. 'I already knew that Arsène had me in mind when he opted to go to Arsenal,' said Vieira. 'Why did I choose England? Because I was lucky and I like the spirit of the English players on the pitch.' In Garde, Vieira found a type of elder brother. 'Rémi Garde . . . I will always remember how he greeted me when I arrived, how he took me under his wing.'

Vieira would eventually follow in the footsteps of Garde and wear the captain's armband at Highbury some seven years later. He would be the skipper developed and forged by Wenger, his form improving immeasurably at the club. The ambitious midfielder had already been dreaming of claiming trophies back in the autumn of 1996, but silverware would prove elusive in that first season in the Premiership. Despite convincing wins against Leeds (3–0), Tottenham Hotspur (3–1), Everton (3–1) and Chelsea (3–0), the Gunners would end this campaign in third place, languishing behind Manchester United and Newcastle. The champions, inspired by Eric Cantona and steered so supremely by Alex Ferguson, claimed a league double over Wenger's side that year, beating them home and away.

Yet, almost unnoticed, Wenger was making his mark. On Saturday 5 April 1997, an unknown was handed a debut for the Premiership game between Chelsea and Arsenal. Nicolas Anelka, at 18, was a new hope unearthed by Wenger who had been prised from Paris St Germain for a bargain £500,000 some three months before. Arsenal won 3–0 at Stamford Bridge. If the scoreline generated the headlines at the time, interest would centre on the striker in the years to come.

Yet that first season was to end in relative disappointment. On 19 April, Blackburn Rovers visited Highbury, and with the hosts ahead late in the game, Arsenal kicked the ball out to allow an opposing player to receive treatment. When play resumed, Blackburn kicked deep into Arsenal's area with Chris Sutton putting Nigel Winterburn under pressure, the full-back duly forced to concede a corner. Arsenal players were still protesting when the visitors equalised from the corner through Garry Flitcroft. The draw, furiously received both in the dugout and the stands, deprived the hosts of two points and would eventually cost Arsenal a place in the Champions League as the Londoners ended up slipping behind Newcastle on goal difference. Wenger was gutted in the aftermath, vowing never to forget the costly loss to Blackburn. But once the feeling of injustice had subsided, he set to work in the transfer market, turning his attentions back to France, and to Monaco, where he set his sights upon signing a rough diamond he had been tracking since leaving the Principality. Emmanuel Petit.

It was 6.30 p.m. on Thursday 17 July 1997 and Arsène Wenger, wearing sunglasses and clad in training gear bearing his initials, strode on to the turf of the stadium in Nyon. The venue was stunning, the Alps visible in the distance and the tranquil Lake Leman gleaming nearby. Opposite stood Uefa's headquarters. In these idyllic surroundings Wenger had chosen to prepare for the 1997–98 Premiership season.

The manager's journal for the three-week stay resembled work notes, with sheets of preparation revealing the huge attention to detail demanded. Wenger left nothing to chance.

At 4.15 p.m., his team reached the hotel. Rooms were allocated almost instantly, with a bite to eat at 5 p.m. before the squad trotted out for training. Ahead of them lay nothing but gruelling work.

Wenger took the training sessions, flanked by his two assistants, and oversaw everything that his players were asked to do. He began that pre-season with 20 outfield players, which would become 22 over the next few days, and three goalkeepers. The exercises that followed, whether physical, technical or designed to be fun, were undertaken with clock-work precision. The warm-up lasted 19 minutes: running, stretching. If mobility is the key to most of the routines, so too is ball work, with the onus placed on feints and footwork. The travelling Arsenal squad played the local Nyon team on 20 July, with the Premiership club fielding a different side in each half. Then, on the following Wednesday, Wenger's side played RC Strasbourg in a friendly, though by then, their ranks had been supplemented.

The two new recruits had been lured from Monaco and would make their debut on the season's opening day at Leeds. Wenger strode off the team coach at Elland Road with two long-established stars at his side, David Platt and Dennis Bergkamp, to be followed by two unknowns, Gilles Grimandi and Manu Petit. The latter, all flowing locks, had departed France wracked with self-doubt but Wenger was intent upon rejuvenating his stuttering career. The team sheet that day showed a multinational selection which, over the course of the ensuing nine months, would establish themselves as a potent force. There were Englishmen in David Seaman, Nigel Winterburn, Steve Bould, Ray Parlour and Ian Wright;

Dutchmen in Bergkamp and Marc Overmars; then four 'Frenchies' in Garde, Vieira, Grimandi and Petit. The game ended 1–1, a promising result early in the campaign, with the Gunners finding their feet in the weeks ahead to sweep aside Coventry (2–0), Southampton (3–1), Bolton (4–1), Chelsea (3–2) and West Ham (4–0).

Even so, the dreary autumn which followed condemned Arsenal to start the new year some ten points behind the league leaders, Manchester United, with the bookmakers convinced the title was to remain at Old Trafford. The Gunners were, apparently, in hopeless pursuit. Frustration spilled over at the club's Christmas Eve party at London's Café de Paris, with Tony Adams venting his anguish to his manager. The centre-half's complaints centred on his assessment that the midfield was not adequately protecting the defence, the celebrated back four of Winterburn, Adams, Keown and Lee Dixon, with Bould as a ready-made back-up. 'He listened to me,' said Adams. 'Obviously, he made his own decisions after I'd said my piece, but he was very sympathetic to his players' point of view. He was very approachable, much more so than Bruce Rioch before him. That day, he took all of our opinions into consideration. I told him what I thought, and that helped us build a more honest relationship.'

Those concerns were related to the midfield shield, Petit and Vieira, and acted as a spur for the remainder of the campaign. The pair never looked back, their form carrying the team to one of the most astonishing late-season revivals of recent times. When one marauded forward, the other sat deep in defence; if Vieira was beaten, there was Petit to quell the danger; Arsenal's back line had their protection. In the blink of an eye, the Frenchmen developed such an understanding that it was as if they could go into battle blindfolded and still emerge victorious. Arsenal were unstoppable in the final weeks of that season, sweeping all before them in the Premiership. Petit, a player who had been so down on his luck when he arrived at Highbury, was reborn to inspire those around him. In April, Arsenal hammered Newcastle (3–1), Blackburn (4–1) and Wimbledon (5–0), though the players themselves levelled credit for their resurgence firmly with the manager. 'What Arsène accomplished with Arsenal that season was huge,' said Petit. 'He propelled the club to first position, and, in doing so, began to establish Arsenal as one of the powerhouses of English football again.'

Petit's own contribution was outstanding, though this was a player whose Arsenal career would eventually end in disappointment, albeit with a lucrative move to Barcelona in 2000 which prompted simmering bitterness. There was a further spell in England with Chelsea, though it was at Arsenal that Manu felt most at home. 'Arsène and I always kept in contact the first year after I left, then gradually we lost touch a little,' he said. 'He is a very busy man. Though, in saying that, when we do bump into each other, we always enjoy talking. I have some powerful memories from those days at Arsenal, like the song the supporters used to come up with for each player. I still know the lyrics to all those songs by heart.'

Back in the spring of 1998, Arsenal won ten Premiership games in a row to whittle away at United's lead at the top. The decisive encounter was to come at Old Trafford in mid-March, with the home side's flair snuffed out by the visitors' suffocating midfield of Petit and Vieira. With ten minutes to go and anxiety sweeping through United ranks, Marc Overmars gathered a pass by Anelka to poke in the winning goal. The doubters who had greeted Wenger's appointment at Highbury recognised the genius at work, this exciting side – a team laced with power and intent – unstoppable. The tables were turning, and as May 1998 came and went, the first signs of a revolution were visible.

Thirty years previously, back in May 1968, French students had taken to the streets to protest in their own modern-day revolution. Yet for one 19-year-old economics under-graduate, the rioting and marches which erupted across the country that year were a mere sideshow. Arsène Wenger was too busy either playing football or serving his apprenticeship watching games across the continent to throw stones against the authorities in the streets of Strasbourg. Back then, he deemed the groundswell of political feeling to be nothing more than a fad. Later, he became politically liberal in his thinking, and overtly 'pro-Europe', but events in Paris in the summer of 1968 rather passed him by.

Some 30 years on, with his chestnut locks long since shorn and greying at the temple, the 49-year-old stood in a pocket of north London and realised a long-standing ambition. His odd collection of nationalities, a mishmash of ages and outlooks, welcomed Everton to Highbury for their last home game of the 1997–98 campaign with Arsenal eager to celebrate a first league title since 1991. The din inside the stadium was of giddy expectation, the celebratory mood typified by supporters wearing traffic cones as hats, passing

cars blaring their horns in pre-match delight, and a stream of
delirious 'Gooners' pouring out of the underground stations
in the area. On Avenell Road outside the ground, the fanzine
vendors were doing a roaring trade, with the match day
magazine similarly selling well. On most of their covers was
Wenger, beaming from ear to ear.

On the pitch, the Frenchmen on show were Anelka, Vieira
and Petit, with six Englishmen – Seaman, Dixon, Adams,
Keown, Winterburn and Parlour – complemented by Marc
Overmars and Christopher Wreh, George Weah's cousin, in
the line-up. This was Winterburn's 500th game for the club.
Just like Adams and Keown, he had Wenger to thank for
extending his playing career. Everton, with nothing to play
for, were swept aside with ease, the hosts already three up
when Adams raced through on goal and slammed in a fourth.
The captain's reward was the icing on the cake. The FA Cup
was to be secured later that month, completing a remarkable
league and cup double, to prompt open-top bus celebrations
through north London. 'All those people waiting for us . . .'
said Petit. 'It was awe-inspiring just to see that crowd
everywhere; it gave us a taste of how things would be at the
World Cup that summer.'

Petit, fed by Vieira, would end up scoring *Les Bleus*' third
goal in the World Cup final at the Stade de France, a euphoric
dismissal of Brazil, in July. In the wake of that triumph, the
Daily Mirror's back-page headline screamed: 'Arsenal win the
World Cup'. Wenger, working as a commentator at the
tournament, had more reason than most to feel proud of the
national side's achievement given the complement of Arsenal
players in their ranks. 'I felt so happy when they scored the

third goal,' he said. 'First of all, because it sealed the fate of the game and I understood right then that we had won. Then because Petit and Vieira knew each other so well. They had been playing together all of the previous year and that goal topped it all off. Manu Petit had a great World Cup, but I was just as happy for Vieira, who didn't get to play much [as a *Bleu*]. It was so symbolic just how those two players shone during their season with Arsenal and achieved the Double. For them to win the World Cup together the way they did was wonderful.'

Back in north London, some Arsenal fans celebrated France's victory as if England had won, such was their affection for the French contingent at the club, with Wenger chief amongst them. 'You could tell Arsène had been under a huge amount of pressure since he had arrived at the club, a year and a half earlier,' said Grimandi. 'When he came in, some tried really hard to hurt him.' The utility player was referring to totally unfounded rumours concerning the Alsatian's personal life; which opposing fans, with the usual delicacy displayed on the terraces, had seized upon and incorporated into abusive chants. Wenger has had to endure chants at away grounds ever since, which made the celebrations shared with his own supporters on occasions such as the Everton rout, with the title claimed at Highbury, all the more special. 'The day we beat Everton, I really sensed how much this title meant to him. He seemed really, really happy, completely contented. So with this first title you could just read the satisfaction of a job well done on his face. I saw Arsène radiating such relief. You could tell how proud he felt just by looking at him.'

'Winning the Premier League, and at home no less, was a great moment,' admitted Wenger. 'This championship was truly the result of a whole year's worth of hard work. I was also the first foreigner to win the English league, which is something I will never forget. As for the day itself, I remember the sunshine, the lap of honour, the noise of people cheering . . .' The trophy paraded around Highbury on 3 May would soon be followed by another, of equal importance – the FA Cup. Indeed, on 16 May at Wembley, Nicolas Anelka truly came of age.

The youngster had been born on 14 March 1979 in Versailles, growing up in the Parisian suburb of Trappes, Yvelines, with Wenger first becoming aware of his considerable talent whilst manager at Grampus Eight. Anelka had made his mark at Paris St Germain, handed his debut by Luis Fernandez on 6 February 1996 at Monaco. But when Fernandez was replaced that summer by Ricardo Gomes, Wenger got wind in Japan that Anelka no longer featured as heavily in the club's first-team plans. 'Allegedly, the reason I wasn't playing was because I was a kid,' said Anelka. 'That was nonsense.

'So I went to see Ricardo and told him: "Coach, I want to play. Trust me." I wasn't asking to be the player the team had to be built around or anything. I just wanted to get a chance to prove my worth. Ricardo replied that I should wait a little, that I should be patient. This went on for three months, and still nothing happened. I couldn't take it any more, so I left.'

Wenger, by then at Arsenal, seized his chance. The relationship between the Gunners manager and the PSG president, Michel Denisot, was one of honest respect, but the

Arsenal boss exploited the French club's relative inertia over their young starlet and a loophole in French law. Anelka, encouraged by Wenger, turned down a six-month contract offered by the PSG sporting director Jean-Michel Moutier and, almost unnoticed, signed for Arsenal on the day the French club took on Juventus in the European Cup. Panicked, PSG suggested they would take Arsenal to the European courts, but it was an empty threat with the so-called Bosman ruling – the 1995 European Court of Justice decision permitting players to move to a foreign club without a transfer fee at the end of their deals – effectively allowing the youngster to move under freedom of contract.

There was fury in the French capital. 'But would it be considered shocking for French parents to send their children to study abroad if the university over there is better than at home?' asked Wenger, justifying Anelka's move. In the end, a compensation settlement amounting to no more than £500,000 was agreed with the French club. Some three years later, PSG spent around £20 million to lure the striker back to Paris after an unsuccessful year at Real Madrid. Indeed, the forward has commanded huge transfer fees ever since his controversial move to Arsenal, even if it could be argued he has rarely made the most of his exceptional talent. 'When you have been fortunate enough to have talented players, all you hope for is that they make the most of that talent and make it big,' admitted Wenger. From PSG to Arsenal, then Real Madrid with whom he won the Champions League in 2000, PSG again, Liverpool, Manchester City, Fenerbahçe and, most recently in the Premiership, Bolton Wanderers, clubs across the continent have warmed to Anelka, with his time at

Highbury having set his career on the right path.

'I have nothing but the highest respect for Arsène because he gave me my chance,' admitted the striker. 'He believed in me and trusted me enough to let me play alongside players like Dennis Bergkamp, Ian Wright and Mark Overmars. This is why I have such huge respect for him. And I am not the only one. Just ask any other young player who has grown up under Wenger. He would tell you: "We know you're good and that you've got the ability required." When you're a trainee and the coach talks to you like that, it does wonders for your self-confidence. He must be really clever because whenever he buys a player they always seem to end up featuring in the Premier League and playing there as if they had been there for five years. It's amazing. He likes to keep things simple, and never complicates his instructions unnecessarily.'

Wenger himself cites his former protégé as a 'tiger' of a player. 'When he goes for it, he can do some serious damage,' he conceded. Anelka departed for Real under something of a cloud, having demanded a higher wage than the club was willing to offer, and is reminded of the fall-out which tarnished his reputation by disgruntled Gooners every time he lines up against the Londoners these days. But the France international nevertheless left a lasting mark on Arsenal. From 5 April 1997 when he first featured in a thumping win over Chelsea, via a debut goal in the 3–2 win over Manchester United on 9 November 1997, to the summer of 1999 when his relationship with the club's hierarchy ruptured, forcing him to Spain, 'Nico' was a searing presence in Arsenal's ranks. 'Anelka was an incredible player,' said the former Arsenal striker turned journalist Alan Smith. 'When he first came to London he was just a kid and had hardly ever played top-flight football, but he got better and better by the day and forged an excellent relationship with Dennis Bergkamp. It was such a shame that he chose to leave the club in the manner that he did.'

Wenger relied upon Bergkamp's guile to supply the livewire striker, who had quickly assumed Ian Wright's mantle as the club's principal goal threat. 'Arsène basically recognised Anelka's strong points and, with Bergkamp's help, made a first-class player out of him,' added Smith. 'It was really shrewd of Wenger to use Dennis as a supply line.' Thereafter, the Arsenal manager would continue to employ a strong forward alongside raw pace, with Nwankwo Kanu, Davor Suker and Emmanuel Adebayor, who was bought in January 2006, lining up alongside Thierry Henry as Bergkamp's role at the club steadily wound down. Yet even now, Wenger would admit to regret that Anelka, poorly advised by his stable of agents, chose to seek new pastures in the summer of 1999, despite Arsenal achieving an astonishing profit on his £23 million sale. (Wenger had wanted Anelka to stay, but he did not try to stop the move when the situation got complicated. For his part, Anelka has good things to say about Wenger: 'I won my first trophy with Arsenal, and it meant so much to me. Moreover, it was all taking place in England, with all the other French! It was the old good times. I've only kept sweet memories of my times at Highbury. It is where it all really started for me. It is where I was taught my football, in many ways. That is where I took off. And Arsène was there to teach me all that. It is the start of everything.')

Back on Saturday 16 May 1998, Arsenal's supporters had

migrated to Wembley confident of securing the second leg of a glorious league and cup double, with Newcastle United waiting in the FA Cup final. The Geordies were a fading force from the side that had challenged Manchester United at the summit in the mid-1990s under Kevin Keegan's stewardship, but still boasted experienced players desperate to secure the club's first major silverware since the Inter-Cities Fairs Cup in 1969. The Arsenal line-up that day included the stalwart English core, as well as the trio of Frenchmen who had already made their mark in the Premiership, with the pace of Marc Overmars and Anelka and the bustling industry of Ray Parlour unnerving the hordes from the North-East. As ever, Vieira and Petit dictated play forthrightly in the centre, and 23 minutes in, Arsenal had their reward. Overmars, racing clear, opened the scoring and the contest, already, was as good as over.

Parlour's slipped pass for Anelka, 20 minutes from time, confirmed the win. With a few minutes remaining, Wenger told Grimandi to warm up on the touchline with the former Monégasque desperate to enter the fray. Unfortunately for him, the Arsenal manager was so lost in his thoughts with the Double so close that he forgot to complete the substitutions. 'He glanced at me when the whistle blew and I understood from his look that he had really wanted me in on the game, but that it had just slipped his mind,' said Grimandi. 'Even if playing for a mere few minutes in a Cup final would have been magical, I don't resent missing out. For him, that was the accomplishment of a brilliant season, and a tremendous achievement.'

It was 27 years since Arsenal had last won the Double and,

although he remained at the club for a further season, that success at Wembley represented the high point of Anelka's stay. His brothers, acting as his agents, persuaded him to move to Real in the summer of 1999 after 23 goals in 65 appearances. He was one of the first *Galácticos* – the perceived best of the best – at the Bernabéu, with the fee recouped by Arsenal allowing them to start work on a new training centre at London Colney. 'But we lost Nico, which was a blow,' admitted Wenger. 'You don't so much forget it as digest it. When you have a player of that calibre you don't want to lose him. Yes, it does hurt, because first and foremost, you're a coach and a tutor. So when things don't go as well for them as you'd like them to, it makes you feel sad. Now when a lad has one or two outstanding years, there's bound to be a trough to follow. I can't think of one player starting out at 20 who just progresses steadily to the top. In order to go back up, maybe it was necessary for Nicolas to hit the bottom at some point.'

The Double of 1998 set the tone for Wenger's reign and was a groundbreaking achievement. 'Back then, to see a foreign coach winning the Premiership was completely unheard of,' he conceded. 'There was this prejudice against coaches from abroad. It was said that a foreigner couldn't possibly win the English Championship. I now feel that I have lost this uniqueness, that is, to be the first foreign coach to win in England, given the successes of others after me.' José Mourinho has achieved similar success since at Chelsea, flushed by Roman Abramovich's millions, but Wenger was a trailblazer.

*

Arsène Wenger's office is his laboratory. London Colney, 'his' training complex, is the Arsenal preparatory base, having been built as per their manager's ideas and designed precisely along the lines he had demanded. This is where his theories are put into practice. His office is about 15 metres square, with windows along two sides to flood the room with light. Arsène set himself down on one of the two small couches across from his desk. There are pictures of his past successes on the wall ('He didn't even choose those himself,' a friend of his acknowledged) which brighten up the understated white paint, and a thin pink carpet.

On the wall behind the sofa, commanding attention over the entire room, hangs a photograph of his flagship team from 2003–04. The Invincibles. A small crystal dish, a delicate glass bird, a wooden apple and a North African-style ashtray litter the coffee table. There is a plant in the corner, token greenery in an otherwise sterile environment. The main window looks out on to the car park, where the players' lavish, fuel-guzzling cars are all neatly parked. The coach's Mercedes-Benz is among them, with its 'W'-branded personalised number plate.

Facing the coach is a small, if slightly bulky, television. There is no hi-tech flat screen or plasma, or even a DVD player, the technology stuck in the 1990s and limited to a VHS video recorder with tapes crammed into a shelf. The only slightly modern item is the remote control for the satellite television box. Arsène has allowed himself the luxury of the plethora of television channels, although the only ones that get much of a look-in are broadcasting games from across the globe: La Liga, Serie A, the South

American or Far Eastern championships. The games never stop.

Outside are the wind-swept training pitches where the manager has requested the groundsman to plant the exact same grass as in Highbury to ensure that his Gunners are able to practise on the same turf. This is where the manager plans Arsenal's successes. 'I spend 90 per cent of my waking hours thinking about football,' he freely admitted. Access to the centre is strictly by invitation only. There are wire fences up around the complex, with security cameras monitoring for trespassers. Those French or Japanese tourists who camp outside the main entrance, clamouring for autographs, might mistake the place for a military compound. Regardless, they are rarely discouraged even by the sign decreeing 'Players are not allowed to sign autographs'.

If Wenger was not responsible for the draconian level of security here, the design and philosophy of the place is completely down to him. The Alsatian was consulted on every aspect of the redevelopment of the London Colney site. Unlike at AS Monaco, where the directors wouldn't let him fulfil his dreams, Wenger has built this complex up from scratch in much the same way as he was permitted to at Nagoya Grampus Eight. 'He has a real passion and high regard for architects, as they make it possible for him to build a training centre just like the one in Colney as well as ensuring a higher level of comfort for his players,' confirms a confidant.

The main building, a two-storey structure of shimmering glass and solid steel, is astonishing. Opened in 1999, the training centre is a white-walled factory. A laboratory where

Wenger-style football is developed. 'This is a labour which began when I first arrived,' admits the Frenchman. 'It took about three years to complete the first phase. The hardest part was to buy the field, the trouble being to find it in the first place, then to acquire it and to obtain the building licence. This is a green belt area and, even though a football pitch seems green, it's awkward to gain planning permission.'

But, as has been proved since, nothing can stop this manager. The Colney site is of key importance. 'This forms part of a club's biggest projects,' he said. 'I've always thought that the quality of the pitches, infrastructures, healthcare, swimming pool and gym is essential to high-level football in this day and age. At the same time, it is an attractive feature when it comes to luring players to the club. It gives off the impression that this club has a lot of ambition.' With that in mind, the plethora of pictures depicting recent triumphs, from the Double of 2002 and the unbeaten campaign two years later, offer a constant reminder of what Professor Wenger has achieved.

The grounds have been heavily influenced by the Frenchman's sojourn in Japan, with streams, small grassy hills, wild reeds in water beds and tiny bridges reminiscent of a Far Eastern garden. The gym area looks out upon this tranquil scene, as if to offer body and mind the chance to unwind. Such is Wenger's desire to keep the whole complex in pristine condition that he requested an extra layer of gravel be laid on the car park used by players and staff so that they did not trample mud from the practice pitches into the main building.

Through the main entrance, the players pass through large

glass doors into a small antechamber where, each morning, they collect their fan mail from large pigeon-holes, each bearing their name. They discard their shoes and head off to the changing rooms and therapy centre. The sauna and pool are reserved for players, whether fit or injured. Such is Wenger's desire to keep tabs on the progress made by those players in rehabilitation that he has even installed underwater cameras in the pool to chart how they run and move below the surface. He also insisted that the floor of the pool be adjustable, so it could be raised or lowered to suit the injured player's particular workout. In this way, the medical team can monitor development and decide on the most suitable exercises to get players back to peak fitness. There are similar cameras in the weights room and gym area, monitoring everything from the exercise bikes to the treadmills, so Wenger can monitor his squad's recovery. It is as if Arsenal has taken a leaf out of *Big Brother*, such is the level of surveillance.

'Arsène's approach is human, technical and scientific,' said Dr Yann Rougier, Arsenal's official dietitian who worked alongside Wenger for a decade. 'You could say that Arsène is an explorer beyond the limits of football but, at the same time, as well as the fact that he used to be a player, you could say that Wenger's intellect aspires to a sort of excellence. Yes, he is technically brilliant, but also has a human touch.'

The bay windows which flank each side of the building allow light to flood in. 'After building Colney, Arsène studied how the sunlight passed through the glass so his players would have the best environment to improve their state of mind as well as their bodies,' added Rougier. 'Arsène wanted the building to be designed in such a way that diffused light enables footballers to maintain good levels of serotonin and dopamine [stress reduction and good mood hormones]. The light is especially important when players are recuperating. His eyes receive the sun, which improves recovery. It's amazing. I have never seen such a high-performing intellectual eclecticism.'

On the first floor, the huge cafeteria is also bathed in light, and there are sofas upon which the players can relax in front of the TV, and round tables around which they chat. Arsène even designed the tableware, or at least approved the knives and forks. 'The qualities Arsène showed at AS Cannes were the same as those on show in London,' said Richard Conte, the manager's friend and permanent confidant. 'The competitor remained the competitor, the winner also. Everything he did was with an attention to detail that really makes the difference. What changed for him was the off-the-pitch work that the Arsenal manager needs to do. His advice is asked in areas which have nothing to do with the game. A new training centre or choice of cutlery – he is asked about everything these days.'

Amongst Wenger's contemporaries, the Colney training complex became something of a Mecca, a place rival managers from Jean Tigana to Glenn Hoddle visited as they sought a blueprint upon which to build their own clubs' training centres. It became a place to seek advice and inspiration. In 2000 the Liverpool manager Gérard Houllier visited the St Albans site while in the process of redesigning his own club's Melwood centre. He asked his compatriot to keep his visit secret at the time, though it is clear from the redesigned training complex on Merseyside just where Houllier was inspired.

Some might be surprised to hear that Wenger threw his doors open to rival managers to inspect his facilities, but they gained no real insight into the Arsenal coach's tactics on their visits. Arsène's tactical nuances placed huge emphasis on the team as a whole. 'We merely ask players to play the way in which they feel most comfortable,' said Wenger. 'Arsenal's game was perhaps more direct before I came – we gradually developed into a more structured game, from the back, and to which players adapted remarkably well. A more structured game that needs to be based on movement and mobility. We achieved this, but it is always dangerous, because you never know too much in advance. The ideal situation for a trainer is to find a system which allows his players to express them-selves as much as possible. Whether you can actually change things little by little, gradually integrating new elements, and be successful is very much down to chance.'

Christian Damiano, briefly Houllier's assistant manager at Liverpool, was invited to watch sessions at Colney for a few days. Once he had entered this 'green factory' with its dozen carefully tended pitches, it was the precise care that amazed him. 'What made me smile was that Arsène had the grass cut by hand,' he said. 'For me that just shows his attention to detail, at all levels. I was an observer, but I often felt privileged as he called me to his side, on the pitch, to discuss positioning problems. He asked me: "How would you solve this or that technical or tactical aspect?" '

Damiano was not alone in coming to north London. Daniel Jeandupeux, Jean-Marc Guillou and Claude Puel all

Wenger (top left) pictured at his first Holy Communion at the church of St Louis in his home town of Duttlenheim. 'I've always told myself that there's nothing in life other than football,' said Wenger the Catholic.

The FC Duttlenheim youth team in 1963, with Wenger the second player standing from the right. Back then, his footballing dreams centred upon forging a career as a player rather than as a manager.

Wenger stands proudly, third from the right, amid the FC Duttlenheim team who won the Bas-Rhin regional Third Division title in the 1968–69 season. He scored 13 goals in 18 appearances that campaign.

The Alsatian's only experience of European football as a player was painful, with a 4-0 defeat at Duisberg in a third-round Uefa Cup tie in November 1978. The first team's regular sweeper was injured, but his deputy failed to impress.

In the colours of
AS Nancy, an ailing
top-flight club, where
the young manager
was given his first
chance to impress
with a three-year
contract worth
£2,500 per month.
Wenger was forced to
wheel and deal in the
transfer market to
keep the side afloat.

At Nancy's Marcel Picot stadium for a game against Girondins de Bordeaux. The relegation
suffered in his third season at the club remains the only demotion of his 30-year
coaching career.

Wenger, flanked by Claude Puel, José Touré and Fabrice Poullain, takes his Monaco squad on a lap of the club's training ground in 1989. The manager always tried to put himself through everything he demanded of his players.

Relief sweeps through the dug out as Wenger celebrates with his assistant Jean Petit. His Monaco side had just secured their first league win of the 1994–95 season with a narrow 1-0 success at Caen's Michel d'Ornano stadium.

Wenger addresses his Grampus Eight squad, his assistant Boro Primorac to the right of the picture, during his second season in Japan. That year (1996), his side would finish fourth in the league championship but would claim silverware with victory in the Emperor's Cup, the equivalent of the FA Cup.

監督
ベンゲール
ARSENE WENGER

The Frenchman is introduced to the crowd on the scoreboard as Grampus Eight visit their fierce rivals Kashima Antlers.

In deep discussion with his good friend Jean-Marc Guillou, under whom he had coached at AS Cannes in the 1980s. Whilst at Arsenal, Wenger has often tapped into Guillou's expertise on African football.

Wenger relaxes with a game of beach football in Morocco.

Tempers are frayed on the touchline. Wenger and his bitter rival Sir Alex Ferguson prowl the technical area as Manchester United visit Highbury. Games between the teams have become increasingly explosive, with relations strained between the two managers.

Wenger acknowledges the Arsenal support in Cardiff after his side had squeezed out United on penalties (5-4) in the 2005 FA Cup final. It was a remarkable fourth FA Cup of the Alsatian's reign.

To the victor, the spoils. Wenger hoists aloft the Premiership title claimed for the second time under his management in 2002. The Frenchman would follow up that success with the Gunners' 'invincible' season two years later.

paid visits and each learned something that would stand them in good stead in the future, whether in European or African football. 'I was lucky enough to have a two-year sabbatical from the game and went on a world tour to observe, meet people, see what was going on, so I couldn't leave Arsène and Arsenal out,' explained Jeandupeux, who today applies some of the things he picked up in Colney with the French First Division club Le Mans. Colney had become the Milanello – AC Milan's celebrated football factory – for the millennium, with Wenger effectively the new Arrigo Sacchi.

'At Colney, I discovered the team spirit that is so typical of Arsène's sides,' said Damiano. 'He always wants to learn from others, and is always asking questions. He is always questioning, modifying, evolving, seeking, all the time thinking of effectiveness. He continuously combines the four main areas – technical, tactical, physical and mental. This is a must for him.'

'Arsène always gave me more than I gave in return,' added Dr Rougier. 'He teaches without taking.' With that in mind, Wenger likes nothing more than to surround himself with specialists so he can refine his own methods. Rougier, in his role as consultant on nutritional biology, was a key member of the manager's coterie. At the request of the Alsatian, who had first worked with him in Monaco, Rougier joined the team of specialists assembled by Wenger at Arsenal.

When he talks about the canteen in Colney, Rougier is passionate. 'The chef, responsible for the food over there, is almost a clone of the Wenger–Rougier spirit,' he said. 'When Arsène wants to prepare a new menu and I go to Arsenal, he asks me thousands of questions, and involves the chef in our discussions, putting our heads together to come up with a dietary plan. And the Colney chef soon adapted to the virtuous circle that I tried to develop. I can confidently say that Arsenal, today, could almost do without me. Between the chef, the physiotherapist and the English doctor, the club has managed to take on board 90 per cent of my 25 years of experience in the game.'

Diet and food hygiene represent between 15 and 20 per cent of sporting performance at the highest levels. For almost 25 years, Rougier has worked as a consultant either to Arsène Wenger or in Formula One, tennis and athletics. At the beginning of each season he prepares a dietary profile for each player. He describes the different dietary and recovery needs and passes a personalised file for each player on to Wenger and the doctor in charge, charting what each player's menu should incorporate.

'When Arsène had arrived at Arsenal, the club had no medical department to speak of,' said Rougier. 'The players' diet was total anarchy, and they'd snack on things like Mars bars during the day. Tony Adams, for example, told me that in the first half this kept him going physically and in terms of calming his nerves, but then he had problems with con-centration, physical strength, recovery, breathlessness. After three months of the new regime, Tony came and told me it had changed his life. It transformed the life of many players, but of course it was only the beginning.

'When a new player arrives, I ask him to carry out a dietary analysis – what does he eat over a fortnight? Is he married or not? If he isn't, the club asks him to eat at the club canteen as often as possible because meals are more nutritionally balanced. I also give him a sheet with the main rules he must follow. The first is never to eat sugary snacks between meals. The next is to always follow the correct structure of a meal, even if eating at a pub or restaurant: start with a raw salad, with a light lemon and oil dressing. Typically English dishes with amazing sauces are acceptable as long as the sauce isn't sweet. Contrary to popular belief, our players' tables have bread, toast with jam and light butter, fruits as well. But these lipids are preceded with yogurt, cheese, a boiled egg, because the protein in these foods blocks sugars. Our aim is for the player to hit the pitch at a stage when he isn't digesting his food or isn't hypoglycaemic. There is therefore a system to follow, rules to apply. Some, for example, used to eat pasta before matches. This isn't ideal because starchy food, to be digested, requires around three hours.'

With Arsène, Rougier adapted, compromised, asking players if they would agree to eat their pasta a bit less al dente to ensure faster digestion. 'We kept the pasta, but changed the way we cooked them,' said Rougier. 'One last small detail: I also asked for the pasta to be accompanied by less Parmesan so the players could completely digest their meal before going on to the pitch.'

Schedules at Colney – whether for meals or training – are calculated to suit the biological clocks of the athletes. Training is set to begin at 10.45 a.m. on the dot. 'Why? So I can keep the players at the hotel for lunch, so they eat properly,' Arsène explained .

Jean-Luc Arribart, a player under Wenger at AS Nancy, noticed the emphasis the manager placed on each player's health and wellbeing from a very early stage in his career. 'At AS Nancy Lorraine, he emphasised healthy living, healthy food,' he said. 'We had seen a dietitian at that time, and he also showed that managers can make a real impact, with their team and their methods.' Even then, Wenger had monitored the players' weight and had cracked down on members of his squad who had put on too much. Everything was geared towards ensuring the players were at peak performance, always within the law.

For Rougier, the dietary techniques employed at Arsenal are, in fact, the opposite of doping. 'The definition of "doping" is the use of substances, physiological or otherwise, in excessive doses aimed at improving performance,' he explained. 'Sure, in the past, there was a type of melting pot, a bit dubious in scientific terms, where you took magnesium and vitamin C, and that became suspect. But a body which recovers quickly is one that has been treated to a proper healthy lifestyle and diet. Indeed, Arsène applies the same rules to himself as he does to others. It's about seeking a balanced diet rather than taking supplements. Arsène always questioned the specialists around him so he could be sure that the methods he employed were the best.'

As at AS Monaco, the manager ate like his players. It was out of the question for the chef at Colney to prepare special treats for him alone. 'Arsène often told me: "I want you to prepare me a menu which is absolutely identical to that of the players. Why? Because if I don't stand shoulder to shoulder with them when it comes to food, how can I ask them to fight for me on the pitch?"' said Rougier. However, the Alsatian had mellowed in some respects. At Arsenal, for example, his players were allowed the odd glass of wine during the season. 'But Arsène would choose the bottle, and he always chose a good Bordeaux,' added Rougier. 'He considered wine, under these circumstances, to be a performance enhancer.

'Arsène is a mate, almost a brother to me. Despite all that, I always feel like I should be respectful to him. He is so sharp when it comes to football techniques that he forces respect, even from his friends. He is the master, someone who always has his eye on the ball. When he sees a meal being served, he will often make a comment like: "But didn't you say that protein should be served before starches? Why did you do it differently today?" And I have to report to him, all the time. He studies the techniques of each speciality, and therefore understands what the specialists around him are trying to achieve. The fact that he keeps an eye on everything means he can respond to the most specific requests from players. Wenger tries to see what works for players, to ensure they benefit from the highest possible energy levels. He doesn't mind players asking questions, observing what he himself can improve, or compromise. What he can't change, he adapts.

'His knowledge is incredible, even in medicine. Arsène knows the difference between a scanner, an IRM, an ultrasound, a fracture, a sprain. He knows about recovery and rehabilitation time. When the doctor announces that he wants to treat a player further, Arsène wants to know, for example, if there is a complication with the bones. He ensures his staff do their very best, as they know he could ask them anything, even when off duty. If the doctor, the physio or the rehabilitation specialist are around a table with him, he can talk to us knowledgeably about all of our specialities. What most surprises me is the intelligence with which he goes to the heart of the matter, and his visionary side.

'The strength of the Wenger method is that Arsène forces people to change without explaining why. He listens, then explains their habits, then he reorganises them. When he arrived at Arsenal, he didn't say to the older members of the squad, those who were 30 or older: "Thank you, but goodbye." Instead, he offered each of them complete respect, whether it was Tony Adams or David Seaman, and merely reorganised the habits of the less productive elements to improve and extend their performance.

'Everything is aimed at the wellbeing of the players. When the team is travelling, when a plane is late and we are waiting for it, Arsène generally takes us to eat in one of the airport restaurants. With his typical phlegm [self-control], he always chooses the one which seems the most appropriate. Of course people recognise him and he signs autographs, then he asks to speak to the chef. The cook arrives, delighted to be hosting Arsenal, and Arsène chats with him for a few moments. In just half an hour, any airport cafeteria becomes an Arsène Wenger restaurant. When coming back from European ties, in planes often full of directors and their families, Arsène will have a few words with the cabin staff, and barely after take-off the stewardesses will start distributing the meal trays at a phenomenal speed to the players. The directors would watch this happening before they'd even received their aperitifs. They were usually famished because they hadn't eaten since the morning, and they normally watched these special "Wenger menus" pass them by up the aisle with a sour expression on their face. But for Arsène, the players came first because they are the soul of his team. Wenger is friendly to everyone, but there was certainly a hierarchy at work. In his way of thinking, it is the player who works, who plays, and therefore who is the priority.'

As well as Yann Rougier, another internationally renowned specialist took up a role at London Colney charged with dealing with the injuries picked up so regularly by the players. Like the dietitian, Philippe Boixel – a celebrated figure in French football who took up a role with the national team on the insistence of Eric Cantona in the early 1990s – would work as a consultant, visiting St Albans regularly but retaining his base in Laval. He played his part in *Les Bleus'* successes at the 1998 World Cup and at Euro 2000 and had long been a friend and confidant of Wenger's. His reputation was forged in that time, with Wenger duly using him extensively at Arsenal as the team's osteopath.

'Arsène knows how to surround himself with experts in their respective fields,' said the former Arsenal midfielder Rémi Garde. 'Philippe managed to combine osteopathy and all so-called "alternative" practices with allopathy. Often, these two worlds compete, but with Arsène, we soon realised that these two areas of medicine were not incompatible.' Boixel cooperated intelligently with the three Englishmen working permanently at the club – the fitness coach, Tony Colbert, and the two masseurs. All in all, Arsenal boasts eight full-time medical staff, including Wenger's own GP, Ian Beasley, and the physiotherapist Gary Lewin, who combines his role with that of England's chief physio, thereby granting the players the best possible care.

Boixel had first worked with Wenger at Monaco and would combine his role with one at Juventus and with his own firm, making him a freelance par excellence. 'I always felt like a member of the team at Arsenal,' he said. 'From the outset with them, I would spend ten days every month in London. In 1996, Arsène suddenly asked me to join his team. He arrived in September and called me in October.'

'Boixel introduced a new method of care to Arsenal, having a very holistic approach to athletes,' said Garde. 'For him, a muscular injury to the leg was the consequence of a lack of balance, of another problem in fact causing this injury. Sessions with him were very long and very interesting, as he sought the origin of the injury itself, but also why it had happened. He clearly got positive and rapid results. I say clearly, because I have always signed up to this method of care. The fact that he got results allowed him to get his way, not only because the manager had decided this, but because he proved the effectiveness of his method.

'He "rebalanced" me. For a while I was suffering repeated muscle pains. It wasn't linked to my diet, because I paid attention to what I was eating. While being treated with Philippe, he noticed that I had microinfections in my gums, under the teeth, which hadn't been causing me any pain, and whose presence I was unaware of. I underwent X-rays and, to my great surprise, my gums and teeth needed treatment. I had root canal treatment, and following that I had no more muscle pain and was able to play practically without any problems. It was Philippe who detected the cause of my muscle problems.'

'Arsène is unique,' said Boixel. 'His vision is succinct and holistic. Every time I went to see him, which was pretty much each week, I reflected: "His curiosity is peerless." He needs to understand how a pathology works to fight it as effectively as possible. Arsène of course wanted to see his injured players recover as quickly as possible, but above all without any repeats of the problem. He was interested in the immediate performance of the player, but above all it was the management of his health in the long term which concerned him. He would leave an important player on the benches if the medical team told him it was a good idea, because he respected the player, the man, so he would listen. Arsène possesses, under his cold exterior, extreme sensitivity. For example, he knows injections can be damaging, and he left the decision, on the advice of the doctor, to the player. He never forced injections even if they were a key element.'

That would explain why Thierry Henry would remain 'unavailable' for a whole month in the autumn of 2005, and again would be absent for much of the 2006–07 season. 'We were able to treat him, he was able to rest,' explained Boixel. 'To be honest, he needed it back in 2005. During treatment, I said in passing to Thierry: "You don't often get a club like this which lets you rest like this, without pressure, with all the peace and quiet you need." Titi agreed. We both knew that this was unique in modern-day football. Despite the enormous challenges of the game today, Arsène would never risk a player – quite the contrary, he protects them. Sometimes he knows that a player wants to return because an important match is coming up, but he has to cool him down. In fact, working alongside him is exciting, because he gives us practitioners the time to work, like with any normal patient. Thanks to his patience we can respect the rhythms and physiology of each individual. This being said, everything is done to get players back on their feet as quickly as possible, because this is what is required for top-level football, but Wenger would never risk the health of the player.'

Maintaining that theme, Arsenal have developed their own weight-training methods designed to maximise each player's potential. 'Unlike at many clubs, where they lift weights to build their biceps, at Colney each musculation exercise is adapted to meet the needs of the particular player,' said Boixel. 'Arsène doesn't get players to work on biceps on their own, but thinks of the physiological unit, so the movements used are important. If he asks such and such a player to do press-ups with one hand, it is because he knows that his position on the field means that at some point he will need to get free from an opponent using just one arm, which is the case with defenders or attackers.'

At times, Wenger has been willing to send his players abroad to receive specific treatments as an alternative to the club's in-house personnel or visiting specialists. At the end of 1997, Tony Adams was treated by Tiburce Darrou, a renowned physiotherapist based in Saint-Raphaël, with the veteran duly benefiting from that treatment during the Double season a year later. 'Arsène insists above all on periods of recovery, because he has an excellent knowledge of physiology,' said Adams. 'He'd place huge importance on these aspects – stretching, massage, diet, nutritional supple-ments – and it's only now that rival managers and clubs are following suit. With him, a great amount of resources were devoted to getting into shape and all these techniques. These treatments suddenly became accessible to all.'

Wenger has never formally studied science. Even so, over the years spent on the bench, he has amassed such a wealth of knowledge of the human body that, according to Rougier and Boixel, he has become the equal of any doctor. Wenger does not agree, but feels that high-level competition, hygiene and health go hand in hand. The application of fine techniques such as osteopathy or nutrition, and the use of the best specialists, represented a significant expense for the club. 'But the players are so expensive these days that anything which improves their performance is worth the cost, even if it seems expensive,' said Wenger. 'The players from big European clubs expect these efforts to be made.'

Tuesday, 23 February 1999. Arsène Wenger strides down the touchline at Highbury to a deafening ovation from the Arsenal supporters. The reception reflected exceptional circumstances: Arsenal were taking on Sheffield United in an FA Cup quarter-final, despite having won the original game a week earlier 2–1. That tie had been controversial and, on Wenger's insistence, was now to be replayed. The tie had been all square at 1–1 when the visitors kicked the ball out of play so that one of their injured players could receive treatment. Upon the restart, Nwankwo Kanu – newly arrived in England and unaware of the tradition of returning possession in such circumstances – kept the ball and fed Marc Overmars who scored what proved to be the decisive goal.

Once back in the changing rooms post-match, with the United manager Steve Bruce apoplectic at the perceived injustice, Wenger had sought out the go-ahead from his vice-chairman David Dein before indicating he was in favour of replaying the tie. The Football Association may have been surprised at the show of sportsmanship, but they – along with Sheffield United – agreed. 'Of course, under the rules the goal was legitimate, but there are times when the spirit is more important that the rule,' explained Arsène. 'If Fifa had ordered the result to be confirmed, I could even have seen us withdrawing from the competition. It would have soured everything, with everyone seeing us as cheats.'

But was the Alsatian's gesture the action of a gentleman or a mere marketing ploy? A PR exercise? Was Wenger motivated by ethics or a desire to preserve the squeaky-clean image of his club? When questioned about his code of ethics, Wenger responded that he was never afraid of being seen as a troublemaker. 'To the extent that I am ready to defend my point of view, yes, the term can be applied,' he said. 'When you are abroad, you need to respect people's way of life, you need to adapt, but on the other hand you don't have to betray your principles and keep quiet in the face of injustice. You therefore need to find the right balance, which isn't easy. Between giving your opinion honestly and clearly and not causing trouble in the country, it is clear that this balance is very fragile and depends on the moment, the way your team is perceived. I don't think we had a choice. You can't survive by giving in whenever you see an injustice.'

Arsenal would progress in the replayed fixture, but 1999 would throw up other obstacles and, ultimately, disappointments for their manager. On the evening of 11 May, Arsenal took on Leeds United at Elland Road with the Gunners level on points with Manchester United at the top of the Premiership. A win against the Yorkshire club would put Adams & Co. in pole position to retain their title. Yet the game was lost 1–0, Jimmy Floyd Hasselbaink converting the only goal four minutes from time after Arsenal had missed a plethora of chances, and with that, the trophy effectively returned to Old Trafford. In the end, the 1998–99 season would be trophy-less, with United sweeping all before them to claim an unprecedented treble. At Highbury, Wenger took solace in the fact that he had at least blooded a few of his young colts – Nelson Vivas, Stephen Hughes, Nicolas Anelka – and, significantly, earmarked the next rough diamond he was preparing to polish.

On 3 August 1999 a short statement was issued to the press: 'Arsenal have confirmed the signing of Thierry Henry from Juventus.' The forward had cost a little over £10 million, the apprentice rejoining his mentor from Monaco where he had first burst on to the scene as a sprightly 17-year-old. At 21, Henry was attempting to rejuvenate his career after a frustrating spell in Turin. 'Thierry will considerably improve our firepower,' said Wenger at the time, even if the statistics of his time at Juve did not suggest as much. Yet Henry arrived with glittering achievements already behind him. He had featured at the 1998 World Cup finals, and had scored three goals in seven Champions League ties in 1996–97 with Monaco. Even so, few could have predicted that, less than six years after arriving in London, Henry would boast an astonishing 186 club goals for Arsenal in just over 300 appearances.

Wenger, assessing the tally after Henry had scored a brace

against Sparta Prague in the Czech Republic, was over-whelmed by the sheer weight of goals. 'It is amazing to consider what he has achieved,' he said. 'Amazing to have scored so many in a little over 300 games. When an attacker scores every two matches, it is already amazing, but with this record, Thierry is really above average. The fact that no one had managed to score so many goals for the club before him shows that Thierry Henry is exceptional in all that he undertakes. His performance also needs to be put into context: when you think that in the last century, in the 1930s, 40s, 50s or 60s, there was a lot less emphasis placed on defence. There was therefore more opportunity than today to score goals. Achieving such a thing in 2005 is absolutely amazing.'

Back in August 1999, Henry was reunited with another celebrated goalscorer from the 1998 World Cup finals, the Croatian international Davor Suker having been recruited from Real Madrid. With Anelka sold and Suker bought in order to support the new recruit from Juventus, Wenger was preparing the way for Henry to flourish. 'Thierry is more extrovert than Anelka,' he said at the time. 'He is a real team player who gives his all for the group. He has a good attitude, a good mentality for a young player and has, what is more, solid international experience for his age. With him we will have several possibilities. He can develop on the flank or the centre of the attack, and technically he is capable of a lot with the ball at his feet.'

Henry's first few months at Highbury were hesitant as he found his feet, the difficulties he had experienced at Juventus still clearly playing on his mind. He had been asked to play on the flank in Italy, but Wenger used him through the centre. Some observers had their doubts over whether he had the ability to excel there, unimpressed by the scoring record he brought with him. Indeed, it was not until 18 September that Henry found the back of the net for the Gunners.

Wenger's support during that awkward period was paramount. 'I have always had a great respect for Arsène,' recognised Henry. 'I can never thank him enough for the support he gave me back then. I owe him a great deal. He reached out to me when I was at my lowest point. Even after my unhappy experience at Juventus, he still believed in me. Unlike a lot of managers, he lets you live. It isn't his style to call you at home and check up on you. He never gives orders, but suggestions. I have to salute his vision, because a lot of people doubted me, a lot of people thought I would never play again as a centre-forward. And I think it was starting to play on my mind. If he hadn't had that idea, I don't know what would have happened.'

Wenger merely resumed where he had left off with Henry at Monaco, using him through the middle to great effect even if the forward needed some convincing initially. 'To finally persuade him to play there, I told him that he had everything to gain by taking on this new challenge,' said Wenger. 'He really needed to bounce back, because he was no longer the killer I had known a few years before. He needed to learn to be a bit more selfish when it came to goal scoring.'

'I have always said that Arsène Wenger is a man who knows exactly when he needs to talk to his players, to encourage them at the right time,' added Henry. 'He knows them by heart, and also knows how to manage the group, even if it isn't always easy. I love playing for Arsenal – the team is like my family. We often meet up when we aren't playing.'

Realisation dawned on Henry as to what he would need to bring to his game if he was to prove successful in the Premiership at a testimonial match organised to pay tribute to Ian Wright, the recently departed Arsenal striker. The celebratory dinner was attended by VIPs and former team-mates, along with the recently arrived France striker. Wright was toasted by the whole of Highbury. Henry, watching from the stands, understood that the secret of his pre-decessor's success was total commitment, and complete self-confidence. It was then that Henry vowed to chase every ball, fight for every pass, and follow in Wright's footsteps.

Wenger understood the need to support the young Henry. Whenever he could, he paired him with the experienced Bergkamp. The first two goals the Frenchman scored at Highbury earned Arsenal a 2–1 victory over Derby County, with Henry supplied by Grimandi and Petit to claim his brace. 'I'm what they call in my country a shadow scorer,' said Bergkamp. 'I try to remain in permanent contact with the scorer, playing freely. I'm not a finisher myself. Neither have I been a midfielder – I am something between the two. Henry has it all. The way he has developed over the last few years is extraordinary. Some players can challenge one or two defenders, but he can pass three or four in a row, which makes the work of the team all the easier. During my career, I have played with those who played with their back to the goal, others who curved their runs, and others who were, well, selfish. Thierry is the most complete attacker I have every played with. He has the speed, he is a finisher, he has a good attitude, he takes free-kicks. He is, in short, exceptional.'

'Thierry is more mature now than when he first arrived at the club,' said Wenger. 'In the air he is unrecognisable because, when he arrived at Arsenal, he hardly ever tried to head the ball. He has made real progress in his movement with the ball, his possession. Playing alongside his team-mates at Arsenal has helped him, and his transformation from winger to centre-forward has been great to behold. He has his future in his hands, but he is on the right track. I think he could still improve by 40 per cent, still.'

The English game is in awe at what Henry has achieved since becoming a Gunner. 'Arsenal players come from another planet, especially Thierry Henry,' insisted Harry Redknapp, who has coached West Ham, Southampton and Portsmouth against Wenger's team. That sentiment was shared by the former Chelsea manager Claudio Ranieri. 'Thierry Henry can make a difference at any moment,' said the Italian. 'He is fantastic. Even when he is having an off day, he can score.'

'He is all-powerful and, for me, is the key player at Arsenal,' said Manu Petit, who played against the Gunners whilst with Chelsea following his brief spell at Barcelona. 'He has a different style from Cantona, who was a great footballer, but Thierry has the capacity to finish off a match on his own, and at any time. You can count attackers capable of doing that on the fingers of one hand.'

At the start of the 1999–2000 season, Wenger had announced publicly that his team would be champions and would suffer no more than four league defeats all term. That had seemed an overly optimistic statement when the Gunners had edged beyond Leicester City 2–1 on the opening day only courtesy of a late own-goal from Frank Sinclair. Henry had not scored that afternoon, but he rediscovered his zest in front of goal over the course of the campaign. He scored 26 times in league and European competition that term – Arsenal finished second, losing nine league games despite the manager's initial optimism – and would go on to become one of the leading lights in the France team that won the European Championships in Holland and Belgium in the summer of 2000. Later that year, on 1 October, Henry scored a glorious goal from 25 yards beyond the Manchester United goalkeeper Fabien Barthez to secure a fine 1–0 victory, an indication of his genuine pedigree.

In his 303rd match for the club in Prague, the two goals scored against Sparta saw Henry overhaul Wright's record of 185 Arsenal goals. On the return flight from the Czech Republic, the French striker grabbed the microphone and expressed his thanks to his team-mates over the cabin intercom. A hat-trick against Middlesbrough in a rousing 7–0 victory in January 2006 would see Henry equal Cliff Bastin's long-established club record of 150 league goals for the club. He would beat that record on 1 February. During the winter of 2006, it was no surprise that Wenger was reduced virtually to begging his compatriot to sign an extension to his contract at the club with rumours persisting that Barcelona, the team who would defeat Arsenal in the Champions League final in Paris, were intent upon luring him to La Liga. The manager asked his forward to trust his club and their ability to remain a dominant force, despite the continued excellence of Manchester United and the emergence of Roman Abramovich's Chelsea across the capital. There would be frustration in recent years, a sciatic nerve problem limiting his impact in the 2006–07 season which he spent largely on the sidelines. When Barcelona's interest re-emerged in the summer of 2007, prompting a £16 million bid, both Wenger and Henry deemed the time right for a separation. The Gunners' leading goalscorer departed for the Nou Camp with words of appreciation for the club he had served for eight years and with his manager's blessing. Arsenal may never see his like again.

Yet, even with Henry in their ranks, Arsenal had not been immune to the odd slip-up in domestic competition. They were eliminated on penalties by Leicester City from the FA Cup fourth round in January 2000 following a 0–0 draw, a defeat which prompted Wenger to bemoan: 'Leicester were only seeking to defend.' Some took that criticism as a sign of sour grapes, that the Frenchman was a poor loser. Others pointed to the fact that he seemed overly reliant upon a 4-4-2 structure which limited his ability to adapt to certain situations and, in effect, denied him a back-up plan. Yet Arsenal had actually played 3-5-2 at times during Wenger's first season at the club and would, occasionally, revert to that system even if 4-4-2 remained the manager's preference.

Gabriele Marcotti, an Italian journalist and a follower of English football for over a decade, considers the Frenchman to be an 'out of the box' thinker. 'Wenger is the Descartes of football, a philosopher of sport who uses rationality not with the aim of winning at any price, but in the service of the beautiful game,' he said. Marcotti wrote a series of books on the great thinkers of football, and interviewed Wenger extensively, accompanied by Gianluca Vialli. 'What most surprised me was his enthusiasm. His face lights up when he talks about his players – he is like a little boy, amazed at the prowess of Henry and Robert Pires. This capacity for wonder is refreshing for someone who has been in the football business for such a long time, and it is surprising.'

How does the journalist explain Wenger's apparent innocence? 'Because he has never been a great player himself. Take Fabio Capello – he observes Henry and understands his technical moves; not Wenger, who reacts like a child when faced with a great player. However, this doesn't prevent Arsène from using his intelligence in the service of football.'

Paul Frantz, the mentor from Alsace, confirms Wenger's methodology has been forged by exposure to 'alternative' ways of thinking. 'What I noticed most was that he was open to all discussions – football, naturally, but also any other discussions,' he said. 'I was a teacher in a regional physical education and sporting centre, the CREPS, and before me I had a young student player who always answered back. It is rare to have such a chance: seeing intelligent players who look beyond the game and have an interest in other problems. In this respect he was really great. Something very unusual happened to me in his company. I was writing my book on football, and Arsène and I were on the train. At one point I came across a statistical problem – it was quite complex in mathematical terms, but I was using it to develop a thesis on the game. And I couldn't work it out – I just couldn't manage it. I asked Arsène to take a look and see if, by any chance, he could solve the problem. I passed him the paper and he returned it just two or three minutes later. Solved. I had taught elementary maths and loved number crunching, but I'd been properly shown up. I was flabbergasted! I took my hat off to him that day.'

This ability to analyse swiftly and accurately has clearly helped Wenger assess his own team and those of his opponents over the years. 'At half-time, he sometimes told his staff: "It's OK, we're going to win,"' said Damien Comolli, Arsenal's head of recruitment and a member of Wenger's back-room staff for almost ten years. 'He said nothing to his players, but he would tell his staff, in the changing room, right before the second half. I saw him after defeats at Arsenal, too. He didn't talk, he didn't eat. Normally – that is to say, when he hadn't lost – he was a nice guy, with a lot of class and restraint. But people knew there was this cauldron inside of him. Arsène in a rage is nothing like the image the public have of him. It is precisely the opposite because he is perceived as detached and lacking passion. In fact, he always gives 200 per cent, and yes, he can explode. I have seen him in some incredible states. I have spent evenings with him after defeats and he wasn't the same guy.

'But the amazing thing is that the morning after a defeat, although he feels exactly the same inside, he never shows it to his players. His body language is normal, and training is carried out as usual. He has this great quality: he can become detached from the event as soon as it occurs. He remains calm and cool-headed.'

Inside, however, the frustration was mounting. Back in the 1999–2000 season, Wenger was aware that his side were slipping behind. 'We are so close to Manchester but not yet good enough,' admitted the Alsatian at the time. His assessment was backed up by the reality of the Gunners' predicament. Between February 1999 and January 2000, the Londoners faced Sir Alex Ferguson's side six times. They would draw 0–0 three times, win once (and that merely the Charity Shield in August 1999) and lose twice, including the memorable FA Cup semi-final in April 1999 when Dennis Bergkamp missed a late penalty and Ryan Giggs inspired United's ten men to improbable victory in extra time.

United were to become Arsenal's major rivals. On Sunday, 25 February 2001 – the day Gérard Houllier's Liverpool would win the League Cup in Cardiff to glean the Frenchman his first trophy in English football – Arsène Wenger's Gunners were preparing to enter the lion's den at Old Trafford. 'We were doing all right in the league, but we knew it would be difficult confronting a team like United who were dominating at the time,' recalled Wenger. 'It is often psychologically hard to say to yourself: "God, they are never going to break, they are always there. We simply have to find a way to beat them." This was the challenge we set ourselves that year. Everyone can win once, but winning every year makes you a real champion.'

Observers predicted this would be a tense, tight contest between the two sides who so often ended the season making up the top two. No one foresaw the display of staggering power from the league leaders which ensued, and the ramshackle manner in which Arsenal would disintegrate that afternoon. Gilles Grimandi and Igors Stepanovs, an unfamiliar and makeshift centre-half pairing for the visitors, were torn to shreds. United were ahead after only 120 seconds, Dwight Yorke opening the scoring. Henry offered a glimmer of hope with an equaliser, set up by Sylvain Wiltord and Robert Pires, but thereafter every time United poured forward, Arsenal creaked to hold them.

On the touchline, Wenger offered only a scowl. Yorke burst beyond Grimandi to restore the hosts' lead, and 22 minutes in, the Trinidadian had his hat-trick. Roy Keane added a fourth before the half-hour, with Ole Gunnar Solskjaer conjuring a fifth, remarkably, after only 36 minutes. 'I was so out of it that I don't even remember what Arsène said to us in the changing rooms,' said Grimandi. Pires, on the right of midfield that day, retains a clear memory of his manager's reaction.

Barely had the dressing-room door been slammed shut when Wenger exploded with rage. For the first time since moving to Arsenal from Japan, the Frenchman lost control. He threw notepads, water bottles and cups. His crestfallen team, 5–1 down and in a hopeless position, were showered in mineral water. 'It's a good job he lost his temper because to be losing by that much at United in a game in which we were hoping to show we weren't that far behind the leaders, well . . . it wasn't good enough,' admitted Pires. 'Even so, we were all taken aback by his reaction. We'd never seen anything like it from him. It was obvious how much it had hurt him. It happened again after the match, so the message really got through to us. This simply wasn't good enough.'

By the final whistle, Arsenal had been humbled 6–1, the substitute Teddy Sheringham rubbing salt into raw wounds with a late sixth. United went on to claim the title, just as they had in 1999 and 2000 with the Gunners forever playing catch-up. After that slaughter at Old Trafford, Arsenal had slipped 16 points behind the league leaders, a gap they would trim to ten by the end of the campaign. Yet, even if the chasm between the clubs had appeared increasingly unbridgeable, the debacle in Manchester would prove to be a turning point for Wenger in England.

Wenger took the defeat personally. He always does. Setbacks such as that have tended to plunge him into uncertainty – he was just as troubled when Newcastle won 3–1 at Highbury in December 2001, after which he conceded that 'We lost the championship this evening.' That proved an overly pessimistic assessment but, for the most part, Wenger did well not to pass on his doubts to his players. Chaos may have been reigning all around, but the Alsatian generally kept his doubts to himself. Regardless, better times lay ahead.

On Bonfire Night 2001, with the scars inflicted at Old Trafford still smarting, Arsenal had a chance to exact some kind of revenge. A young United side travelled to London for a League Cup tie – only Phil Neville and Yorke of the seniors were included by Sir Alex Ferguson that night – and the Gunners, fired up and intent upon biting back, tore into them. The hosts were 3–0 up at the break courtesy of a Sylvain Wiltord hat-trick and ended 4–0 winners, with Grimandi putting in an assured performance against the visiting kids. 'Arsène is my mentor,' said the defender, now working with Arsenal's scouting department in France. 'I worked with him in Monaco 20 years ago, and today I am still there with him. I have great admiration and respect for him, and if he wasn't there today, I don't know if I would still be in football. I have realised recently that the people who worked with him at Monaco are all working at the highest level: Claude Puel, Dominique Bijotat as well . . . Loads of former players are trainers today.' Arsenal, at the end of that autumn, had progressed into the fourth round of the League Cup – a lesser competition, admittedly – and Ferguson, for once, had been dismissed from Highbury with aplomb. If nothing else, the psychological balance had been redressed.

The psychological struggle between Arsène Wenger and Sir Alex Ferguson did not date from the League Cup humbling at Highbury, or the 6–1 thumping at Old Trafford, but from the very day the Frenchman had arrived in the Premiership. Up until then, the title race had been dominated by Scottish managers – Kenny Dalglish and George Graham in the 1980s and early 1990s, then Dalglish again with Blackburn in 1995. Only Howard Wilkinson's Leeds United, in 1992, had broken this monopoly, with Ferguson and United the dominant force from the first year the reshaped top flight was introduced. Ferguson was not knighted until 1999, but he was already established as the best manager in the Premier League when Wenger arrived on the scene in 1996. When Wenger – an outsider – achieved the Double in 1998, the established order was shattered. Add to that the new man's refusal to share a post-match drink with Ferguson at Old Trafford and, already, this smacked of division.

The English press asked Wenger about his reluctance to share a glass with his opposite number, with the Frenchman explaining that he did not drink whisky. The irony, of course, was that Ferguson preferred to share a glass of fine wine with opposing managers in Manchester. Perhaps the lack of empathy between the pair stems from a misunderstanding of each other's approach. Wenger, certainly, enjoys sharing a glass of wine with friends. Indeed, having planted himself in front of the television to watch Manchester United take on his former club AS Monaco in the Champions League in the spring of 1998, Wenger had drunk a little too much as he celebrated the goal from David Trézéguet which served to eliminate United from the competition. The next day, the manager was so hung-over that he cancelled training after only 45 minutes with his head pounding and stomach churning.

Yet Wenger would clearly never uncork a bottle in Ferguson's company. 'Out of all the managers in the Premiership, Wenger is the least popular,' insisted a long-time observer of the English game. 'None of the other coaches really like him. They don't appreciate the fact that Arsène is a bad loser and never joins in with their activities.' These 'activities' range from a shared bottle of wine after matches to functions laid on by the League Managers' Association, which Wenger does not hold in high regard even if he is a member. Wenger preferred not to socialise with his rival managers. He was dedicated to the profession, but something of a loner in his approach to the game. He may not have intentionally cut himself off from his contemporaries, but he had no great desire to join in.

Until the emergence of Chelsea under Roman Abramovich in 2003, Wenger appeared to reserve most of his criticisms for United, with his verbal spats with Ferguson duly becoming the sideshow to every meeting between Arsenal and the Red Devils. When Wenger was publicly critical of the use of replays in FA Cup ties, Ferguson asked the watching world what the Frenchman knew about English football. Later, the Alsatian was deliberately inflammatory when commenting on the potential use of new technology in football. 'It is vital we introduce video replays on key decisions as quickly as possible,' he said. 'If we take the example of Manchester United, they would be mid-table [rather than top] if referees could use video evidence to check on their decisions.' Ferguson, of course, was quick to respond.

The Scotsman from the shipyards of Govan has little in common with the Alsatian from agricultural Duttlenheim, and their antipathy has deepened over the years. Ferguson, with his team at the height of their powers, took huge pleasure in sowing the seeds of doubt in Wenger's mind as the Frenchman attempted to play catch-up. Perhaps their animosity reflected deep-seated rivalries between the clubs themselves, and certainly Ferguson recognised Wenger as a threat to his team's dominance. Regardless, the verbal jousting made for great entertainment. 'I respect Alex, but I don't understand his comments, or what he has to say about Arsenal,' said Wenger.

When United were granted special dispensation by the Football Association to travel to Brazil in January 2000 to compete in the Fifa World Cup Championships, waiving their right to defend the FA Cup in the process, Wenger was incensed. The Frenchman described the trip to South America as a 'holiday', a 'welcome break' in a long hard season. He argued that, by allowing United to drop out of the FA Cup, the FA had handed them an easier schedule for the season's final weeks and an opportunity to concentrate solely on the defence of their Premiership title.

That placed further strains on the pair's relationship, with the deterioration maintained the following season. Defending his own side's style and potency, Ferguson dismissed the notion that Wenger was a technical and tactical genius, which provoked a response from Wenger, who notoriously claimed: 'Every man thinks he has the most beautiful wife.' 'Arsène doesn't know me well enough to judge me,' retorted Ferguson. In March 2002, Wenger's response was succinct: 'Ferguson's only weakness is that he doesn't have one.'

At the turn of the century, the pair's regular tête-à-têtes sustained interest in a league that had become a two-horse race between their sides. Ferguson was due to retire at the end of the 2001–02 campaign, only to have a change of heart in February and extend his contract at Old Trafford. 'What would I do if Sir Alex wasn't there?' asked Wenger at the time, his comments dripping with sarcasm. 'I would have no one to keep my feet on the ground, no one to quarrel with. So, of course I am delighted that he has changed his mind – I appreciate our rivalry. It is good for Arsenal, good for United and in the end good for both of us.'

In May 2002, Ferguson took charge of his 1,000th game for United. Wenger was asked whether he would attempt to emulate that achievement with the Gunners. 'I will try. At the moment I can't imagine leaving the club. I have always wanted to stay on here, but 1,000 matches is a huge amount. I am sorry that, sometimes, my emotions get the better of me after matches, but that is just an indication of my frustration that things don't always go exactly as we have planned. Often it is more like heaven than hell, but I am always delighted to work here. I think of myself as a calm person, but when I watch the TV and shots of me at a match, then I think I might be wrong.'

The sight of a scowling, anxious Arsène on the touchline does not suit his image as a football thinker, though the suggestion is that Ferguson does get under his skin. The Scot may have taken some pleasure from events at the FA Cup final of 2001, even if Liverpool – United's bitter rivals – ended up claiming the trophy. Arsenal dominated at the first final at the Millennium Stadium in Cardiff, yet succumbed to two goals from Michael Owen late in the game. Quizzed subsequently about Ferguson's constant sniping, Wenger snapped. 'He can say what he wants,' he said. 'I think it is what you English call "putting a cat among the pigeons". I have no diplomatic relations with him. I never want to talk about that man again. He has ruled the roost in England, and he should try his luck elsewhere and see how he is received.'

That tirade was delivered with little show of emotion, the Frenchman maintaining his sang-froid, fuelling the argument that the public spat may merely be for show. 'Look, we both want to win,' added Wenger. 'Neither of us is hiding the fact that he wants to beat the other. We never meet in our day-to-day lives, but we do occasionally see each other when we are "on tour", particularly abroad. Sometimes it feels as if it is "us against the world".'

'Wenger certainly shares that mentality of "us and them" that has served Ferguson in such good stead,' said the journalist and biographer Jasper Rees. 'Wenger has instilled that into Arsenal. When he came in 1996, this feeling was already at its budding stages within the London club, but he really brought it out and turned it into a strength, a motivation, even. The aim when he teamed up with the Gunners was to knock Manchester United off their pedestal and he achieved just that, sometimes by adopting Ferguson's very own tactics. Yet, behind the verbal barbs and their hysterics, it is obvious that they respect one another's careers and the results reaped by the other. I remember once asking Ferguson about Wenger and his tactical sense whilst in Manchester. Fergie suddenly grabbed the salt and pepper shakers from the table in front of him, moving them around like crazy to show me how Pires moved on the pitch and handled his assailants. Ferguson was obviously impressed by the Arsenal offensive unit and had clearly studied it in spite of anything he might say.'

Pires had become key to Arsenal's approach by then, the man nicknamed d'Artagnan having recovered his poise after a difficult first season in the English game to fulfil the potential spied early in his career by Wenger. For that, the midfielder owes his manager much. 'Honestly, Arsène Wenger is such an easy person to talk to,' said the France international. 'He is really approachable and makes players feel like they can tell him about all their niggles, and certainly whatever is troubling them.'

The midfielder's career had been stagnating at Olympique de Marseille when Wenger came to the rescue. 'Arsène called me himself during Euro 2000,' he recalled. 'For me, the message was pretty clear and it was a very good sign. That he would contact me in person was really significant, a sign that he wanted me to play for him. He wanted to find out what my situation was and see what I wanted to do. The president of my club, l'OM, granted me the right to leave. It was written black on white; it was OK for me to go. Real Madrid wanted me to sign but, after speaking to Wenger on the phone a couple of times and hearing how interested he was in me, there was no choice to make.'

Pires had ended Euro 2000 by supplying the pass with which Trézéguet scored France's golden goal against Italy to claim the trophy. A private jet chartered by Arsenal awaited the Marseille captain at Rotterdam airport, with Wenger desperate to conclude a transfer and buy his replacement for the departed Marc Overmars. 'The role Wenger envisaged me playing on the pitch gave people a lot to talk about,' said Pires. 'But I liked his speech because it expressed just how much the club wanted to sign me.' So speedy were negotiations over the contract that the France midfielder was able to return to Paris that same afternoon to celebrate his country's European triumph: he may have left Holland as a Marseillais, but he arrived back in France as a Gunner.

It was Adams who christened Pires 'd'Artagnan', amused as he was by the thin goatee beard sported by the Frenchman which was reminiscent of a Musketeer. The new campaign, Pires's first in the Premiership, began at Sunderland, the thunderous pre-match din in the Stadium of Light reverberating through the arena and into the dressing rooms below. Pires was to start on the bench and, while he was perplexed at first, he soon realised this was a protective measure rather than a punishment. The tackles flew, crunching challenges biting all over the pitch. 'Every player hates being left on the bench,' admitted Pires. 'Obviously, we all want to play, but Arsène explains the reasons why you're omitted to you, so you always know why you're on the bench. This is a healthy relationship between the coach and the players. I really don't think any old coach would bother doing this.'

Pires emerged from the substitutes' bench in the second period but Arsenal, with Vieira sent off, succumbed 1–0. The Frenchman realised even then that he would have to adapt his game if he was to flourish in England. Wenger made it clear he would need to toughen up, with the winger condemned to hours on the weight machines improving his upper-body strength. In training, the likes of Tony Adams and Martin Keown charged into challenges and Pires, slowly, learnt what it would take to make his mark on the Premiership. By the end of his first season, he winced at a disappointing tally of four goals scored and seven key passes delivered. A year on, by May 2002, he had established his quality: nine Premiership goals, 15 decisive passes and a reputation forged. It was a tally on a par with David Beckham, with Bergkamp and Ryan Giggs playing catch-up.

Wenger had helped reinvigorate Pires. The Frenchman had endured a torrid spell in an underachieving side at Olympique de Marseille, where the supporters had been so disillusioned with the team that they had even attacked them at the club's training centre. Arsenal offered an exit, an obvious choice in July 2000, just as it had offered Wenger an escape route some four years previously. Yet the best was still to come from Pires. Through the 2001–02 and 2002–03 campaigns, the Gunners were propelled by their Musketeer.

'Arsène wanted me to recover my self-confidence,' he explained. 'He placed an emphasis on the basics of my game and my instincts, coaxing them out of me. He made me work on collecting and controlling the ball, on my forward runs and dribbles. He underlined my strengths by making me work on them, by pushing me to provoke a better response, over and over again.'

By the end of his time at Arsenal, Pires was averaging nearer 15 goals per season, such was his level of improvement, in a side renowned for its attacking flair. He spread his wings during 2001–02, with his glorious lob over Peter Schmeichel in a fine 2–1 victory at Aston Villa in early March arguably his finest flash of brilliance. Yet there was a sting to the campaign's tail. On 23 March, Arsenal hosted Newcastle in the FA Cup quarter-final at Highbury. The game was barely two minutes old when Pires slapped the home side ahead with his 13th goal in all competitions of a productive season. Soon afterwards, his cross supplied Bergkamp with a second to establish the home side's ascendancy. Then the Frenchman leaped to vault over Nicos Dabizas's challenge near the goal-line and as he landed awkwardly, his knee buckled beneath him. The anterior cruciate ligaments of his left knee had been torn to shreds.

The following day, Wenger dispatched Pires to Strasbourg to consult Dr Jean-Henri Jaeger, a respected knee specialist. He confirmed the worst and, in the blink of an eye, Pires was forced to come to terms with the reality that he would not only play no part in Arsenal's run-in in pursuit of both the FA Cup and Premiership title, but would also miss France's defence of the World Cup in Japan and South Korea. On the day the title was celebrated at Highbury, Arsenal's players knelt in homage to Pires's contribution and the midfielder briefly relinquished his crutches to hold the trophy aloft. While France toiled in the Far East, d'Artagnan spent his summer in rehabilitation in Saint-Raphaël, where Arsenal players from Tony Adams to Martin Keown, via Rémi Garde, had convalesced under the watchful eye of Tiburce Darrou.

The consultant is one of the few employees at Arsenal who feels confident enough to contradict Wenger if he feels it is necessary. 'It isn't so much that I give him advice, but I do anticipate and visualise things for him. I'd never say: "Arsène, you're wrong. You should do as I say on this matter." But he trusts my judgement and our relationship is pretty close.

'Arsène may have put Tiburce on my case, but he acted like my own personal physiotherapist and psychologist during that summer on the Côte d'Azur,' recalled Pires. 'I remember my mobile phone going off at 4 a.m. once, waking me up – I'd made the mistake of leaving it on – and it was the boss, all calm and relaxed, just checking up on me. He was the last person I expected to call me at that time in the morning. He just asked me how I was, how the rehabilitation was going. I replied, in this raspy voice, that I'd been fast asleep when he'd called. "Oh, did I wake you up?" he asked. I should have pointed out to him that it was actually four in the morning and most people are asleep at that time, but I nearly said he hadn't bothered me at all and that he'd interrupted me playing tennis . . .'

Wenger, acting as an expert summariser at the World Cup finals, had lost track of the time difference between the Far East and France. 'It's actually quite funny when you think about it,' added Pires. 'When I told Tiburce about it the following day, he wasn't in the least bit surprised. He knows what Arsène is like. I returned the favour later. I called him one day and asked if I was disturbing him. He said I wasn't and that he was just watching a football match. That didn't surprise me but, all the same, I asked him which one he was watching. He was actually in Switzerland watching FC Thun play. That just shows how much he loves his job. He could have sent someone over there to watch a team like that, but he wanted to go himself. He's completely obsessed with football.

'Everyone knows his qualities – he has proven them in France and in England. But his strength is that he really protects his players. He always keeps up to date on injured players' progress and for us to know that, to feel it, really helps your confidence. It almost serves to inspire. He also keeps track on players who interest him. Apparently, Arsène first spotted me when I was at Metz and had tried to sign me then. When I went to Marseille, he just kept tabs on what I was doing. He was disappointed when I went to l'OM because he had really wanted me at Monaco, but I felt at the time that the fan base in Marseille, compared with that in the Principality, was just on another level. It was a setback for him, my going elsewhere, but it was wonderful to know that, two years later, he still wanted the chance to work with me.'

If Pires had been instrumental in hoisting Arsenal to within sight of another League and Cup Double, then it would fall on another of Wenger's players to edge them over the finishing line. Wenger felt he had a player already in his ranks who could fill the void left by d'Artagnan's absence. On 4

May 2002, with the Premiership within their grasp even if two fixtures remained, Freddie Ljungberg, who had joined the club in 1998 from the Swedish side Halmstads, would make his presence felt.

The scene was the Millennium Stadium in Cardiff, with a confrontation against Chelsea in the FA Cup final ahead. Claudio Ranieri's side may not have benefited yet from Roman Abramovich's arrival – the footballing landscape in the Premiership would not be transformed until the summer of 2003 – but they were awkward and dangerous opponents with the likes of Marcel Desailly, William Gallas, Frank Lampard, Emmanuel Petit and Eidur Gudjohnsen in their ranks. Arsenal's players had glided beyond all comers to clinch the league. Against their London rivals, they selected a familiar XI: Seaman; Lauren, Campbell, Adams, Cole; Wiltord, Parlour, Vieira, Ljungberg; Bergkamp; Henry.

If Henry and, more latterly, Pires had been this side's star performers, then Ljungberg had also established his quality. The Swede patrolled the left flank with real industry and, increasingly, a potent eye for goal. 'Arsène Wenger taught me a huge amount,' he admitted. 'The most amazing thing he did was to convince me that I was a winger. Under his tutorship, I learnt to cross, and to get beyond a defender. I could mix my game up and not be limited to one position. I'm so proud of the fact that I can play forward and also protect the flank during the same match. It isn't always easy to play a double role like that for someone in this position. It was Arsène Wenger who taught me this technique.'

Ljungberg was something of an old hand having joined the club in 1998, but it had taken him time to find a niche in the side. 'When I was younger, I'd played much higher up the field, right behind the attackers,' he said. 'When I came to Arsenal, Arsène told me that I could hold the flank, and I said: "Me, a winger? But I have never played this position in my life." I couldn't imagine myself as a winger. I wondered whether I had the pace to do it, and whether by playing there I would ever have the chance to score the goals I knew I was capable of.

'I'd usually played as an attacking midfielder, possibly on the right side of two central midfielders. But, from my very first training session, the boss had me playing right on the wing. On the touchline. That was my designated role. It was an enormous change. I needed to learn all the tricks you need to do well out there, but I took them on board, listened to what he wanted me to do, and it paid off. Nowadays, I feel comfortable wide. It didn't bother me so much playing on the left wing, either, because that gave you the opportunity to cut inside and shoot at goal. And that, after all, is what I was bought to do for Arsenal.'

In front of some 73,965 spectators in Cardiff, Arsenal waited until the 70th minute before their probing finally pierced Chelsea courtesy of a splendid goal from Parlour. Then, ten minutes from time, the travelling Gooners were treated to Ljungberg's best impression of Pires. Avoiding Gallas and then Lampard before leaving the tiring Petit in his wake, the Swede bore down on goal and lifted a cheeky shot over Carlo Cudicini to confirm Arsenal's Double. Those fans who had been bellowing 'Super, super Rob [Pires]' a few weeks earlier were now chanting 'We love you Freddie' with gusto.

'I'd gone through the same work-outs as Robert in terms of building up my upper-body strength after I signed for the club,' admitted Ljungberg. 'The manager taught me to develop the technical aspects of my game and, because in England it's more of a contact sport, he explained that I needed to be much more of an aggressive player. The first time I met him was at Sopwell House. Before I signed, I'd wanted to find out a few things about Mr Wenger, principally how he saw his team playing football in the future. It was really important to hear his responses. He explained to me how he saw football, and I realised that we had an identical vision. I'd signed the contract in no time.'

Wenger chose a type of man as much as a player profile. By nature optimistic, he loves expansive sportsmen and would not be fazed by Ljungberg's occasional flamboyances, from hairstyles to underwear modelling. Some managers might have been put off by such a player. 'But I'm someone who doesn't see danger coming around every street corner,' admitted Wenger. 'I trust other people. I believe in them. As a manager, my job is to say to a group of guys: "Look, my fate is in your hands. I believe in you." I believe my players will do their utmost for the team. I have a positive image of human nature, and that is really important as a manager.'

Wenger had told Ljungberg that he envisaged playing a 4-4-2 system favouring 'individual freedom' to allow particular players to bloom. The Swede was to enjoy a mouth-watering start to his career in England. 'My first match was against Manchester United. I don't think I needed motivation on that day for what was the biggest match of my life up to then. But Wenger spoke to me before the match. He just told me do what I knew best on the pitch.'

Back in May 2002, the Arsenal fans in the Millennium Stadium were basking in their 2–0 victory as Wenger, his tie removed and top button popped open, held the trophy aloft in the sunshine. Arsenal's season was not yet over, with two pivotal league fixtures remaining and a key clash at Old Trafford to come in four days' time. 'You know, a cup is a cup,' offered the manager. 'It's great for glory, and you are happy to win it. But a team's worth is proven in the championship. Everything else for me is secondary – I have often repeated it, and I am convinced it is true.'

The Gunners were unbeaten in 25 matches stretching back to their 3–1 home defeat to Newcastle in December 2001 and travelled to Manchester aware that a victory would secure them their Double. That evening at Old Trafford still represents the highlight of Ljungberg's Arsenal career. There was tension, there was controversy, but above all there was a victory to savour and a league title to celebrate in their bitter rivals' backyard. 'For me, personally, that season was a complete success,' said Ljungberg.

The honour of scoring the title-winning goal fell to a player much maligned in an Arsenal shirt, but whose worth was appreciated by his manager. Sylvain Wiltord had cost some £10 million in signing from Bordeaux, his reputation forged by a season in French football when his 22 goals had carried *Les Girondins* to the title at the expense of Pires's l'OM. He had arrived in August 2000 with a reputation as a hothead and troublemaker, born of his time at Rennes, but Wenger refused to believe that a player is ever untameable. Privately, Wiltord was admonished when he was late for training at Colney. Publicly, his manager never swerved from supporting him and deflecting the criticism that came his way.

Wiltord was never prolific, scoring eight goals in the Premiership in his first year, ten in his second and a disappointing 13 in each of his last two years at the club. But his presence was beneficial. Wiltord was arguably the Ian Wright of the Arsenal dressing room, a livewire presence with an extrovert personality. Asked how you control such players, Wenger offered a smile. 'There is no miracle cure,' he said. 'It is just like any other type of management. You need to respect people, make clear demands, act with a certain amount of consistency, and do everything you can so that they can express themselves, both in terms of the game and as people. Apart from the fact that players are celebrities, management issues are the same, though people perhaps forget sometimes that players are maybe more sensitive.'

Wiltord, sensitive to the fierce criticism he endured in the press with much made of the large fee it had taken to secure his services, was continuously protected by his coach. On the pitch, Wenger little by little transformed the centre-forward into a winger. Just as with Pires and Ljungberg, the transformation was a success. 'I felt the potential of the team grew when Pires and Wiltord came into their own,' Wenger said. 'I felt a soul, a spark. It was important not to make a mistake – I had lost Petit and Overmars to Barcelona but, in fact, the real challenge was, little by little, how to replace Lee Dixon and Nigel Winterburn in defence: with the arrival of Sol Campbell [from Tottenham, in 2001]. The old guard had been the cornerstone for years. Everyone said: when they've left, Arsenal is finished. This was quite a lot of pressure to deal with.'

Nevertheless, that evening at Old Trafford represented a turning point for Wiltord. 'Nino' had scored his first Arsenal goal against Coventry in a 2–1 victory back in September 2000. Some two years later, he had been converted into a potent threat from wide midfield. Against United, he competed willingly as the elbows flew through the first half, a game of rugged tackles still level at the break. Yet the hosts' desperation to edge back into the title race demanded they take more risks thereafter and, with more space to exploit, Arsenal seized their opportunity. Wiltord wriggled through, squeezing the only goal into the corner, and the title was theirs. Pires, in the south of France, leapt from his barstool forgetting he was on crutches. The corner where the away fans were crammed erupted in delirium. The home supporters swallowed their pride to applaud the victorious Londoners through their post-match celebrations. 'People tell me that United have 52 million supporters in the world,' offered Wenger in the aftermath. 'Perhaps it's symbolic, then, that we won this title here in Manchester. To have the belief and strength to come here and win shows we deserve it: this is our time.'

A few weeks after that heady night, David Dein invited his manager to a party. 'I can't tell you anything other than that your presence is vital,' he told a quizzical Wenger. In reality, it was an awards dinner where the Arsenal coach was to be crowned manager of the year. 'I wasn't really keen on attending, thinking it was just a normal party and not really being into such things, but David just asked me what else I would do if I didn't go,' recalled Wenger. 'I think I told him I'd be at home, watching [the French football weekly magazine programme] *Jour de Foot* on Canal+. Still, it was a nice evening in the end and a great surprise and honour to be given the award.'

In truth, that Double in 2002 was a triumph of science, applied by Wenger after hours spent devising a master plan in his laboratory at London Colney. It was based almost entirely on guaranteeing, as well as he could, the wellbeing of his squad – all the care put into infrastructure, diet, osteopathy and tactical planning ultimately paid off to sweep Arsenal's rivals, and United in particular, out of the Londoners' way.

Arsène Wenger spread his arms, pointing his fingers obligingly for the cameras with his feet planted firmly in the mud. This was Wenger the project manager, Wenger the foreman, all smiles for the flashbulbs as he stood by the building site that would soon be transformed into Arsenal's new stadium. His wellington boots covered his suit trousers, a red safety helmet on his head and the fluorescent yellow parka slightly too big for him. In it, his wiry body was almost lost. Among the towering cranes, the mounds of dirt and soil, and with the concrete mixers whirring at his side, the Arsenal manager posed, somewhat uneasily, for the press. The shirt and tie made him look even more uncomfortable, a businessman perched on an oil rig. Behind him stood the huge sign with its red slogan declaring boldly: 'Emirates Stadium – the new home of football'. This was to be a new 60,000-seater home for Arsenal Football Club, due to be opened in August 2006, offering a neat symmetry for Wenger on the Frenchman's 10th anniversary in charge at the club. But this was the spring of 2004. Wenger, the man who had redesigned Arsenal's training complex and had sculpted various teams during his time in north London, was now helping to oversee the construction of this club's new home.

Wenger's vision extended beyond the new stadium. Back in May 2002, he had already stated in *L'Équipe*: 'I am very proud of having developed the training centre at London Colney and helped encourage the building of the new stadium, but that isn't enough. It is necessary to intervene in the lives of players, to participate in their development. In England, a manager is often judged by what he leaves behind him. For me, that legacy is very important.' True, the manager's regime would be characterised by the '*grands projets*' such as Colney and the brand-new stadium, but his true legacy would be the silverware he had claimed during his tenure. It is by trophies that managers are measured.

On 16 April 2003, Arsenal welcomed Manchester United to Highbury. After their first Double under Wenger, secured in 1998, the Gunners had failed to mount a sustained and successful defence, succumbing once more to United in the pursuit of honours. Ultimately, Arsenal struggled to compete with Manchester United's financial clout and depth of squad and ability – it was a scenario which eventually convinced them of the need to move from Highbury to the Emirates Stadium in 2006 as they sought to match their rivals' greater buying power – with Sir Alex Ferguson effectively operating on another level. In 2003, having led the table convincingly at one stage, their season was threatening to unravel yet again in the spring. Valencia had already dismissed them from the

Champions League, and they had to win this match if the Premiership was to remain theirs. Wenger recognised that only by defending the trophy could Arsenal claim to be the dominant force in English football. This was to prove a frustrating night.

Ruud van Nistelrooy had given the visitors a lead which they held, comfortably, until early in the second half when Thierry Henry equalised six minutes after the restart. Then, some 11 minutes later, Henry – suspiciously offside – raced clear to ease the hosts ahead. Highbury was still celebrating what they had hoped would prove a pivotal goal when United broke downfield virtually from the kick-off, Ole Gunnar Solskjaer wriggling free to centre with Lauren, Ashley Cole and Martin Keown unable to offer their rookie home goal-keeper Stuart Taylor any protection. Ryan Giggs, nipping in challenged, equalised again. In the time that remained, frustration boiled over with Sol Campbell dismissed for an elbow flung at Solskjaer, earning the centre-half a suspension from the FA Cup final. Two key points had been frittered away.

Wenger had been seething on the bench at his side's inability to stride clear in the title race long before this game, but Giggs's equaliser prompted fury. The final score annoyed him, perhaps even hurt him. Didier Roustan, a long-standing friend of the Arsenal manager, claims that it can take him up to a week to recover from a result such as this. 'Watch the match again . . . you can see Arsène on the touchline, and when Giggs equalises, he is absolutely furious,' said Damien Comolli, who was working as Arsenal's chief scout at the time. 'You can read his lips. He screams: "Fucking hell!" I went up to him after the game and tried to console him. "Don't worry," I said. "So you swore on live television. It's not so much of a problem. The match was only being broadcast to 150 countries around the world, after all." He had to laugh.'

Yet that frustration was born of Wenger feeling powerless. The succession of errors leading up to United's second goal had undermined his hours of preparation, all that time spent on positional technique and tactical awareness. A lapse of concentration for a split second had rendered all that utterly pointless. A year previously, after Wiltord's goal had won the title at Old Trafford, Wenger had admitted: 'I didn't want to see a second-rate mentality taking root at Arsenal. You needed to risk everything to be number one. Players had to be given a conscience. We have a team with a fantastic core – when I think that we went to Manchester with Bergkamp on the bench, and without Henry or Adams . . . that says it all.' Yet his side's failings in the drawn game at Highbury, most notably their lapse in concentration, had undermined his long-term hopes.

In the immediate aftermath of the 2–2 draw, a result which had handed United the advantage in the title race, Wenger had refused to point the finger of blame at any of his defenders specifically. 'But he was furious,' admitted Comolli. 'He had a right go in the dressing room after the match, but he didn't ever go up to the guilty players after the game and say: "What did you do that for? You've cost us our title." He has never behaved in that way, and never will. Generally, Arsène waits 24 hours before debriefing his players, going over the game and the positive and negative aspects that he has witnessed.

He likes the dust to settle, the emotions to calm, before he scrutinises the performance. But even in that debriefing, he wouldn't point fingers even if, inside, he was still fuming.'

'The "morning after" analysis sessions were actually always pretty calm,' said Daniel Jeandupeux, who spent time at Colney experiencing Wenger's management techniques. 'That had an excellent effect on the players. It influenced me and how I do things now, but I couldn't copy Arsène even if my ideas are now pretty similar to his. There is only one Arsène Wenger, after all.'

The 'no blame' culture encouraged might not guarantee immediate recovery from defeats in the next game, but it did at least help stabilise the squad and create a convivial atmosphere at training. On 26 April, Wenger took his side to Bolton Wanderers and the title edged even further away. Arsenal needed to win this game to stay in touch with United, resurgent and untouchable, but the Reebok Stadium is no easy venue from which to escape with victory. For weeks, since their elimination from the Champions League in Valencia, Arsenal had been treading water with energy draining from their limbs. Even when Wiltord and Pires handed the visitors a 2–0 lead, the sense persisted that Wenger's side were vulnerable even against opponents labouring against relegation. Pascal Cygan and Freddie Ljungberg suffered at the hands of the hosts' rugged tackling, setting a troubling tone, before the away team succumbed.

Youri Djorkaeff, a player Wenger had groomed at Monaco as a youngster, clawed one goal back with 16 minutes remaining. Then, with Arsenal forced further and further back into grim defence, Martin Keown nodded inadvertently into his own net with six minutes remaining. Wenger, exasperated on the touchline, did something that, for him, was extraordinary – grimacing, he took his tie off. As a statement of dismay, that was telling. Thereafter, he stood with arms folded in his technical area, head occasionally bowed, as the minutes ticked away. Confirmation that there would be six additional minutes at the end barely registered. The sending off of Bolton's French centre-half Florent Laville in the dying seconds did not prove the catalyst for an Arsenal revival. This draw was as good as a defeat. 'When you manage at a great club like Arsenal, you know that you have 150,000 to 200,000 people in London following the results of your team,' he offered. 'So, when you lose, you go home and tell yourself: "I am responsible for the unhappiness of 150,000 people tonight."'

Arsenal's title defence, fractured and on the verge of failure, would ultimately hinge upon the visit of Leeds United on 4 May. Just before kick-off, Wenger went down the long tunnel at Highbury leading out on to the turf and experienced the chants drifting across the pitch from the Clock End. Anything other than a victory that day would see Arsenal surrender their crown to United, who had beaten Charlton 4–1 the day before to move eight points clear at the top with one fixture remaining. The Gunners had three games to play – Leeds, Southampton and Sunderland – but Arsène, like the vast majority of the 38,000 spectators taking their seats, knew the implications of failure.

Wenger wanted to believe in miracles, clinging to the conviction that nothing in football – particularly in England – is certain until the final whistle. 'For a manager, the game in England is so different to anything we see in France,' said Christian Damiano, who experienced the British game whilst at Liverpool and Fulham. 'There may be so many foreign players at Premiership clubs, but they are playing in a country where there are three fundamental values which are different to those on the Continent: that, in England, you respect and never question the manager's role; you stick to the discipline laid down by the club, whatever, whether it is politeness or punctuality; and, thirdly, you buy into the reality that football is combative. The English players are naturally combative.'

Wenger had bought into all three principles. 'The fact that the manager is given the freedom to dictate his work and do his job buys into my idea of the role,' he said. 'And the passion that motivates everyone is also something that sits well with me. It suits my personality down to the ground.'

But this optimism was to no avail. Leeds, struggling against relegation and a club about to career headlong into a slide that would see them relegated to League One, flickered one last time on the big stage with Harry Kewell scoring a stunning goal and Mark Viduka, two minutes from time, notching the decisive goal in a 3–2 away win. Henry and Bergkamp both scored to give the home side hope, but could not restore parity and with Arsenal needing to win, the game was up. Some 200 miles away, United could celebrate a title without having kicked a ball as Wenger saw his dream of defending the championship evaporate once again.

However, such was the sense of unity established in the squad and the strength of the coaching staff assembled at Highbury, there remained grounds for optimism for the future even with their title surrendered. Arsenal might have had a largely foreign team and an Alsatian manager, but they remained an English institution. The language used in the dressing room was always English, while Wenger leaned heavily on Pat Rice – an Irishman – and Gary Lewin on the bench. 'Wherever I've worked, whether it was in Monaco or Nagoya, the common denominator I've had is that I could rely on a really skilled staff and support team,' recognised Wenger. 'The people I worked with on a daily basis were of exceptional quality. At Monaco, Nagoya and here as well I think that, above all, the manager is dependent on people he works with on a day-to-day basis. If you come to a club and have a poor entourage, you have no chance.'

The hierarchy within the coaching staff at Arsenal resembles a pyramid. At the summit is Wenger. At the base are 16 Arsenal scouts, spread around the globe and charged with unearthing the next generation of talent. Between these two levels, some 18 members of staff are under the manager's control. They vary from Liam Brady and David Court, who are in charge of youth development at the training centre, to the goalkeeping coach Gerry Peyton. There is Steve Bould, the former centre-half turned youth team coach; Steve Rowley, the chief scout; John Kelly, the masseur; the coach Neil Banfield. Arsène is surrounded by an extensive team but, ultimately, the buck stops with him. 'At 34, with Nancy, I was just a trainer,' he said. 'Now I manage everything, from the cutting of the grass to the washing of kits, but we are a team, not to mention the scouts who work for us. I am therefore very well supported. Also, my deputies have always been vital to adapting to a new culture. For example, in Japan it took me three or four months to understand how people reacted.'

But Arsenal isn't Nagoya, and the Gunners are not the Princes of Monaco. 'I grew to understand that in England, unlike in France, they don't understand why players need to take a break. On the contrary, to manage moods, you need a single decision maker in the team. I spend a lot of time solving psychological problems, talking, and maybe that's why it's been important for me to learn several languages in order to communicate on a proper level. In saying that, I still surround myself with interpreters.'

Players are always treated as responsible adults. Wenger has never admonished one of his squad in front of everyone else, never moved to humiliate one of his players. If a player insisted on eating eggs on toast before a match, the management allowed him. If Martin Keown was not performing an adequate warm-down session at the end of a training session, Wenger turned a blind eye. If Sylvain Wiltord arrived late to training several times in a row, the manager took him into his office to have a quiet word rather than making a public show of his displeasure. 'I don't think people get away with things,' said Wenger. 'I try to be quite open and tolerant, but not lax. It is always a matter of degrees. It is often necessary to be tolerant, because you have to be patient in order to allow people to express themselves, to develop. But tolerance also has its limits.

'Abroad, it is always necessary to find a balance between openness of spirit and the desire to contribute ideas. The first is necessary to adapt to the local culture, the second allows you to survive while contributing something of yourself. If

you behave like the guys on the corner, you aren't contributing anything new. I started to worry about being too
calm, at times. It is probably my Germanic side which was
most upset. I wouldn't have been able to behave like this 20
years ago, but I have become more tolerant with age. You try
to think of what others might think. If I had come to Arsenal
20 years ago, I would undoubtedly have failed. I was too
demanding, really intolerant.'

Within Wenger's hierarchy, the kit manager has as
important a role to play as the masseur, but one job is critical:
that of the scout. 'If the recruitment department does not
function smoothly, it is the manager whose neck is on the
block,' said Wenger. 'If the manager does not have the final
say on a player, the writing is on the wall. In England, the
pressure is greater to get it right than it is in France, but at
least you have the ultimate say. On the Continent, some clubs
have technical directors who are in charge of transfer policy.
That cannot work in England.' For Wenger, recruitment is
key. It is something he loves. After all, this is a manager who
once went incognito to a lower-league game in Holland,
complete with false moustache, to spot a young talent.

Among the many stories about Arsène's ability to persuade
players to join his revolution at Arsenal, one is particularly
significant. One night back in the summer of 2001, Wenger –
accompanied by Dein – spoke passionately about the club
and his vision for the season ahead. He was addressing a
player who had become his absolute priority in the transfer
market that closed season, but also a player who he knew
would buy completely into his way of thinking. It took hours
of negotiations but eventually, and with dawn about to break,

the duo from Arsenal convinced their man. At about 4 a.m., the trio signed a contract. Who was this key player? It was Sol Campbell, the rock upon which Arsenal's bitter rivals Tottenham Hotspur were built, but who had now been persuaded by Wenger and his vice-chairman to join the enemy.

Damien Comolli, the former chief scout at Arsenal who has since moved in the opposite direction to become sporting director at White Hart Lane, explained the way Wenger approaches such negotiations: 'Arsène looks for four qualities in terms of his recruitment: he looks for power, for pace, for technical ability and for an intelligence in the guy he's considering bringing in. If a player lacks one of those four strengths, Arsène drops his interest. That is his rule. That's why, at Arsenal, there is a team brimming with world-class talents, all quick, powerful, technically brilliant and physically imposing. Players like Thierry Henry or Kolo Touré, Gilberto Silva or Emmanuel Adebayor.'

It is the keenness to recruit intelligent players that perhaps catches the eye most of all. 'His scouts find out everything about a player, watching promising youngsters in training and how they carry themselves off the pitch. They scrutinise their reactions, their temperament, their game awareness. Just because a player is physically impressive or technically adept doesn't mean he's necessarily going to fit in.' Assimilating a player into an established squad, allowing him to flourish in an environment that suits him, is essential. Only players who will fit in are pursued, these factors making up the profile of the player Wenger will target in the market.

'In terms of bringing people, Wenger has very clear criteria and particular ideas,' said Claude Puel, coach at the French club Lille who, as a relatively small provincial outfit, rely upon unearthing young talent which they develop and eventually sell on to survive. 'He's very precise with what he is looking for in terms of a potential new signing's physical and technical strengths.'

'His approach to recruitment is in his own image,' added Max Hild. 'Arsène takes on players with potential, players he can mould, but also players who can fit in with what he already possesses and play in the style he demands of his side.' In that respect, the prodigious Arsenal second string, built up of players recruited from around the world and all boasting glorious natural talent and temperament, appears set to flourish in the years ahead. The image of their swashbuckling 6–3 Carling Cup victory at Liverpool in January 2007, the home side's worst defeat at Anfield in 77 years, is seared on the memory, though it is significant that that very strategy – seeking out the best young players for the future – was actually born out of frustration at being unable to compete at the top end of the transfer market.

Back on 11 May 2003 at Sunderland's Stadium of Light, Arsenal brought the curtain down on their season with a rampant 4–0 victory courtesy of a Ljungberg hat-trick and a goal from Henry. The visitors were untouchable, though that was little consolation for Wenger. His side had lost their title, surrendered to Manchester United, and the manager recognised a new approach was needed. He may have been exhausted after a lengthy and draining campaign but, disappointed by the young players emerging through the club, Wenger's mind was whirring. He didn't retire to bed until almost 2 a.m. after that victory on Wearside, and he was up barely two hours later and en route to the airport, bound for the Côte d'Azur and a meeting with the parents of a player in whom he was interested, and a player whose arrival would set the tone for future transfer policy.

'He was up at 4 a.m., even though he'd just seen his side lose their championship, to go and meet a kid of 17 who'd been playing in the French National Division [the equivalent of the Third Division] at AS Cannes,' recalled Comolli, who had set the talks in motion. 'I knew he'd hardly had any sleep and I remember asking him why he was putting himself through this. He just replied: "I'll stay up around the clock if I can sign a good young player." Gaël Clichy had only played 15 matches for AS Cannes in 2002–03, but we wanted him at any price because we knew he had a phenomenal natural talent and huge potential.'

The young full-back certainly met all Wenger's criteria: he was strong, quick, technically sound and bright. 'When my parents told me that Arsenal wanted to sign me, I told them they must be joking,' said Clichy. 'But the next thing I know, Arsène Wenger is on the phone and asking to meet me in a restaurant in Cannes.'

On 12 May 2003 the young defender found himself sitting at a table with the former Monaco coach, as if he was living a dream. 'I was with my parents and, a few times, I had to pinch myself that here I was, face to face with Arsène Wenger.' The discussions centred on football, but doubts remained for the youngster. 'To be honest, both myself and my parents weren't sure whether it was a good idea to up sticks and move to a new country. It didn't seem to be the best thing to do. In fact, our preference was to keep progressing through the French system, through the National league to Division Two and then Division One, because that way at least I would get to play senior games rather than being forced to play in the reserves.'

But Wenger insisted that the youngster could maintain his development, quietly and steadily, at Arsenal and that the doors to the first team at Highbury would, in time, open to him. 'He assured me that I would feature in at least five matches in the senior side over the course of the next season,' added Clichy. 'In fact, the outline he gave us of his long-term vision for me and my career sounded more and more interesting.'

There was real competition for Clichy's signature in France, with interest swollen by his displays in the handful of appearances he had made for Cannes that season, and French clubs duly came out of the woodwork to express an interest in signing him. They made contact with the youngster's parents, and he visited the managers and coaches who wanted to take him on. But, in the back of his mind, it was always Wenger who had made the greatest impression. 'None of those talks I had with other managers and at other clubs were as inspiring as those I'd had with Arsène Wenger. He'd sold his club to me and there was only one choice. Arsenal.'

The youngster, just turned 18, moved across the Channel that summer and was installed immediately as Ashley Cole's understudy at left-back, though his new manager was forever offering him indications that his chance would come to play in the first team. 'He'd won so much already,' said Clichy,

who arrived aware of Wenger's achievements and was relish-
ing life as a member of the squad the manager had assembled.
'What he'd done for these players was extraordinary, notably
with Thierry Henry, Patrick Vieira, Robert Pires and Sylvain
Wiltord. The confidence he had instilled in them was
unbelievable. In return, all these players gave him everything.
When Thierry Henry says in the newspapers that he doesn't
want to leave Arsenal and his heart is at the club, that just
makes you want to work harder and do the same, achieve the
same, as he has.

'It was difficult at first, coming into that dressing room full
of star players, the Harlem Globetrotters of football. I didn't
really know how to approach them, even speak with them,
and I was a bit nervous and overawed by it all. But I realised,
all the same, that I had been brought there for a reason. That
Arsène thought I was good enough to join this group. The
other players welcomed me and looked after me. I'd sit there
talking with Edu [Eduardo César Gaspar] before games and
he'd help me get over the butterflies and the pre-match
nerves.'

It was on 22 November 2003, at St Andrew's, that Wenger
decided the time had come to blood his protégé in the
Premiership. Clichy started against Birmingham City and,
thanks to a riotous attacking display allied to a steely defence,
the visitors ran out comfortable 3–0 winners with the
youngster – starting in a more advanced role ahead of Cole
on the flank – enjoying almost an hour. 'There were so many
people there,' he recalled of the crowd of almost 30,000
who witnessed the rout. 'At the end, I wasn't particularly
happy with the way I'd played. Wenger told me I'd played

almost within myself, possibly because I wasn't used to that kind of atmosphere. He asked me whether I'd dreamt of playing in front of a packed arena, and of course I said I had. He just replied: "You mustn't let what you dreamt of as a kid inhibit you and stop you playing." He was right, and it helped.'

Clichy has matured since with Wenger good to his word; the left-back went on to play 13 times for the Londoners that season, then 17 the following year, including twice in Europe. Foot injuries may have frustrated his progress over the next few years, but the former Cannes youth-teamer has become an essential part of Wenger's new-look Arsenal set-up, particularly since Cole's controversial transfer to Chelsea in the summer of 2006. Clichy's tale is indicative of Wenger's thinking – there is long-term strategy in his outlook. It is no coincidence that Arsène first became aware of and attracted to Robert Pires when the midfielder was a youngster at Metz and Wenger was at Monaco. These days, the Arsenal manager's net is cast wide – he returned to Cannes to pluck Carl Parisio, a young defender aged 16, under freedom of contract. The youngster is currently developing his talents at London and awaiting his first-team opportunity. One suspects it will eventually come.

Of course, Wenger has endured failures as well whilst attempting to lure players to London. In the summer of 2005, after months of delicate negotiations, the Brazilian Julio Baptista rejected a move to the club from Sevilla. 'When you miss out on good players, it's always frustrating,' said Damien Comolli, who had tracked Baptista's progress and was dismayed ultimately to see him opt to move to Real

Madrid instead. 'Does that get to Arsène? Definitely. He's always under pressure to deliver. When you are manager of a big club, you have 18 or 19 internationals in your squad, your every move is scrutinised by the players. You're obliged, therefore, always to be positive and proactive, to forever be moving forward. It's an awkward balance. You have to make out to the players you have that they are the best, and you can't let the odd failure in the market cloud your outlook.'

The Brazilian did eventually move to London, with his options limited under Fabio Capello at Real, and featured heavily during the 2006–07 campaign, memorably scoring four times and missing a penalty in the staggering 6–3 Carling Cup rout of Liverpool at Anfield. Yet his year-long loan was unconvincing, and in May 2007 Baptista returned to Madrid having failed to secure a permanent move. There are others who did get away, from Vicente Rodriguez – the Spanish attacking midfielder who came up through the ranks at Levante – to Chris Sutton, the former Norwich and Blackburn striker who ended up joining Chelsea and then Celtic ahead of Arsenal. Added to them can be figures like Rivaldo and Wily Sagnol, who were priced out of moves to Highbury, with the relative lack of funds at Wenger's disposal – certainly when compared with Roman Abramovich's Chelsea – making his achievements all the more remarkable. In the summer of 2006, in the wake of defeat in the Champions League final to Barcelona, the Alsatian expressed publicly his hopes that the move to the Emirates Stadium would hoist Arsenal to the next level and allow him to spend substantial fees on established talent to challenge the likes of Chelsea and United. Still, the ability to compete remains

Arsenal's biggest problem of recent years. The board have proved resistant to attempts by an American billionaire, Stan Kroenke, to buy the club when some among the hierarchy – and David Dein in particular – believed it was vital that outside funding be brought in. The refusal by Peter Hill-Wood and Danny Fiszman to deal with Kroenke directly prompted Dein's departure from the club in the spring of 2007, forcing Wenger to extend his policy of unearthing young talent.

Yet while Wenger is acknowledged as a superb talent-spotter, there have been failings. 'I don't want to come across as someone who's always pointing out faults or mistakes but, while a lot of players have been signed in the last few years and have proven themselves to be of an international standard, Arsène has had some failures with those he's recruited,' reminded Manu Petit. 'At the moment, we're only seeing the ones that paid off. The ones that fell away are no longer at the club . . .' The German defender Stefan Malz and the England international striker Francis Jeffers, a pricey failure at £10 million after signing from Everton, are best forgotten as Arsenal players, while others have gone on to flourish elsewhere, such as the Brazilian Silvinho in La Liga with Barcelona.

The veteran Croatia striker Davor Suker or the Latvian Igors Stepanovs, who both enjoyed brief spells at Highbury under Wenger, will not linger too long in the supporters' memories with the former a spent force and the latter not up to the Premiership. Similarly, English players such as Stephen Hughes, Matthew Upson and David Bentley have been allowed to leave, prompting some resentment at the club's

academy amongst home-grown talent who have only witnessed Ashley Cole progress into the senior set-up in recent
years. That feeling of uncertainty has been heightened by the
influx of young foreign talent, after Clichy, into the club.

There are also accusations that Wenger's eye for a player
does not necessarily extend to goalkeepers, something often
drummed up by the press. Reporters point to the fact that
since the retirement of David Seaman, no keeper has truly
proven himself as Arsenal's undisputed No. 1. Some even
doubt Jens Lehmann's qualities despite his performances en
route to the 2006 Champions League final. It seems the
biggest problem confronting Wenger is the need to recruit
players capable of flourishing in the physical English game. 'I
would never tell Arsène that he's made a mistake in buying a
player, such as José Antonio Reyes,' said Tiburce Darrou,
Wenger's friend from the south of France. 'But I would
sometimes point out to him that a player like Reyes will not
develop as well in England as he would if he stayed and
played in Spain, purely because of the type of football he's
going to have to be playing.'

Regardless, Wenger remains admired and respected for
what he has achieved in the transfer market, particularly at
Arsenal. He is fussy in terms of what prices are paid, he can
sniff out a bargain and he knows which talents he can revive
and take to new levels. They are qualities which set him apart
in the main when it comes to unearthing the world's best
players. Players scouted by Arsenal are examined, assessed
and considered in competitive action tens of times before the
club make their move. The manager's policy of recruitment
reflects his greatest quality: hard work. 'I remember Arsène

interrupting a family holiday in the summer of 2005 so he could go to Brazil and look at a player,' recalled Damien Comolli. That trip lasted two days but, as far as Wenger was concerned, was worth it on the off-chance that he might uncover a jewel of a player. Everything, it seems, is a pursuit of a Holy Grail. 'He's an innovator,' added the English writer Jasper Rees. 'That's the only way to describe what he does, whether it be the way he tracks players, the way he prepares for games and his whole philosophy for the game. They have all changed the way the game is played in this country, in the same way that the attacking football his team plays has changed attitudes in England.'

Early afternoon of 17 May 2003 at the Millennium Stadium. Wenger strode out of the tunnel, past the banks of empty seats, and on to the turf where his players claimed the FA Cup a year earlier. Cardiff had welcomed the Gunners back, this time to defend their trophy against Southampton. As the first supporters began drifting into the arena, some two hours before kick-off, Arsenal's players, dressed in their swish Cup Final suits, ambled around the pitch taking in the atmosphere. They trotted out again an hour later for their warm-up. Tony Colbert, the fitness coach, Boro Primorac, Wenger's right-hand man, and Pat Rice took charge. On the edge of the pitch, Fabrice Dubois marvelled at the thoroughness of the routines and exercises which the players were put through. Dubois was a 'friendly spy' at Colney, invited over from Monaco to see how Wenger ran Arsenal. 'When I met him again in London, Arsène was with his assistant, Boro, who is omnipresent,' said Dubois. 'It's Primorac who carries out the physical preparation of the team, such as the pre-match warm-ups . . . Then Arsène takes control when it comes to technical or tactical work with an eye on small details which will make a massive difference at the top level.'

Just before 3 p.m. that afternoon in the Millennium Stadium, Wenger – a flower in his buttonhole – announced the side who would be challenging Gordon Strachan's Southampton that afternoon. The team line-up was given: Seaman, Keown, Luhzny, Cole, Lauren, Pires, Ljungberg, Parlour, Gilberto, Bergkamp and Henry. Outside, 73,726 fans were bellowing impatiently. The Arsenal fans, the Gooners, knew that winning this trophy would offer some consolation for the team having surrendered their league title. This Cup would be Wenger's third. Against a weaker but determined team, the team-mates of Henry and Pires chattered nervously amongst themselves, self-doubt creeping into their preparations, while the manager waited for his moment to speak.

Typically of Wenger, his pre-match ritual went unchanged: he would keep his words to a minimum, but what he said would be hugely significant. The voice that rang out, screaming for quiet, was that of Pat Rice, Wenger's No. 2 since his appointment in the autumn of 1996. But, if Arsène relied on his assistant to shut the side up, it's always clear just who is giving the orders. That day, his players' fears that they might let the FA Cup slip through their hands as well as the Premiership were to be allayed. Wenger would not have allowed them to be defeatist. Subsequently, the manager gave a rare insight into his thinking. 'I'm certain of one thing,' he said. 'I could not bear to sit on the bench with a team who won't play and who gives up. But, on the other hand, if I was obliged to shut down a game and squeeze the life from it to save my team, I would. But to say at the start of a season: "This year, we're just going to keep our heads down and out of the firing line," that's not possible.'

When the game kicked off, Arsenal played without fear. Victory was secured by one of their French contingent, Robert Pires capping a fine move with a tidy finish in the 38th minute to secure a 1–0 win. It might not have been the most expansive of performances, or the most entertaining of finals, but Arsenal won the day and the fact that Sylvain Wiltord came on with 13 minutes remaining (the Frenchman replaced Bergkamp) confirmed that the manager had been true to his attacking instincts. Southampton were an inferior side, and limited on the day, and the Londoners held sway until the final whistle. Wenger departed Cardiff that afternoon with his third FA Cup.

Despite his side leading for so much of the game, he kept encouraging his players forward and ensuring they did not sit back on their lead. He hadn't forgotten the lesson of a match against Leicester City on 27 August 1997, when his side dominated and at one stage led by two clear goals. 'At 2–0 up, I sat back on the bench assuming the game was won,' Wenger once admitted to his friend Daniel Jeandupeux. 'I took off a player who was tiring and introduced a defensive player, rearranging the team to hold what we had. We ended up drawing the game 3–3. The experienced players in my team were furious with me, accusing me of having cost them the game. Perhaps they weren't wrong . . . even if no one would have come to that conclusion.'

Jeandupeux has been analysing how Wenger runs his Arsenal side for almost ten years now. 'I asked him once: "Arsène, over the course of a season, are you always in complete control of the squad? Don't you get the impression that, now and again, things get away from you a bit?" It wasn't supposed to be a naive question because a coach surely loses control of his players once in a while. Sometimes he clicks his fingers and they all fall into line. Other times, he argues with them until he's blue in the face and that relationship between the coach and the player concerned, albeit normally temporarily, is wrecked.

'But a coach can't acknowledge that he's not in control. That would just be too dangerous and would undermine his authority. And yet I remember Arsène's response quite clearly. "Yes, my team slips away from me each year. Even in the best seasons, I sometimes get the impression that I don't have any influence on them." As an admission, that was incredible.'

Graham Rix, who played at Caen when Wenger held sway in the French league championship, gave his own assessment of the Arsenal coach. 'When he arrived at Highbury, that team had a reputation for a long-ball game and a reliance upon the offside rule,' he said. 'Today, under Wenger's influence, the team is spectacular.' If the narrow victory in Cardiff, courtesy of Pires's goal, hardly holds up that assessment, the FA Cup claimed that day did prove to be the catalyst for an incredible season ahead.

In the summer of 2003, with the FA Cup in the bag from the previous campaign, the Gunners travelled to Peterborough

United for a pre-season friendly. They lost 1–0 and Wenger appeared at the post-match press conference with the gaggle of reporters dispatched to London Road. 'Arsène was smiling,' said Daniel King, a journalist on the *Mail on Sunday*. 'He sat down and, without anyone asking a question, said: "Well, at least I can't tell you we'll manage to go through the whole season unbeaten!"' King believes that Wenger, at that moment, still believed his team capable of remaining undefeated throughout the campaign, even if he did not say so publicly. 'Wenger remembered at the time that it's best sometimes to keep your true thoughts to yourself, just in case what you say in public comes back to haunt you.'

After all, it had done once already. Some ten months earlier, in the autumn of 2002, a journalist had asked Wenger a question that, at the time, had come almost out of left field: 'Would it be possible for Arsenal to win the title without losing a single match in the Premiership?' 'Yes, of course, it's possible,' had come the manager's reply. 'I have a good team, a good squad, and we possess the quality to achieve that.' The headlines in the newspapers screamed out the next day: 'Wenger believes the title can be won without defeat'. By the end of that season, Manchester United were Premiership champions at the expense of Wenger's side.

Yet the 2003–04 season would prove to be the stuff of dreams. Wide-eyed in amazement, with mouth gawping at the splendour of it all, England witnessed the implausible that year. Up and down the land, the Gunners were untouchable. Whether they were sweeping aside inferior opponents or emerging unscathed from combustible face-offs with their nearest challengers, Arsenal carried all before them. If the big guns such as Vieira and Henry led the way, then the emerging talents of Kolo Touré and Lauren, Ashley Cole and Gaël Clichy, took up the challenge.

Whatever magic spell Wenger had cast, he was keeping it a secret. 'A coach tries above all to create an ambiance and group in which young players who like to play football can do what they do best. I am there to try and create an environment in which the players can express themselves out on the pitch.' The team which tore through all comers that season boasted a young average age, but it was anything but naive in its approach. Indeed, it proved itself to be enterprising. Lauren, Touré, Cole, Fabregas and Reyes were the bright young things combining so wonderfully with the old guard of Pires, Ljungberg and Henry. They seared their way through the new Premiership season, their rhythm unchecked by the break, while their challengers dropped like flies. The only minor wound that could be inflicted on the Arsenal machine came outside the Premiership, when Manchester United knocked the holders out of the FA Cup in the semi-final at Villa Park. Otherwise, this team proved indestructible.

On 9 April 2004, the side beaten in the FA Cup the previous week welcomed Liverpool to Highbury as the run-in to the Premiership season began. Sami Hyypia caught the home side off guard early on, easing the visitors ahead. The home fans crammed into the stadium, so unused to seeing their side in arrears, were stunned by the concession. On the pitch, Wenger's side seemed gripped by self-doubt: where they were usually so sharp on the break, biting deep into their opponents, now they rather laboured, their customary flowing football running aground on Liverpool's rugged defence.

The Merseysiders led until the half-hour when Henry, so often the saviour, equalised only for Michael Owen to score in the 42nd minute. At the interval, Liverpool led 2–1 and the Gunners, heads in their hands, feared the worst. Had the Cup elimination knocked the stuffing out of Arsenal's Premiership challenge? Were their title aspirations also to be ruined at the last? Was their unbeaten run to end here, with Nottingham Forest's record 42-match streak without defeat from the 1970s to stand unchallenged?

Doubt drowned the home dressing room but it was there, in that room with its white tiles and wooden benches and windows looking out on to the street, where Arsenal teams had changed since 1936, that Wenger restored calm. It was the coach, as quietly spoken as ever, who reminded his side of the basics, reassured them that this would not be the end, and cleared their heads. His team talk was brief, succinct and delivered almost without emotion. That, he left to Patrick Vieira. The captain suddenly roared at his team, yelling at the other players that 'We are not going to lose this!' One by one, his fellow senior players were shrugged back out of their shells. Edu, Pires, Henry, one by one, they took the younger players under their wings, and by the time the team tore out of the changing room for the second half, Liverpool's chance had effectively gone. Certainty had returned to the home side's game, authority sweeping through their play, and the visitors were brushed aside. Pires equalised, with Henry scoring twice more to complete his hat-trick. Arsenal had won 4–2 and Arsène realised, for the first time, that no one would beat his class of 2004.

On 16 April 2004 the Gunners hosted Leeds United. At

Newcastle, five days earlier, the Londoners had emerged unscathed with a 0–0 draw to stretch their unbeaten sequence. Fans, sensing the team were reaching their peak, flooded into the ground with the party atmosphere reflecting as much. Leeds, the side who had denied Wenger his title the previous year by winning 3–2 in north London, were then subjected to the 'Thierry Henry show'. Robert Pires had opened the scoring six minutes in before Titi took over. His first was pilfered just before the half-hour, his second plundered from the penalty spot after 33 minutes. His hat-trick was chalked up five minutes into the second half with a fourth goal, just for good measure, secured after 67 minutes with the party in full swing. The scoreboards at either end of Highbury burned brightly: Arsenal 5 Leeds United 0. Highbury roared its approval, though the cherry on the cake was achieved across town at White Hart Lane, home of their bitter rivals, some nine days later.

It was at Tottenham Hotspur that Wenger's untouchables secured the Premiership, dominating the match with goals from Vieira and Pires even if Spurs equalised with a penalty in the last minute to make the game 2–2. Still, a point was enough. White Hart Lane emptied. Those who remained were crammed into the away section, the Gooners celebrating raucously with their little pocket of the ground jumping up and down in delight. Their heroes celebrated with them, holding aloft in turn an inflatable Premiership trophy tossed to them by one of the supporters. Neither their next visitors, Birmingham City (a 0–0 draw to reflect the anticlimax with the title claimed), nor Portsmouth (1–1) could check Wenger's champions. Fulham (1–0) and

Leicester City (2–1) were duly beaten in the final fixtures of the season, the latest victims of the fluid, attacking football with which opponents simply could not cope. The Invincibles became, according to some commentators, The Immortals that year. Europe was gearing itself for Euro 2004 in Portugal, where the likes of Holland, France, the Czech Republic and Greece would offer plenty to dazzle and admire, but the only truly thrilling football played that year was witnessed at Highbury.

Arsenal had become one of the few teams in the modern era to go a whole season unbeaten. The others have all become the stuff of legend: AC Milan in 1991–92 had done likewise, with Ajax Amsterdam emulating the feat in the Eredivisie in 1994–95. But Milan had not been able to compete in Europe that season, due to suspension, and Ajax compete in a championship that most consider to be sub-standard when compared with the Premier League. Indeed, Wenger's team were following in the distant footsteps of only one English side: the original Invincibles of Preston North End who, in 1888–89, had emerged from a season without defeat. Yet even this is an unfair comparison to draw. Back in 1889, the league season was made up of 22 games. Some 115 years on, Arsenal's achievement in a hugely competitive division made up of 20 teams and 38 fixtures was startling. The bare statistics remain astonishing: 26 games had been won, 12 drawn, with 73 goals scored and only 26 conceded. The Gunners ended up with 90 points, 11 more than second-place Chelsea and 15 more than third-placed Manchester United. Wenger had realised one of his dreams. To be unbeaten. 'People laughed at me when I said it could be done, but I saw it was possible despite what everybody was saying . . .'

Even Alex Ferguson, albeit grudgingly, lent his voice to the chorus of those ready to praise Wenger's achievements that year. 'I have to admit that Arsenal have been better than us this season,' he said at the time, aware that his Manchester United team had arguably come closest to deflating the Gunners only for Ruud van Nistelrooy to miss a contro-versial late penalty at Old Trafford which allowed the visitors to escape with a 0–0 draw. 'The fact that they've been unbeaten in the league all season is, quite simply, astonishing because the Premiership is such a difficult league in which to compete.' That game, so tight and tense, actually offered a glimpse of the ugly side of Arsenal with their players, incensed at the award of a penalty after Van Nistelrooy's tumble, jostling and shoving the Dutchman in the wake of his miss. The striker was visibly shocked by the reaction, the sight of Martin Keown celebrating manically within inches of his face an image that did Arsenal no favours. The enmity between these two clubs deepened that day, though Arsenal remained unbeatable.

Kevin Keegan, then coach of Manchester City, added: 'Arsenal are so happy when they've got the ball, particularly if they're ahead. You just can't get possession back off them. Even when they don't play quite at 100 per cent, they are still capable of winning a match. That is the mark of greatness.' 'When you play against Arsenal, you can't afford to slip up even for a split second,' added the Everton manager David Moyes. 'They will punish even the slightest mistake.' To understand the Arsenal winning machine assembled by

Wenger, it is necessary to appreciate the hold he has on his players, even from a distance, and the permanent protection he offers them.

On 16 May 2004, the streets of Islington and those around Highbury in particular were heaving with joyous Gooners heralding their heroes as they undertook a victory parade to celebrate their Premiership title. The flags fluttered, the fans chanted as the open-top buses rolled past, the hamburger stalls on the street corners did a roaring trade and this pocket of north London ground to a halt. There were two red buses crawling through the streets carrying the Invincibles before their people. On the sides of the buses, the face of each player who had played his part that season stared out. Wenger savoured the scene. The Dein family – David, his wife Barbara and their sons Gavin and Darren (Thierry Henry's friend and lawyer) and daughter, Sasha – mingled with the players in the open air. Arsène was wearing a grey suit, but had taken off his tie in the spring heat, lifting up the Premiership trophy to the delight of those watching from below. Behind his smile, his mind was clearly moving on already. His expression bore the worry lines of so many past battles, and an appreciation that many more lay ahead. While those around him celebrated gleefully, holding aloft their season's plunder, the Alsatian already knew that the delight would not last. He would not be able to rest on this achievement in the days to come, but would have to set new goals, find new motivation, to rekindle the desire of his squad for what would inevitably be greater tests ahead.

'As people say in England: "Who motivates the motivator?"' explained Wenger. 'You always want your players to perform better, and your team to be perfect. However, that actually only happens at most once or twice in a season. I can excuse myself the frustration which I show when that doesn't happen.' The new season would offer him another chance to shape his squad and mould them into that 'perfect team'. Before that, though, was a summer of planning, of squad strengthening and renewing players' contracts, or even letting some of his side leave. Rather than dwelling on what has already been achieved, Wenger is forever thinking ahead, planning for the short and long term, and for future conquests, thinking about his next squad. He is planning ahead, moulding his next side of combatants. It is no surprise to learn that when Wenger's youthful team reached the Carling Cup final in 2007, he admitted the team had been 'five years in the making'. In that time, other Arsenal sides had claimed the title and reached the Champions League final but, while he received plaudits for those achievements, the manager had been moving unnoticed behind the scenes to create a new, progressive side.

This aspect of Wenger the organiser, forever distracted by strategic decisions, is gently reinforced by Dennis Bergkamp. 'The reality is that Arsène is the only coach in the world who spends more time talking with agents than he does with his own players,' said the Dutchman. In fact, even on that victory parade aboard the open-top bus, the impression remained that Wenger was keeping himself slightly separate. He didn't stand alongside the likes of Vieira or Henry, his arms aloft on the top deck in celebration once the photocalls had been undertaken. Wenger may consider himself an equal of his players on the training pitch, always working as hard as they do, but off the field he does not attempt to be like them. He has established a hierarchy with his troops; the master doesn't mix with his students when they are playing, for the sake of keeping a little distance and maintaining a sense of authority.

'The considerable distance he keeps from his players off the field melts away when in training,' said Daniel Jeandupeux. 'But, still, he completely separates his private and professional lives.' Jean-Luc Arribart, his former team-mate in the French university side, has noted two major changes in his friend over the years. 'When I knew him back then, he was a practical joker,' he said. 'He'd love to fool around, all the time. Now, though, he seems to stay quite cold, serious and detached, certainly on the outside. I'm sure he's still mellow inside, but he's so used now to transmitting to his players that he is in charge and must be taken seriously. That's one of his character traits: he doesn't let himself get worked up into a panic or get consumed by worry. He doesn't really do angry or annoyed, and if he does it's very rare. That's an important factor in his management. It's almost as if I've seen the two sides of Arsène. Back when we were at university together, he never gave us the impression that he'd turn into this hugely professional person, or indeed would feel so passionately about his job.'

Those who experience Wenger's unemotional managerial style would be surprised by this revelation. The manager is capable of both tolerance and intransigence, but is able to get the best out of his team. 'These days, if some of my players aren't paying attention or mucking about when we do our stretches at the end of training, I just turn my head and don't say a thing,' confirmed Wenger. 'I'm not going to get angry with them over such small things. On the other hand, I will come down on them hard if I feel their attitude is affecting the way they play in a match.

'A manager has to work out what his priorities are, where the line must be drawn in terms of focus and preparation, and not be distracted by little, unimportant irritations. It's about the bigger picture. Once a coach has worked out what type of football he wants to play and how he wants the team to be structured and organised, as soon as he knows his approach, he mustn't stray too far from that path he's set himself. There are danger signs a trainer must be wary of, such as becoming annoyed with his players over small things, tiny aspects that will detract only one or two per cent from their game, and to dismiss them as bad players as a result.' The other risk is the wearing effect of being in power. An old enemy is always lurking around the next corner ready to end a winning or unbeaten run, as Arsène is well aware.

But the constant desire to move on to the next challenge and potential success is healthy. 'I forget quickly what I have achieved,' admitted Wenger. 'I don't really linger on any memories of the titles, cups or victories I've enjoyed in my career. I'm sure my winners' medals are somewhere in my house, but I haven't got a clue where. All that I'm concerned with, all that matters to me, is what I'm facing up to next. I live my life thinking about the future and constantly looking forward. Any competitive person does, with their focus on the competition to come. I'm like someone betting in a casino, only ever thinking about the next hand . . . The present is shaped by the players, the future by their coach.'

*

Sunday 24 October 2004. Old Trafford. The Theatre of Dreams opened its doors to Wenger's Players of Pleasure. Since Wenger took the reins at Arsenal, the Londoners' encounters with Manchester United had effectively been transformed into a derby, with the thrill of anticipation heightened for this fixture. The Gunners had eclipsed Nottingham Forest's 42-game unbeaten run by beating Blackburn (3–0, on 25 August), having recovered from 3–1 down three days earlier to beat Middlesbrough 5–3 at Highbury. Arsenal arrived in Manchester knowing they would become the first team in history to go 50 league games in a row unbeaten, etching their names into the record books, if they avoided defeat at Old Trafford. Faced by his old adversary Sir Alex Ferguson, Wenger wheeled out his big guns: Lehmann in goal; Lauren, Campbell, Touré and Cole across the back line; Ljungberg, Vieira, Edu and Reyes in midfield; with Bergkamp drifting in behind Henry up front. The champions had begun the season as they had ended the last, certainly in terms of the results they accrued if not always the free-flowing attacking football. They were unbeaten after nine matches and strode out against the Red Devils poised for the phenomenal 50.

As was to be expected, the game was fierce. Ruud van Nistelrooy and Patrick Vieira, in particular, went out of their way to wind each other up, a legacy of past encounters; Rio Ferdinand crunched into an eager Freddie Ljungberg, while Ashley Cole sent Cristiano Ronaldo flying, with the full-back later fouled horrendously by Van Nistelrooy . . . Every centimetre of turf was contested, every blade of grass fought for, and the score remained level. The Londoners were clinging to their invincibility. On the touchline, Wenger's mind was a whir. Was his tactical plan coming off? In the 70th minute he made his move, introducing Robert Pires for Reyes. But just three minutes later, Arsenal's world imploded. Wayne Rooney tumbled in the area under a soft challenge from Sol Campbell. Television replays appeared to show that the defender had pulled back his leg just before the striker fell, but the referee Mike Riley pointed straight to the spot. The game had turned in the blink of an eye, with Wenger, alongside Gary Lewin and Pat Rice, still protesting vehemently as Van Nistelrooy converted the penalty. The game plan had been wrecked, and as the game lurched into added time with Arsenal pressing frantically for an equaliser, Alan Smith and Rooney mounted a counter-attack with the latter duly adding the killer second.

Vieira and his team trudged off the pitch, their heads in their hands and their shoulders hunched in defeat, denied two notable records: their 49-match unbeaten run was over, as was their equally impressive 27-game undefeated sequence away from home. Arsenal had not lost since they had hammered Southampton 6–1 in May 2004, a few days after surrendering their title to Manchester United. The visiting players smouldered with injustice as they headed back towards the changing rooms. Wenger, furious at the award of the penalty and what he perceived to have been United's underhand tactics during the game, waited in the corridor leading to the home players' dressing rooms. Rooney and Van Nistelrooy, in his eyes, were hardly knights in shining armour and, enraged, he sought them out to tell them what he thought of them. The clamour rose as the arguments began and, hearing raised voices, Ferguson emerged from the home dressing room to have his say. In the mêlée that followed, a food fight broke out with Ferguson pelted with pizza and soup, food which had been there for the players to eat post-match. With the scene submerging into farce, United's security staff were forced to intervene before it got totally out of hand.

The Battle of the Buffet, as it was christened in the press, was followed by a war of words between the managers. Ferguson, having changed clothes, wasted little time to have his say, telling the television cameras at the ground: 'They are the worst losers I've ever seen. They don't know how to lose graciously. They'd probably only behave like that against Manchester United because, other than against us, they don't lose that many matches.'

'I'm not interested in what he says at all,' retorted Wenger a few days later. 'I don't want anything to do with him. I'm not going to respond to his provocation from now on in.' When pushed further, the Arsenal manager added: 'Ferguson is finished, he's lost all sense of reality. He seeks out confrontation and, when he finds it, he expects the other man to back down.' 'It's unthinkable that a manager wouldn't apologise for the poor behaviour of his players,' added Ferguson for good measure. 'It's disgraceful, but I'm hardly waiting on an apology from Wenger. He's not the type of man to apologise.'

English football was up in arms at the spat between two of the game's most prominent and respected figures. The Football Association, who would go on to charge Wenger for implying that Van Nistelrooy was a 'cheat' in his post-match interviews, attempted to instigate calm, though their efforts were in vain. Gérard Houllier, the former Liverpool manager and now coaching Olympique Lyonnais, attempted to defend Wenger with tongue firmly in cheek. 'I've dined with Arsène enough times to know that he loves pizza and he'd never want to waste it. Seriously, people say that Arsène is a bad loser. I'd say to him: stay as you are!' One of Wenger's close friends says: 'I wouldn't describe Arsène as a bad loser. He is a winner. But he has this incredibly competitive mind. When we played beach soccer, three against three (with Jean-Marc Guillou and Boro Primorac), everyone was fighting so hard!'

Others, even if they admire Wenger as the master tactician, felt his part in the tunnel fracas damaged his reputation. 'I believe that Wenger lost a bit of the dignity for which he had become renowned in that incident,' said Daniel King of the *Mail on Sunday*. 'Perhaps he had good reason to point out that Manchester United had been overly aggressive that afternoon out on the pitch, but his players might have lost a bit of the confidence and respect they'd always placed in their manager seeing him behave in the manner in which he did, losing his head in the way he did. Looking back, I think that defeat had much to do with Arsenal failing to retain their title that season. They suffered a huge setback against United, and not just in terms of the result.'

There were disappointments to come. A failure to beat Chelsea either at Highbury or, critically, at Stamford Bridge in April 2005 handed the Blues the advantage in the title race. Arsène, as frustrated as he was, realised the balance of power was shifting. Back in pre-season in 1997, Wenger had issued a warning to his side. 'You have to be up for the fight in each match,' he had stated, 'because confidence drains away so quickly.' Those words proved prophetic in 2004–05, particularly after that defeat at Old Trafford, with the team stuttering thereafter. The three clubs eventually relegated – Southampton, Crystal Palace and West Bromwich Albion – all took points off the Gunners in the wake of that painful defeat. The side which had swept all before them so gloriously had not only slipped up but, ultimately, fallen by the wayside. They lacked focus and confidence as they ambled to the season's end in a hopeless game of catch-up with Chelsea. To restore order and revive the side, Wenger embarked upon a new project, turning his attentions back to youth recruitment to generate a new side, that would require patience before it bore fruit. It was a move that would require all his skills as a motivator and man-manager if it was going to prove successful.

By 11 May 2005, the title had been claimed by Chelsea for the first time in 50 years. Everton, visitors to Highbury that night and themselves confirmed in an impressive fourth place, bore the brunt of the Gunners' frustration at being dethroned. The Dutchman Robin van Persie scored for Arsenal after only eight minutes, with the visitors drowning in an avalanche of goals thereafter. Pires put the hosts two up after only 12 minutes, Vieira adding a third eight minutes before half-time, with Pires again, Edu, Bergkamp and finally Mathieu Flamini completing the rout. The 7–0 scoreline was Arsenal's best ever in the Premier League and, even if the result meant nothing in terms of either side's aspirations that season, one had to doff the cap to Wenger, the brain behind this swashbuckling Arsenal team. The motivation remained, even with the title lost, to put Everton to the sword and his enthusiasm had not been dampened by a difficult season. 'To be a manager in England suits me,' he said. 'I like the fact that it's so hands-on here. Of course, the flip side is that it involves so much work, demands so much energy, and you can get tired sometimes. But everything is in your hands. You make the key decisions. It's a fact that 90 per cent of players owe their careers to what they achieve with the club where they play.' In other words, nine out of every ten players who have featured for Arsenal have enjoyed a successful career as a result of the club and, moreover, having worked with the manager. Adams, who would begin a second football career as assistant manager at Portsmouth, comments: 'If we hadn't met, I would be dead now. Once I was familiar with what the Professor wanted of me, the six years I played for him were easy. He made them easy.'

The last game of that season, on 15 May 2005, was lost 2–1 at Birmingham to a last-minute goal. The campaign had seen its ups and downs, the team flitting between the superb football witnessed against Everton and disappointing performances in the wake of their defeat at Old Trafford. Yet, even after finishing second, a distant 12 points from Chelsea, faith remained in the manager, and in his managerial style.

Adams describes him as 'a man of few words. He doesn't speak just for the sake of speaking. I remember noticing how he loved to walk everywhere, how he was constantly on the move. While we were training, he'd leave us sometimes to stride off into the distance to check on the under-17s on a pitch at the other end of the training ground. And, while he walked, he was lost in his thoughts.'

The manager laughed when that aspect of his personality was pointed out to him, but he admitted that his ability to shut himself off in his own thoughts was actually one of his strengths. The calmer the manager is, the more confidence is transmitted to his team. As an indirect result, the more simplistic a coach's approach, the more responsibility is accepted by his team. 'It seems to me that this isn't just my approach, but it's the only approach,' said Arsène. 'I have always thought that, when you prepare a team, you have to give them guidelines to get across how you want the side to play. I've always told myself: it's not really that important what the manager has to say. What is important is what you instil in the players' heads. What they take on board and then instigate amongst themselves. That's what I mean when I say that you have to make sure the players are under the impression that they are playing and struggling for themselves. Point them in the right direction and then allow them to express themselves. If they do that, they can move mountains.'

It is for that reason that in every side Wenger has put out, there have been players selected not necessarily for their ability alone but for the way in which they affect the rest of the team. From Rémi Garde to Gilberto Silva, Tony Adams to Gilles Grimandi, these water carriers have effectively transmitted Wenger's message to their team-mates out on the pitch in much the same way as Arsène himself, never the most gifted of players, had been the eyes and ears of Max Hild or Gilbert Gress on the turf during his own playing career. Paul Frantz admits as much. 'He was my general out on the pitch because he understood what I wanted the team to do and he instructed those around him when the game began,' he said. 'I do find it amusing now to see him, now as a coach, doing exactly the same in all his sides, with certain players filling the role I made him play back then . . .'

His disciples, the players upon whom Wenger relies, aren't necessarily his blue-eyed boys, but they are key members of the team. 'Our work cannot rely completely on one player alone, but the goal is to develop a state of mind,' he explained. In the same way that he does not adhere necessarily to a strict hierarchy in terms of his management style, he does not like the idea that his team is made up of a few leaders and plenty of followers. Certainly, players like Patrick Vieira or Martin Keown are more vocal than Kolo Touré or Cesc Fabregas, but everyone is part of an overall system.

Except in his first season at Arsenal, when he opted occasionally to use three centre-backs, Wenger's Gunners have mostly followed a strict formation of four strung across the back, four in midfield and two attack-minded players. This rigidity and refusal to consider using other systems has prompted criticism from certain quarters over the years. One of the presenters on *TalkSport*, one of the most listened-to sports radio stations in England, once christened Wenger 'The Ayatollah of 4-4-2'. The critics point to the fact that it's impossible to improvise when there simply isn't a 'Plan B' given the manager's complete reliance upon 4-4-2. When he heard that scepticism, Damien Comolli insisted that his former boss at Highbury actually has plenty of other options in his locker should he have to use them. 'I'd point out to the doubters that Arsène won his last FA Cup in 2005 in fact playing 4-3-3, or 4-5-1, with Dennis Bergkamp playing through the centre on his own. That's the first thing I'd say.

Secondly, I'd add that it simply doesn't interest Arsène to win without playing well. That's why, over the years, he hasn't changed either his basic tactics or his style of play.' In other words, for the Arsenal manager, 4-4-2 has proved itself to be a winning system and an attacking formation, as is backed up by the honours Wenger has accrued playing it.

Whether he is perceived as a champion of attacking football by his admirers or a coach capable of only robotic tactics by his critics, the Gunners boss remains ever conscious that neither praise nor flak should be taken too much to heart. Rather, it is a matter of keeping his feet on the ground. Hearing people describe him as a genius prompts a predictable response. 'I find that not only an exaggeration, but also ridiculous,' he said. 'We have had successes, sure. But people's passion for football is so deep-seated that when you do well, they go overboard in their praise. But, of course, there's a flip side to that . . . There is such a pressure in-built in English football that takes its toll on managers. They are the people who suffer. The passion and desire to do well from supporters to club chairmen means there is constant instability amongst managers, who lose their jobs when things go even slightly badly but are hailed as conquerors when things go well.'

For his part, Christian Damiano believes that the formation favoured by his compatriot offers him some sense of security in an increasingly unstable environment. 'We, as coaches, are always asking the same questions and are all craving answers. But the reality is that only those right at the top of the game ever really stumble upon those answers. Arsène falls into that category. For Wenger, 4-4-2 has proved itself to be reliable, and therefore his answer. In this line of work, there's a certain logic to sticking with what you know because it does offer some sort of stability. I get the impression with Arsène that, while he explores new ideas and methods which he might take on board, he doesn't really want to revolutionise what he does. He knows what works and, essentially, he'll stick with that. Of course Arsène is curious, as any good coach should be. The day you stop being curious is the day you should pack this job in. You have to be innovative and seek ways of keeping things interesting, but he's got a base to work on and that will always remain.'

Rémi Garde, the first Frenchman to have experienced the Wenger way on this side of the Channel, believes his mentor finds satisfaction in the little adjustments he makes to his famous 4-4-2 system, just as an engineer in Formula One would revel in the tweaks he makes fine-tuning his car. 'The day before every game, he'd explain to us the things we needed to work on in our game, taking into account what we hadn't produced in recent games and what hadn't worked well previously. There was always something he wanted us to fine-tune, something he thought we should attempt to improve ahead of the next game. I'm not going to say that, by doing this, he changed the face of every match that I played for him, but it's fair enough to say that, with certain players, he was very shrewd and perceptive on a tactical level to get the best out of them.' Looking back, the former France international and captain of Olympique Lyonnais credits the 'long-term job' instigated by his manager at Arsenal above his desire to tweak small details.

But if Wenger was always keen to grease and oil the engine

of his team, he was also a mechanic eager to lean over and advise those driving his machine and tell them what direction to take. 'The day when he asked me to fill in at right-back to replace Lee Dixon, who was injured, was the first time in ten years as a professional that I'd been asked to play in that position,' said Garde, who had been brought up through French football's youth system and into the professional game as a central midfielder. 'I said to him: "Arsène, I don't think I would know how to play there. I've never played there in my life." He just replied: "Rémi, you've been working with me for two years, so you know what I expect of a right-back in my system!" At the end of the game he came up to me and just said: "There you go. It's not all that complicated, is it?" '

Back at the Millennium Stadium, on 21 May 2005, the Arsenal line-up for the FA Cup final broke away from the traditional 4-4-2 and, instead, crammed five midfielders (Fabregas, Vieira, Gilberto Silva, Pires and Reyes) into the centre and used a solitary forward up front (Bergkamp). Confronted by Manchester United, the back line comprised – unsurprisingly – a four-man unit (Lauren, Touré, Senderos and Cole). This unusual 4-5-1 formation, prompted undoubtedly by the absence of Henry through injury, was designed to protect the goalkeeper Jens Lehmann as well as offer a means of piercing the armour of Sir Alex's Red Devils. The first part of the plan worked well, but Bergkamp – eventually replaced by Ljungberg after 65 minutes – was ineffective.

Arsenal were devoid of bite up front, even if their feverish work in midfield and defence nullified the threat offered by their opponents. At the break the game was scoreless. The match meandered in much the same way after the interval with few opportunities gleaned by either side to score. Indeed, so anaemic was the contest that Wenger could not completely curb his natural instinct to attack, replacing Fabregas with Van Persie four minutes from the end of normal time. Even so, it was 0–0 at 90 minutes. Edu came on for Pires after 105 minutes, but the game spluttered out into the inevitable drab goalless draw. The resultant shoot-out went Arsenal's way, the captain Patrick Vieira scoring the decisive goal to claim the Cup 5–4 on penalties, securing Wenger's seventh major domestic trophy since his arrival in London some nine years previously. One Arsenal fan wrote at the time: 'It was a day when we were forced to wait for our expectations to be realised. The newspapers had declared this game was going to be a clash of the Titans of epic proportions in Cardiff. In reality, it turned out to be 120 minutes of tedium followed by five minutes of blind excitement at the end.'

Beyond the basic smothering tactics put in place to obtain the result, the composition of that victorious Cup team in 2005 was imbued with the footballing philosophy of the European from Duttlenheim, the man born near the German border who grew up not far from Switzerland. The Gunners who claimed this fourth FA Cup of the Wenger era resembled an international brigade fighting under the colours of the Wenger Republic. England was represented by Ashley Cole, France by Patrick Vieira and Robert Pires. Also among the 'United Colours of Arsenal' were the Dutch, with Dennis Bergkamp and Robin van Persie, and Germany in Jens Lehmann. The Spanish were present courtesy of José Antonio Reyes and Cesc Fabregas, the Swedes via Fredrik

Ljungberg. There were South Americans in Edu and Gilberto Silva from Brazil, and Africans in the Cameroonian Lauren and Kolo Touré of the Ivory Coast. This was a global team, reflecting the only criteria Wenger bears in mind when it comes to recruitment: the quality and potential of the player in question. At the risk of infuriating the patriots, as far as Arsène is concerned, nationality is irrelevant when it comes to unearthing and signing new talents.

With free movement in mind, Wenger still asks himself why people take umbrage at the sight of players leaving their native country and coming to London to play for a big club. Arsenal's professional squad list for the 2005–06 season was 29-strong and, just like that at AC Milan or Real Madrid, read like the make-up of the council of the United Nations: three Spaniards, three Dutchmen, a German, an Estonian, two Swiss, five Frenchmen, two Ivorians, an Italian, two Brazilians, a Belarussian and two Swedes. In this melting pot of nationalities, there were three Englishmen of whom one, the 22-year-old defender Ryan Garry, started only once for the first team in the Premiership.

Arsène, speaking in Hagueneau, responded to his critics at the time. 'Even if some of the characteristics of the game have changed – football's played more on the ground than it was, what with the turf being of better quality these days – and the fact that the players come from different countries, we retain the particular Englishness of our game at Arsenal in the fact that the crowd is always pushing the team forward in attack. The English want their players to work flat out. They don't care about their nationality. In my cosmopolitan side, four cliques were forming themselves so I had to try and find a common identity – a cultural or European identity – to unite the team and the spirit of the club. We have achieved that. It is not long ago that, at Racing Club de Strasbourg, we insisted that only players from Alsace should represent our club. Then things changed and evolved, despite people criticising it at the time, and we allowed players from other French towns to come and play for Racing. Nowadays, visit the ground and there are players from around Europe wearing the club's colours. In the youth academy at Arsenal, the kids are 60 per cent English and 40 per cent French, and all our work is conducted with an eye on us being a European club.'

English supporters still point out that opportunities are limited for British players to make their mark in the first team at Arsenal, while the sceptics back in France cite Jérémie Aliadière, a precocious talent who was initially brought over in 1999 with his grandparents and installed in a house in north London, as an example of promising youngsters failing to live up to their potential when flung into life in a foreign country. On the other hand, the likes of Fabregas and, for a while, Reyes fulfilled their potential with the Gunners. 'The top level fashions the footballer and a foreign country shapes the man,' concluded Wenger, widely travelled as he is. Country boundaries mean nothing to him, just as they don't for Chelsea whose arrival on the scene as a financial force suddenly threatened Arsenal's dominance not just in the Premiership, but also in the capital itself.

Sunday, 21 August 2005. Arsène Wenger was preparing to celebrate his 500th match in charge of Arsenal, with his team travelling across London to Stamford Bridge. To have clocked up so many games demonstrated remarkable longevity and a splendid record, with under 100 of those lost en route in nine years in charge. 'I look forward, not back,' insisted the Frenchman when asked to reflect upon those dizzy statistics. 'I have never been one to scrutinise my results like that. You have to keep looking forward in this job, always setting yourself new targets to meet. You do that so often, you simply don't have the time to look back at what you have already achieved.' Yet, in west London that afternoon, Arsenal were to endure a sign of those times ahead.

There was an acceptance at the beginning of the 2005–06 season that this would be a transitional period for Wenger. His team had never lost to Chelsea in the Premiership but, beaten 2–1 by José Mourinho's team in the Community Shield earlier in the month, they still stepped off the team coach at Stamford Bridge betraying a certain apprehension as to what lay ahead. Those from north London were not as confident as they had been in recent years. Thierry Henry and his team were a pale shadow of the Invincibles of 2004 and actually made the short journey as underdogs. Around the stadium, the impromptu souvenir stalls groaned with memorabilia commemorating the previous season's title success, Chelsea's first championship win in 50 years. There were blue and white flags, T-shirts from which stared John Terry or William Gallas, and everywhere constant reminders. Chelsea – champions 2005. Wenger and his players had spent the night in a luxury hotel on the banks of the Thames, a Conran hotel in Chelsea Harbour, but the task awaiting them was daunting.

In the dressing room, Wenger scribbled the team on the

whiteboard. Lehmann; Lauren, Senderos, Touré, Cole; Ljungberg, Fabregas, Gilberto Silva, Alex Hleb, Pires; Henry. The plan was to suffocate midfield, marking Hernan Crespo and Eidur Gudjohnsen tightly and preventing Claude Makelele from dominating. Then attacking Paulo Ferreira at right-back in an attempt to unnerve the Chelsea goalkeeper, Petr Cech. What transpired was very different. Wenger was, according to the *Guardian*, 'the very picture of discontent on the touchline, muttering, frowning and gesticulating in exasperation'. That Arsenal, a team renowned for their attacking flair, had resorted to playing one man up front was also noted with interest.

The first half petered out without a hint of a goal, but Arsenal had been too disjointed for comfort. Robin van Persie, on for the injured Ljungberg, forced a save five minutes after the restart, but Wenger was still agitated as if sure of the blow to come. Some 73 minutes in, Frank Lampard's free-kick flew into the area and Didier Drogba, playing off the last defender and perilously close to being deemed offside, touched in the winner. Thereafter, Senderos and Ashley Cole may have threatened reward, but the hosts held firm. Arsenal were hesitant, unsure and deflated. This was no occasion to befit Wenger's 500th game in charge and felt rather more like the end of an era.

The defeats suffered by the Alsatian by the Blues could be counted on the fingers of one hand, their string of solid victories only rarely interrupted down the years. Back in November 1998, in a fourth-round League Cup tie, Chelsea had triumphed memorably 5–0 at Highbury, but they had confronted virtually an Arsenal second team. A year later, at

Stamford Bridge and on Wenger's 50th birthday, the hosts had roared into a 2–0 lead. The home side, masterminded by their French spine of Frank Leboeuf, Didier Deschamps and Marcel Desailly, were comfortable but, with 15 minutes remaining, Nwankwo Kanu wriggled free to spark a remarkable comeback. The Nigerian, bought for virtually nothing from Inter Milan, scored a 15-minute hat-trick, including one from the acutest of angles tight to the goal-line, in a display of such virtuoso brilliance as to render the home fans utterly speechless in their misery.

Wenger admitted at the time that he felt more like 60 after that turnaround. He was also quizzed about his retirement plans. 'I would like to work for my entire life,' he said. 'For example, I admire [the pianist] Rubinstein, who is still giving concerts at 83 years of age. I have a horror of retirement. And I have a horror of the thought of being in a job I have to give up at a certain moment of my life, despite working at full capacity. For example I wouldn't like to be in the place of some friends of mine who work in a bank and are forced to retire in their prime, at 55. That is unfair.'

Roman Abramovich's arrival on the scene had others crying foul. On 12 December 2004, Mourinho's Chelsea visited Highbury and trailed 2–1 at the interval courtesy of a brace from Thierry Henry. The French striker's second was a cheeky free-kick, curled over the wall while Cech was still organising the defenders in front of him. The visitors had reacted furiously, crying foul, but had their revenge barely 30 seconds into the second half when Gudjohnsen capitalised on indecision between Touré and Manuel Almunia to claw his side back to parity.

The game ended 2–2, with Clichy having been replaced by Reyes and Van Persie taking over from Bergkamp with eight minutes remaining. Those changes were heavily criticised by sections of the media and a good number of the supporters present. The changes had been, apparently, too little too late. This, after all, had been a game Arsenal had been desperate to win with the Blues some five points better off in the build-up; the draw maintained the feeling that the title might have been surrendered before the season had reached its midway point. Arsenal were unbeaten in 30 league games at Highbury, stretching back to that defeat by Leeds in 2003, but there was grumbling discontent. Some observers and commentators were questioning Wenger's ability to hold a result. Was he making, after all, the right substitutions at the right time?

Wenger weathered the storm. 'No one is perfect, least of all me,' he said, arguing that his substitutions were made for a reason. He took to sheltering his team from the criticisms, allowing the media and supporters to aim their displeasure at his broad shoulders in an attempt to protect his squad from the flak. As it was, Chelsea won the league that year, though it was not until 22 August 2005 that the Frenchman sensed Arsenal's long period of domination in London had truly come to an end.

Between 1996 and 2005, a series of Chelsea managers had come up short in Premiership confrontations with Wenger – Ruud Gullit, Gianluca Vialli and Claudio Ranieri had all tried but failed to undermine their north London rivals, and Arsène always had the measure of the man. José Mourinho was different. The English game had been deeply affected by Abramovich's purchase of Chelsea in the summer of 2003 but, while Ranieri had reached the Champions League semi-finals in the ensuing season – defeating Arsenal en route – it was only when Mourinho entered stage left that Chelsea boasted a manager as potent as their owner. The Portuguese had just claimed the Champions League with Porto, a remarkable achievement. Piercing eyes, fiercely arrogant and utterly driven, Mourinho would take the English game by storm.

Wenger, such a gentleman outside his duels with Sir Alex Ferguson or, more recently, Sam Allardyce whilst the Englishman was managing Bolton Wanderers, observed the new kid on the block with a certain suspicion. 'Before Mourinho arrived, the stage was only just big enough for two – Wenger and Ferguson,' said Jasper Rees. 'With Mourinho, the third man, space became really tight, and this is why Arsène and Fergie are so irascible. Mourinho is, as a rule, less affected by criticism. His arrival changed Wenger the man and manager. The psychological war with Ferguson was more or less over. End of play. Now, with José, things got serious.'

Mourinho's arrival seemed to rile the established order, and profoundly transformed Wenger. Suddenly, the Frenchman was happy to talk about the huge sums of money being invested by Chelsea – £500 million and counting – which had turned the English game on its head. Wenger argued that it would have serious repercussions for the team and beyond. Some suggested such criticisms were born of jealousy, though Wenger has always encouraged free competition.

The problem was that the figures invested by Abramovich were so startling, the oligarch's bottomless pockets effectively ensuring that other clubs could not compete for the players established at the top of the world game. Instead, Wenger was forced to rethink his transfer policy. 'For us, competing with Chelsea financially and ruining the club in the process would have been senseless,' he explained. 'But there are loads of players out there, and they can't buy them all.'

In May 2005, the Arsenal manager warned football to 'keep an eye' on Chelsea. 'The club is financially doped up to the eyeballs,' he said. 'It improves performance with the help of unlimited financial resources, which is a form of doping, as it has nothing to do with their real resources.' Some six months later, his rivals' approach still grated. 'There are two transfer markets,' he said. 'The one in which Chelsea participates, which is active, and the one in which they have no interest, which is sluggish.'

Wenger clearly has no love of Abramovich and his wealth. 'When I came to England, I was happy to discover the culture of a country that wanted club owners to be English,' he said. 'This seems to be changing.' Indeed, by the end of the 2006–07 season, Liverpool, Manchester United and Aston Villa were all in American hands with Stan Kroenke, another businessman from the United States, having bought heavily into Arsenal. The landscape was changing around the Alsatian. 'Now it is foreigners who are buying up clubs to hire the English. For me that isn't a problem, but it is important that the values of the game remain the same – that they are respected and admired everywhere.

'We, as a club, are stable because we trust people. We don't get rid of five players and pick up another five because we didn't win the championship one year. No, we continue. This form of recognition – which is reciprocal – helps us protect our values. It is like that in families: values are spread through people who are identified with the club. If they change every year they have no chance of integrating these values. Here a player can be told by others: "Watch out mate, you're at Arsenal now – we don't behave like that. Others were here before you and this is what they would do in this situation. You can't give the club an image like that." If players are always coming and going and mucking about, you will never have a club culture. At Highbury, we mould and keep; at Stamford Bridge, they pass through and cash in.'

In reality, Arsenal and Chelsea are contrasting clubs. 'Arsenal are a club belonging to the establishment, very British, where the idea of heritage is important,' said a source close to both who wishes to remain anonymous. 'It is a sort of aristocracy where nobility is passed on. They see themselves as the master of the place and feel superior to others. However, although they are condescending, they treat others with respect and consideration, as long as they know their place. Chelsea, on the other hand, are the autocrats, the Genghis Khan of the Premier League. One thing is sure these days: money talks. Chelsea has bought its way to success and Arsenal, who resent their neighbour's rise to prominence, would argue that Abramovich isn't playing the game.

'Chelsea rather sneer at the natural order. But Arsenal aren't whiter than white either. They can also get their way around the law, as long as they aren't caught, or there is nothing major going down. The Arsenal board are typically English in that they don't like being told how to behave. They have had to be dragged into the modern era of football, and some would accuse them of seeming arrogant and distant.'

The verbal jousting between Wenger and Mourinho soon degenerated into personal attacks, in the same way that the Portuguese steadily fell out with Rafael Benitez and Sir Alex Ferguson at Liverpool and Manchester United respectively. There is a financial gulf between the two: Mourinho is the second-best paid manager ever to have graced the English game, after the former national coach Sven-Göran Eriksson. He earns four times as much as Wenger. Yet, for Rees, the Frenchman was never jealous of the Portuguese's pay slip. 'Arsène felt he had got one up on him not in the war of salaries, which he wasn't interested in, but in the construction of a team,' he said. 'Before the arrival of Mourinho, and without benefiting from the funds the Chelsea manager has at his disposal, Wenger had held his own in the transfer market and occasionally pulled off a coup. These days, Mourinho is the biggest obstacle he has had to overcome to maintain that approach.'

The pair have squabbled over numerous issues, some more significant than others. Wenger was not amused by his opposite number's insistence that a defeat on penalties to Charlton in the League Cup did not actually constitute a loss. 'If you are eliminated from a competition, that is because you have lost,' said the Frenchman. His biggest gripe remains that Abramovich's power off the pitch has effectively loaded the dice against all comers on it. In sporting terms, Arsène the motivator knows how to ensure his squad stay on their toes and take the fight to opponents. But economically, what can really be done if the other side holds the purse strings and dominates the transfer market? Wenger's exasperation took him to breaking point: 'I just think that if you give success to stupid people it makes them more stupid sometimes, not more intelligent.'

Mourinho heard those comments and, incensed, offered a riposte. 'We have, at Stamford Bridge, a file of quotes from Mr Wenger about Chelsea Football Club,' he said. 'It is not a dossier of five pages. It is a file of 120 pages.' The Chelsea manager's suggestion that Wenger was a 'voyeur', someone 'who likes to observe others' from afar, prompted a more furious reaction.

'It is disrespectful and out of order,' said Wenger. 'I will see whether I take any action about that. I don't know yet, but I leave that door open.' The image of Wenger peering through a telescope with the simple headline 'Voyeur' appeared on the back of *The Sun*. Mourinho is understood to have kept a copy of that back page, so amused was he at the furore he had helped to whip up.

The pair did not stop bickering there. 'He talks, talks and talks again about Chelsea,' said Mourinho. 'It is important to talk about rivals, to put them under pressure and give them the message. But when you are always looking in the same direction . . . They [Arsenal] need to work harder and try and improve their own performances. I don't know if he [Wenger] wants my job. But he is obsessed with Chelsea.' Wenger, infuriated, suggested Mourinho was 'out of touch with reality'.

It took the intervention of Peter Hill-Wood, Arsenal's long-standing chairman, to bring the spat to an end by reminding all parties that they had a duty to maintain cordial relations. Had he not made his point, the Football Association would have intervened, so strained had relations between the managers become.

'I don't know what I said that was so wrong,' added a reflective Wenger at the time. 'I am not obsessed with Chelsea. I am very happy to be working for my current club. But I will always say what I think because I have a strong personality. I never seek to hurt anyone. I don't especially enjoy talking about Chelsea. When people ask me about them I respond honestly, as I hope any other manager would if they asked him about Arsenal. When someone at a press conference asks me for my opinion, I give it. Sometimes people agree with me and sometimes not. He [Mourinho] says he hopes Manchester United finish second in the championship. I have nothing against that – it is his opinion and I respect it.'

At the end of November 2005, Arsène confirmed he would not be pursuing Mourinho through the courts. 'I will not be bringing any legal action,' he said. 'I haven't changed my opinion of the matter, but after reflecting on the matter I have decided not to go any further. It is ancient history and now I want to concentrate on what is important for me and Arsenal.'

Given the tense nature of the pair's relations, it has been hard for either to compliment the other in public, though, reading between the lines, a mutual respect may exist, if only deep down. 'Chelsea are like a matador,' said Wenger back in January 2005. 'They wait until the bull is at its weakest until they kill it. They have the patience to outwait even the most experienced team. When the bull has lost enough blood and becomes unsteady, they finish it off.' 'But,' as Jasper Rees neatly summed up, 'it's a lot harder for Arsène: Arsenal built a stadium while Chelsea was building a team.'

'Back at the beginning of the 2005–06 season, a meeting was organised between Mourinho, his chief press officer and several newspaper journalists and editors,' said the journalist Daniel King. 'Some time beforehand, Mourinho had decided to stop talking to the media, so this meeting was essentially aimed at improving the relationship between the press and the Chelsea manager. Mourinho was like a spoilt child. He didn't smile. He simply frowned his way through. Suddenly, he said to all those present: "Above all, nobody loves Chelsea, and especially you journalists. You prefer Wenger. You love Arsenal but you hate Chelsea." We were all taken aback, not really knowing how to react or whether he was joking or not. The bottom line, though, is that the only reason journalists like Wenger is because every Friday he attends a press conference organised by his club, while Mourinho acts like a child.'

That behaviour was repeated at Highbury on 18 December 2005 when Chelsea won 2–0 to continue their inexorable march on a second successive league title. Mourinho marched off down the tunnel at the final whistle without shaking Wenger's hand. The Frenchman, as unamused as he was, made a point of stating that the snub was unlikely to keep him awake at night. Instead, with Chelsea's dominance clear, Wenger turned his attentions instead to creating a new generation of Arsenal stars: to shape this club's future without the funds at Chelsea's disposal, it was time to cultivate a crop of young players to carry the Gunners forward.

The building blocks were already in place. That season, the likes of Mathieu Flamini, Robin van Persie, Philippe

Senderos, Cesc Fabregas and José Antonio Reyes made their mark. These were the bright hopes of Arsenal's future but, waiting in the wings, there were others ready to step into the breach. All had star quality. 'In the summer of 2005, Arsène asked me several times what I thought about the idea of making Senderos captain,' said Tony Adams. 'In the end he chose Thierry Henry, but it is only a matter of time.'

Perhaps most impressive of the crop was Fabregas. On 26 November 2005, with Blackburn Rovers visiting Highbury, the young midfielder – 18 at the time – proved his pedigree. 'Arsène had wanted, from the beginning, to give the kid a chance,' added Adams. 'But the experience that Fabregas acquired would never have been possible if Vieira had stayed.' The former captain had completed a move to Juventus that summer, severing ties with Arsenal with his manager's blessing after a glittering nine years in London. He had left a void in midfield that some questioned whether Arsenal could plug, but it had always been Wenger's intention to use Fabregas in that role.

'I don't like being compared with Patrick Vieira,' said the Spaniard at the time. 'He is a great player, one of the greatest in Arsenal's history, and I am just an 18-year-old, who had been plucked from Barcelona's youth teams and lured to England. I still have a long way to travel, and all I can promise is to do my best to help the team. I play football because I love it, and that's what I want to get across to the fans.'

Against Blackburn, Fabregas proved he was more than a footballer. He, like Vieira before him, was a leader. His 30-yard opener, flashing beyond Brad Friedel, was stunning to behold. Pires's pass for Henry on the stroke of half-time allowed the France international to notch up his 100th goal at Highbury before the break, with Van Persie adding a third in the last minute. There had been criticism of Wenger's policy to blood his youngsters, particularly after a sluggish start to that campaign, but the quality they possessed was already clear. This was a new Arsenal team taking shape.

'A lot of people criticise Wenger for his philosophy, but he doesn't have a conventional view of football,' said Fabregas. 'He prefers to lose three or four matches and see that his young players are developing rather than lining up 11 veterans and leaving the youngsters on the bench. He would rather choose a team of kids and see them lose 2–0 than draw 0–0, or even win 1–0, with a team full of old men. But, in that side, there were experienced players alongside the kids to offer guidance and stability. It is completely normal for Henry and Pires to be the manager's spokesmen out on the pitch. They speak the same language, like Xabi Alonso did for Rafael Benitez at Liverpool. It isn't just a question of language – they are all French, but they are also great men on the international stage. Wenger did not choose them because they came from the same country as him, but because they are all extraordinary players.'

Fabregas's first meeting with Wenger had come back in June 2003. 'The first time I saw Arsène was the month after my 16th birthday,' he recalled. 'I had gone to London to visit the Arsenal ground, and that is when he made his offer. They told me the manager wanted a meeting with me. When I saw him, he was very clear and honest with me. We sat down and he said he would try and play me as soon as possible. I was flattered: Arsène Wenger wanted me in his XI! He wanted me, a 16-year-old player, to join the team as soon as possible.

'People accused him of poaching me from Barcelona, but things had become difficult with me and Barca. I had been about to sign for Espanyol a year earlier but, in the end, Barcelona offered me new terms. I was happy to stay at the club, but things changed. I'd never have moved to Arsenal, otherwise.' Professional terms were signed at Highbury on 11 September 2003. In the little Catalan, Wenger spied a genius. A future giant. His first appearances in the first team proved him right.

On 2 December 2003 he became the youngest scorer in Arsenal's history, at 16 years and 212 days, with a goal in the 5–1 League Cup rout of Wolverhampton Wanderers at Highbury. The following August, his goal against Blackburn (a 3–0 win) established him as the youngest league scorer for the club – at 17 years and 113 days – beating Nicolas Anelka's previous record. He completed the hat-trick on 7 December 2004 by registering in European competition in the 5–1 victory over Rosenberg. At 17 years and 217 days, he was the youngest to score for the club in Continental competition. What made it all the more remarkable was that the youngest Arsenal player ever to feature in the Premiership was not a striker, but a midfielder.

That youth should be given its chance at Arsenal under Wenger should not come as a surprise. 'Throughout my career as a manager, I have always followed one strict belief: children play football for the pleasure of playing, for the love of the ball,' said the Frenchman. 'You won't be playing catch-up for long if you carry on remembering that really is the main motivation of your players.'

'It is clear that Wenger was key to my decision to sign with Arsenal,' added Fabregas, who had been watched by scouts from Manchester United, Rangers and Celtic during the European under-17 championships in the summer of 2003. 'But I didn't play well overall – I wasn't good. Despite that, the Arsenal recruitment manager and his representative in Spain, Francis Cagigao, insisted to Wenger that I was worth pursuing, saying I was worth it, and luckily he followed their advice.'

Fabregas, already a full Spain international and compared favourably with Barcelona's brilliant Argentinean midfielder Lionel Messi, has always admired the Arsenal manager's calmness. 'Wenger is very relaxed in the changing rooms,' he said. 'He is always attentive to the smallest detail, for example asking injured players how they feel. He talks to them and shows he has their interests at heart. When we go to the weights room he is rarely with us. He prefers to stay outside with injured players or new recruits, making them feel part of what's going on. He looks after both categories. That really helps young players to become part of the team. He wants people to gain as much experience as possible, and he is always there to support us.'

There have been accusations over the years that the Arsenal camp is split, between the 'young' and the 'experienced', the 'British' and the 'foreign'. It was once written in the English press that the French members of the team only spoke with their fellow countrymen, and that the English players kept themselves to themselves. Wenger would deny that. 'Arsène surrounds himself with players of different ages and different nationalities, sure, but we are very united as a team,' added Fabregas.

The manager was criticised fiercely for uprooting the 16-year-old Spaniard. 'A coach tries, above all, to work in the best interests of the sport and to let youngsters who love playing football grow,' said Wenger. 'I like to allow players to express themselves out on the pitch. People called me a troublemaker, a nuisance, for uprooting players like Cesc, but that's a bit strong. In any event, I hope that's not what I am.'

'It was him who placed his trust in me, and Arsenal the club which gave me the confidence I needed,' said Fabregas. 'Other teams talked about taking me on, but none of them did. Now it is my turn – I want to give something back. I want to stay in this city and play for Arsenal. I want to help construct the future team. This is where I matured, and for me that means a lot.'

In the winter of 2006 Wenger added another 16-year-old to his ranks in the exciting young Southampton forward Theo Walcott. The winger had long been considered the great English hope of his generation. Wenger savoured his signing, in face of stiff competition from Chelsea and Liverpool, as a considerable coup. 'Theo is a very young player, but he had already proved with Southampton that he had a lot of talent and immense potential,' said Wenger, who would watch the forward travel with the national squad to the World Cup finals that summer, even if he did not make an appearance. 'This is an enormous bonus for the team.'

Some £5 million was spent initially to secure Walcott, a

sum that would climb to nearer £13 million depending on future honours and appearances for the youngster. 'There is still a risk when you sign a young player,' added Wenger. 'But I am ready to take it.' The forward's signing was complemented by that of Vassiriki Abou Diaby, a 19-year-old midfielder built like a young Patrick Vieira and plucked from AJ Auxerre, and the Togolese striker Shey Emmanuel Adebayor, 21, from AS Monaco. The trio boasted an average age of 18, but they represented the future. A thrilling new side was emerging at the new Emirates Stadium, with Van Persie, the Belarussian Alexandr Hleb, Mathieu Flamini, Fabregas, Clichy and Emmanuel Eboué all making their mark. With such talents coming through, Wenger was able to sanction the sale of Vieira and, more reluctantly, Ashley Cole in the knowledge that alternative talents remained at the club.

Others are yet to make their mark. Throughout 2006, Wenger was tracking AS Cannes's Carl Parisio, a 16-year-old defender tipped for great things and, under freedom of contract, eventually lured to London. Arsenal compensated Cannes for 'training costs' incurred during Parisio's development – technically, the Premiership club need not have offered any financial remuneration, but, for the sake of building up 'special relationships' with certain clubs, they were willing to comply. 'What impressed me most about what Arsenal did with their youth policy was that they did not really need to break the bank to succeed,' said Alan Curbishley, who managed Charlton against the Gunners before joining West Ham in late 2006. 'The club saw long-term progression, and they accepted that as a positive policy. Bravo to Arsène Wenger for that.'

The reality was that, with work ongoing on the Emirates Stadium, Wenger did not have the transfer funds to compete with Chelsea, Liverpool or Manchester United at the top of the Premiership, and therefore shifted his emphasis towards (cheaper) youth. Inevitably, a team in transition had its high and low points. On Saturday 14 January 2006, Highbury roared its approval as their favourites subjected Middlesbrough to a 7–0 hammering, a result they had achieved the previous spring against an Everton side who had finished in a lofty fourth place. In central defence, the Swiss pair of Johan Djourou and Philippe Senderos, with a combined age of 38, excelled in front of the veteran Jens Lehmann. Djourou's tackling brought the house down, while Senderos ventured forward to score his second goal of the season. Further upfield, Reyes, at 20, ran rings around Boro's beleaguered defence. Henry, who notched a hat-trick in the rout, was a constant menace while the experienced Pires, Gilberto and Hleb – who each scored one – lapped up the atmosphere.

Then came the flip side. A few weeks later, the same players and supporters who had rejoiced at the dismissal of the Teessiders were grimacing through a home defeat to West Ham United. Arsenal lost 3–2 to slump into sixth place in the league, 26 points behind Chelsea and, more depressingly, four behind Tottenham Hotspur in the last Champions League qualification place. Even Wigan Athletic, newly promoted but punching above their weight, were above the Gunners in the table. Head in hands on the bench, Wenger suffered. Sol Campbell, one of his most experienced players, was suffering such a crisis in confidence that he was substituted at the interval for Sebastien Larsson (20) and departed the stadium. Yet, amid the turmoil, the management still had faith in the bright young things. Flamini, Senderos, Kerrea Gilbert, Fabrice Muamba, Nicklas Bendtner, Djourou, Diaby and Van Persie would make their presence felt.

There were painful times to endure until they did. While the League Cup offered the youngsters a smoother route to progress, their Premiership form was haphazard. The team was capable of the scintillating, such as the 4–1 dismissal of Fulham in the autumn of 2005, but also the mystifying. They lost 2–1 at West Bromwich Albion, a side who would be relegated at the end of the campaign. 'These were matches that used to be our strong point,' pointed out Wenger at the time. Breaks for international matches had not helped, the team's rhythm too often fractured, but it was November until Arsenal won an away game. That constituted their worst start to a Premiership season away from home since Wenger had assumed the reins at the club. The victory, a thrilling 3–2 success at Wigan, was a pointer to the quality this side, deep down, clearly possessed.

There were defeats to endure at Bolton and Newcastle, awkward venues for youngsters to find their feet, though the FA Cup defeat at the Reebok in late January was particularly hard to take. 'There has been an injection of youth into our side, added to injuries to key players, and that has led to inconsistencies,' said Wenger, attempting to come to terms with his side's inability to scale the heights of previous years. 'That has, inevitably, led to some self-doubt within the squad. But I will stick with this side. You cannot just show young players the door. You have to have faith in them, and that is what we will do. What I would say, though, is that to be successful these days you need a side with an average age between 24 and 30. Ours is below that. At the moment, we have a team that is [as] capable of winning 3–0 as it is of losing 1–0.'

Slowly, around the corner from Highbury, the Gunners' new home was emerging in Ashburton Grove, a 60,000-seater arena to replace the 38,000 at Arsenal's old home. For the club, those extra 22,000 spectators in the Emirates Stadium every other week would constitute around £1 million every home game in added gate revenues, not to mention the money to be generated through sponsorships and executive boxes. Over an entire season, Arsenal's home games would be watched by 1.14 million people compared with the 722,795 who had visited Highbury. The construction site, a £390 million development, spread across seven hectares with over 1,000 workmen piecing together the club's new home: 60,000 cubic metres of concrete, 10,000 tonnes of steel. The elliptical roof of 30,000 square metres, rising more than 40 m from the pitch, was reminiscent of the Stade de France. The stadium with its glass-clad façades was designed by the architectural firm HOK Sport, which also designed Stadium Australia in Sydney, and the new Centre Court complex at Wimbledon.

But Wenger played his part. As with the centre at Colney, the manager would follow the project through from beginning to end. He, like his board of directors, was determined that some of the atmosphere of Highbury be retained at Ashburton Grove. 'I intervened quite a bit, even down to the choice of carpets in certain parts of the arena,' he said. 'When all is said and done, functionality boils down to small choices.' Wenger insisted that the grass in the new stadium was of the same high quality as that at Highbury. That, in itself, demanded huge time and efforts were taken in examining whether enough sunlight would reach the pitch, whether there would be enough ventilation at ground level . . . and all was undertaken under Wenger's watchful eye.

The dimensions of the pitch were to be bigger than at Highbury – 113 m by 76 m, rather than 105 m by 70 m – though Wenger relished the chance to lead his team out in the sparkling new arena. 'I am impatient to bring the team there, before 60,000 Arsenal fans,' he said as the 2005–06 season drifted towards its climax. 'That will be great. The stadium and the team are moving in a positive direction, and that is why I want to stay at this club. The entire team management have made an enormous effort, and I think we have thought of almost everything.' (There had been rumours that Wenger might leave the club, on two occasions at least. One was in the summer of 2004, after the Euro Championship: Jacques Santini has just resigned as France's head coach in order to join Spurs. The other time was in 2007, when his friend David Dein resigned. 'I always honour my contract, and I always see the end of it,' says Wenger.)

'The new stadium was absolutely necessary for the club to move forward,' said Liam Brady, the former Arsenal midfielder turned youth team coach. 'Highbury was part of my life, but that feeling is counterbalanced by my desire to see Arsenal compete with the greatest clubs in Europe, and this involves the construction of a bigger home. A lot of our fans couldn't get tickets when matches were held at Highbury. Leaving the stadium was heartbreaking, and it was therefore important to stay in Islington. We didn't change our home, just our house.'

Damien Comolli, by then at Tottenham, watched the Emirates grow with a mixture of admiration and jealousy. 'Now they have the stadium, they have huge resources,' he said. 'They will be able to rival AC Milan, Manchester United . . . Arsène felt a certain frustration with the results of his team, but is also proud of what he has constructed, having bought guys on the cheap, and making them into world-class players – all the young players he has brought on board, and who will play on a national and European level. When they pipped us to the Champions League at the end of the season, it secured a 10th consecutive season in European football. That goes to show that Arsenal are now a top-level team.'

So, in the summer of 2006, Arsenal bade farewell to their home of 93 years and moved a few hundred yards around the corner to the glittering Emirates Stadium. Leading them in their journey was Wenger, the club's most successful manager since Herbert Chapman and a figurehead steering a young team towards new heights. Arsenal had claimed three Premier League titles and four FA Cups under the Frenchman at Highbury. The hope was that, at their new home, the team would rise to even greater levels of achievement.

Yet, with the emergence of Chelsea and the renaissance of Manchester United – Ferguson's side were all but untouchable in claiming a ninth league title in 15 years in 2006–07, despite losing home and away to Arsenal – Wenger has had to rejig his priorities. These days, his inability to secure the Gunners a first European Cup clearly plays on his mind and the sting in the tail to the 2005–06 campaign still smarts.

Back on Friday, 16 December 2005, the Arsenal manager had faced the small crowd of journalists intent upon gleaning his reaction to the day's Champions League knockout draw. Arsenal had drawn Real Madrid and, while that was not necessarily as daunting a tie as it might have been a few years earlier when a Zinédine Zidane-inspired Real had swept all before them, the worry was that the Gunners' inconsistencies could undermine their challenge. In the preceding nine years, Wenger had seen his side stumble infamously to Galatasaray in the Uefa Cup final, Dynamo Kiev and Valencia in high-profile European ties. Now the *Galácticos* barred passage into the quarter-finals.

Bizarrely, Europe offered Arsenal light relief during that troublesome domestic campaign. The Gunners had claimed their six-match qualifying section with an impressive 16 points, a tally that only Olympique Lyonnais and Barcelona could match in the other groups. Real, as runners-up in their group, were to welcome the Premiership side to the Santiago Bernabéu on 21 February. But already belief showed in Wenger's eyes. 'I saw enough during the group stage to suggest we can come through this tie,' he said. Time would prove him right, though, for Arsenal's manager, European competition had long proved a tricky nut to crack.

Wenger's travels have taken him to all corners of the continent. 'Some matches come back to me immediately, but I need a context to remember others,' he admitted. 'Sometimes, rather than the game, I'll remember small details like a hotel room or a view, over Odessa harbour, for instance.

That's where *Battleship Potemkin* was filmed, and we were staying just above the port.' His memories are jumbled, reflecting the reality that he has been involved in European ties since his days as a player with Racing Club de Strasbourg.

Monaco provided him with his first taste of Continental competition as a manager and it was under his stewardship that the Principality side made it beyond the first round of the Uefa Cup for the first time. 'I think it was in Iceland,' he recalled. 'We lost 1–0 against . . . some Reykjavik team. Valur. In those days, back in 1988, French clubs found it hard to get past even that early stage, and for Monaco to be at that stage was definitely a first. We lost over there but won the return leg 2–0 thanks to a goal scored by George Weah. That was progress.'

The foundations had been laid. Wenger's Monaco would beat Swansea 8–0 at the Stade Louis II in the first round of the 1991–92 Cup Winners' Cup, eventually progressing as far as the semi-finals before Sampdoria proved too strong. 'The amazing thing was that Monaco, a club who hardly attracted any fans to home games, would always get to the latter stages of these competitions, whether it was the quarter-finals or the semi-finals of the Champions League or Cup Winners' Cup,' said Wenger. 'Then there was that final in 1992 which we lost in the aftermath of those terrible scenes in Bastia. We had managed to give the club a real presence in European football, and that was no mean feat. We were really close to winning that final, but then we lost George Weah just before we played that game against Werder Bremen.

'A club like Monaco still struggled to hold on to its best players, especially the young ones, and we couldn't keep hold of George. The frustration was that no French team had won a European competition and we could have become the first that day. But that final in Lisbon was the only game we lost in Europe that season.'

There were other close calls. In 1994, Monaco reached the Champions League semi-finals against Milan only to succumb 3–0 at San Siro, having been reduced early to ten men. 'They had three shots and scored three goals,' bemoaned Wenger. Milan went on to steamroller Barcelona 4–0 in the final.

Yet in 1996 Wenger arrived at a club who had European pedigree having won the Inter-Cities Fairs Cup in 1970 (against Anderlecht) and the Cup Winners' Cup against Parma in 1994. That victory was secured by a stunning Alan Smith goal in Copenhagen. 'But although the club had potential, it had no Champions League history as such, and in order to make a name in Europe, you have to feature in that elite competition regularly,' said Wenger. 'That made the challenge so much more worthwhile. It is something that still remains the challenge. I suppose one of the reasons we haven't won a Champions League is that we've not been good enough. Yet, when people say that we're not tactically good enough, I'd say that's nonsense: we have a proven track record in terms of our ability to qualify, year in, year out. Arsenal are up there amongst Europe's elite these days, even if we haven't claimed a European Cup as yet. We've consistently qualified for the knockout phases. Sure, we've not yet won it, but there are about 20 other teams who find themselves in the same position.

'To be honest, when I first arrived what I really wanted to

do was to win the Premier League. I have always had the
utmost respect for coaches who win the championship. This
is the truth of football. You can win a European Cup if you
have a stroke of luck, or the draw goes for you. But to win the
Premiership is a different ball game altogether.'

Early ventures into Europe with Arsenal were painful.
There was elimination to Borussia Mönchengladbach in his
first game as coach and, the following season, to the Greeks
of PAOK Salonika. The 1997–98 Double finally thrust the
Gunners into the Champions League, with Arsenal playing
their home games at Wembley so as to maximise gate receipts
and allow as many supporters as possible to witness their
European campaign, yet Wenger's side struggled to impose
themselves at their adopted home. Panathinaikos were edged
out 2–1, but Dynamo Kiev held the Londoners in the capital
and then beat them soundly back in Ukraine (3–1). Defeat in
Lens confirmed elimination and rendered the return win in
Greece a hollow victory.

'I felt we were missing something in Europe,' said Wenger.
'Every time we played on the Continent, we came across a
completely different football style. We couldn't quite make
sense of what was going on. The style was so different to what
my team were used to in the Premiership. It took us time to
adapt our game for that. In England, we knew what to expect
and came prepared accordingly. Not so in Europe. It was a
steep learning curve, and it took us time.'

Fiorentina eliminated Arsenal from the Champions
League in 1999–2000, winning 1–0 at Wembley in the key
group game. 'That was hard to stomach,' said Wenger. 'We
should have won over there but ended up drawing 0–0.

Losing at home to Barcelona [2–4] was just as painful, but finishing third left us in the Uefa Cup that year.'

In the lesser competition, there was progress to be had. Nantes were seen off 6–3 on aggregate, and in the fourth round Arsenal truly found their bite with a 5–1 first-leg thumping of Deportivo la Coruña. 'That was one of our most impressive ever results because we were up against a very skilful Spanish side,' said Wenger. Werder Bremen were brushed aside in the quarter-finals, with Ray Parlour scoring a hat-trick in the 4–2 win in Germany. 'That was a great match, particularly given the trouble we'd had winning away from home in Europe for such a long period of time. It changed our perspective: we realised that it was possible for us to win away from Highbury. That was arguably our turning point.'

Wenger's compatriots Lens awaited in the semi-finals. The 1–0 first-leg win courtesy of Dennis Bergkamp's early goal left the Arsenal manager unimpressed; the return was more productive, the Londoners prevailing 2–1 to secure a place in the final against Galatasaray. This was a chance for Wenger to make his mark after seeing his Monaco side choke in Lisbon having progressed to their showpiece final, but yet again he was to be frustrated. The Turks had already claimed their domestic league and cup Double. In the Romanian Georgi Hagi they boasted one of the game's greatest ever playmakers. Yet what should have been a mouth-watering occasion was overshadowed, inevitably, by the repercussions of the violence in Istanbul ahead of Gala's semi-final first leg against Leeds, when two English fans had been stabbed to death. The police presence in Copenhagen for the final rather snuffed the enjoyment from the occasion.

'We went into the Uefa Cup final feeling like we were going to war,' recalled Wenger. 'There was military and police security everywhere. The final should be a celebration for both teams, but even restaurateurs shut their establishments down for fear of vandalism. The organisers lost sleep over a repeat of the ugly scenes in Turkey. Of course, coaches have a responsibility to control the behaviour of their players, but it is a limited responsibility because their impact is minimal. In any case, such violence is a product of society. It isn't football that causes violence.'

The final would prove a huge anticlimax. The 90 minutes went by almost without an opportunity for either side to open the scoring, even if the contest did open up more in the extra period as energy drained from the players' legs. Hagi's dismissal for throwing a punch at Tony Adams suggested it was advantage Arsenal, but Thierry Henry failed too often to convert the chances that came his way, the Brazilian World Cup goalkeeper Taffarel proving his nemesis. The game drifted to penalties and, inevitably, to ignominy for the team that had dominated for so long. Davor Suker struck a post, Patrick Vieira thumped against the crossbar, and Gica Popescu – a former Tottenham midfielder – rammed in the decisive penalty to see the Turks home 4–1. 'It was painful,' said Wenger in defeat. 'We felt as if we'd been robbed of the cup. The Turks may have wanted the cup more than we did; teams who consider themselves to be underdogs have nothing to lose, and thus more mental freedom.'

'After that game, the boss was a very angry and disappointed man, even if he wasn't directing that frustration at his players,' said Gilles Grimandi. 'It was the fact that we should have won that really got to him. That's what makes him really, really upset. I had already seen him like that at Monaco. But back then he was more prone to flying off the handle, whereas at Arsenal you got the impression that he wouldn't allow himself to behave like that. He controlled himself so much better in London. He is a very calm person, but at any given moment he can become irritated and scare people, including his players. One of his goals was to claim European silverware and getting that close but still ending up with nothing really hurt him. I don't think he blamed his players . . .'

In truth, the Champions League – and its associated television revenues – was far more of a priority than the Uefa Cup, a competition Wenger has long seen as devalued by Uefa's qualification system. In 2000–01 there was another chance to progress amongst the elite, with the group stage negotiated and, eventually, a place in the quarter-finals gleaned. There were ups and downs to endure, from scintillating victories over Sparta Prague and Shakhtar Donetsk to a damaging 4–1 defeat to Spartak Moscow. This was still a side adapting to the demands of the competition. 'There were similarities at Arsenal to what we had to impose at Monaco,' said Wenger. 'The Champions League was still something new and I felt like the team wasn't handling it as well as we did the Premiership. Little by little, though, it became a kind of habit and now we actually handle Champions League matches just like Premiership matches.'

The quarter-final against Valencia proved they still had plenty to learn. Trailing to Roberto Ayala's goal four minutes before the break at Highbury in the first leg, Arsenal had stormed back to score through Thierry Henry and Ray Parlour around the hour mark. However, critically, Henry missed an excellent late chance to secure a more resounding 3–1 success to take to the Mestalla. Typically, the second leg was remarkable only for John Carew's goal, Valencia prevailing courtesy of their away goal. 'Some fleeting memories come back to me of that night,' admitted Wenger, 'of missed opportunities, and that goal we should have avoided conceding. I can still see Carew edging in front of Adams to convert. He may be huge, but Carew never scores with his head. That image will haunt me for the rest of my life.

'Valencia was a huge disappointment. At one point, with 15 minutes or so remaining and the game in Spain goalless, we'd thought we had one foot in the semi-finals. Then, out of the blue, they score, we lose 1–0 and we're out. I suppose it teaches you what your limits are. Whereas in the Premiership there are usually extenuating circumstances if you don't do well in a particular game – players tired after international duty, for example – and you can't expect to be at your best over 38 league games, in the Champions League every tiny error is punished.'

The same shortcomings continued to undermine Arsenal's challenge. In 2001–02 there were the early shocks of defeat at Real Mallorca and subsequently at both Schalke and Panathinaikos, even if all three were swept aside in London to secure progress. By the time the European campaign resumed for its second group phase in the new year, the inconsistencies had well and truly set in. There were glorious highs – 'The displays against Leverkusen [4–1] and Juventus [3–1] were truly extraordinary,' said Wenger – but in general they were outweighed by desperate lows. Deportivo la Coruña beat the Gunners home and away, and convincingly, while Juventus's victory in Italy in the final game ensured there was no progress to be enjoyed.

Indeed, the only positives were to be had in the steady development of the team. Lauren, a Cameroonian full-back, excelled, while the Brazilian Edu provided a striding presence in central midfield. Others had to be convinced that they boasted the pedigree to flourish. On occasion, flattery proved a useful tool. 'Sometimes you have to prove to them just how good they are,' explained Wenger. 'Just like with a beautiful woman . . . if you don't keep telling her, she can forget just how beautiful she is. A team is the same: if you don't tell them how good they are, they sometimes forget. When a group has been together for a number of years, players tend to accumulate a certain number of references which help them believe in their own worth.'

In the end, even if there was no place for Arsenal in the knockout phase, there was the display against Leverkusen to cling on to. The German side would finish the season in the final, but they had nothing positive by which to remember their trip to Highbury. Robert Pires had set the ball rolling, sprinting from inside his own half, with Thierry Henry and Dennis Bergkamp acting as decoys at his side, before spearing the opener. That set the tone, maintained a few minutes later as Patrick Vieira, Bergkamp and Sylvain Wiltord combined to liberate Henry, whose finish was emphatic. Vieira and Bergkamp, scoring a beautiful goal set up by Wiltord, completed the hosts' romp in the second period and rendered Sebescen's late consolation irrelevant. At that stage, Arsenal believed there was a place to be won in the quarter-finals, loitering as they did behind Deportivo in second place. Instead the Spaniards' 2–0 win at Highbury a few weeks later was followed by defeat in Turin and elimination.

Wenger greeted this latest disappointment relatively calmly. 'It wasn't so much that he was indifferent,' said Daniel Jeandupeux. 'He does have his own methods, the way he deals with things, but most of all he has an astonishing ability to analyse why things like that happen. I called him one morning before a European Cup game. I was fortunate to get him as he tends to be impossible to reach, but we spoke about the match he was about to play. He told me it was going to be difficult for whatever reason. So I said to him: "Forewarned. A coach is always forearmed." It's a simple enough phrase. So he says, scared: "Actually, a coach is always on the edge!" That's typical Arsène. Just like everyone else, he must have panicked at some point during a match, but he used his experience to analyse the situation and to help himself avoid stumbling over the same obstacles twice. Arsène has a talent when it comes to keeping things simple.'

Yet that gift hardly guarantees his side success. The following season, Wenger celebrated his 100th European Cup tie – the first French coach to do so – in the group game against Borussia Dortmund. 'To achieve that is an enormous surprise,' said the Alsatian at the time. 'I had begun my career as a coach working in an academy. If I had been told then that I would be coach for 100 European Cup matches . . . I'd have thought that would have been impossible back then. These days, there are more games each season in the European Cup of course, but it is true that I gain immense pleasure from having achieved it. It shows I've had the opportunity to work at the highest level for 15 years. I know of good, even great coaches who have not had that opportunity. The 100 matches make me realise I have enjoyed a very privileged career.'

Arsenal duly trotted out to win 2–0, following up that victory with a rousing 4–0 win at PSV Eindhoven to buck their depressing trend away from Highbury. Auxerre were defeated 1–0 in France, though then came the hiccups. October 2002 brought drizzle and dejection at Highbury, Guy Roux's Auxerre triumphing 2–1 with Olivier Kapo and Khalilou Fadiga scoring the decisive goals. A few hundred yards from the ground, a table had been set at the San Daniele to celebrate Wenger's 53rd birthday, though it remained empty all night. Perplexed in defeat, the Frenchman opted against a post-match celebration and shut himself away with his thoughts in his office.

In the end, progress into the second stage was only secured with a tense and unconvincing goalless draw against PSV Eindhoven in London, with the inconsistencies rife in Wenger's side maintained into the second phase. Thierry Henry's stunning performance in the Stadio Olimpico secured a 3–1 win at AS Roma, though the mediocrity of the draws home and away against Ajax and the return match against the Italians was more in keeping with Arsenal's European form. A 2–1 loss in the final group game, against Valencia again, jettisoned the Gunners from the competition for another year. 'Some of our performances left deep wounds that year,' said Wenger. 'I have to force myself to forget the damage done so I can concentrate on the future.

The scars left by Europe stay with me far longer than those inflicted by defeat in the Premiership.'

Wenger's biggest problem was raised expectation. Having triumphed in English domestic football, supporters and board members expected more coherent challenges in European competition than the team appeared capable of producing. 'There is a new level of expectation,' conceded the manager. 'Perhaps it sounds arrogant, but for us not to win the Champions League is a disappointment each year. But there are seven or eight other teams out there who feel the same. What we can't afford is to sit back at the end of each season and say: "Well, we've learnt this or that, so we've made progress." We need tangible progress.'

But the setbacks continued. The 2003–04 season began with a thumping 3–0 home loss to Internazionale, the Italians running rings around Wenger's side while the manager stood dumbfounded on the touchline. This would be the Invincible season, though the sight of Andy van der Meyde plundering did not bode well. Dynamo Kiev and Lokomotiv Moscow proved awkward opponents. By the time Arsenal travelled to the San Siro for their final game, they needed to secure victory against the side who had dismantled them so emphatically in the opening group game to stand any chance of progress into the second phase. This was a daunting task.

Yet, by the end of November, Arsenal were entrenched in their unbeaten domestic run. That occasion in Milan would be one of Wenger's finest moments. Before kick-off, the manager had stood alongside his coach Boro Primorac and scout Damien Comolli in an executive box looking out over the turf as his players went through their pre-match stretching routines. 'It was a long time before the game was due to start,' said Comolli, recalling the scene. 'We could see the warm-up from this box, looking out through the windowed front. We knew that if we lost the game, we would definitely be eliminated. But Arsène was a picture of calm, sipping his coffee and surveying the pitch.

'It was amazing just how calm he was. The side we had to put out that night was crammed with youth, with the likes of Jérémie Aliadière and Graham Stack on the bench. These were the players we would have to turn to potentially if things weren't going our way. They were still kids. But I remember Arsène turning to us and saying, perfectly calmly: "I've got a feeling we're going to win tonight." It was unbelievable. This was Inter Milan we were talking about, with Christian Vieri, Obefani Martins, Javier Zanetti and Francesco Toldo in their side.'

At least the first team sent out boasted sufficient experience, the likes of Sol Campbell, Ray Parlour, Pires, Kanu and Henry all keen to impress. Immediately it became clear that Arsenal's pace had the potential to tear the Italians apart. Midway through the first period, with the game goalless, Ashley Cole and Pires combined slickly for the England full-back to square and Henry to convert. It was a lead the visitors merited, even if it was not to be preserved until the interval. Campbell's inadvertent own goal drew the Italians level against the run of play, and as the teams retreated, the sense was that Arsenal's chance might have gone.

No one was prepared for the rout that was to follow. Wenger had stressed to his team in the interval that they still had Inter in the palms of their hands, that the key would be to shift play from either flank, stretching the hosts and tapping into the pace the Londoners boasted. Zanetti, said Wenger, was Inter's weak link and should be targeted. It was a tactic that yielded immediate rewards. Ljungberg and Henry countered at speed, the striker progressing smoothly down the left flank before supplying the Swede to force the visitors ahead again. Gilberto Silva's introduction with 15 minutes remaining offered some much needed steel to Arsenal's centre just as Inter attempted to rally, but Wenger sensed that the home side would be vulnerable on the break in their desperation to conjure an equaliser. Sure enough, Henry broke from an Inter corner, used Pires's run as a decoy before wriggling into the area and, from an acute angle, spearing a glorious third.

Wenger sprang from the bench, fists in the air in celebration. Edu, converting Henry's cross after Ljungberg had air-kicked, duly plundered a fourth, but Arsenal were not finished. With Inter smarting and Henry substituted, Aliadière found Pires who swept in a fifth. The San Siro, with an exception of a small pocket of delirious Arsenal fans, was rendered speechless. 'In the changing rooms after the game, Arsène stressed that the key had been to target Zanetti and the space he was leaving behind him,' added Comolli. 'We scored four of our five goals with that in mind. Tactically, the manager had got it exactly right.'

The performance in the San Siro had been an indication of Arsenal's capabilities, though the flip side was exposed in Galicia at the first knockout stage. Celta Vigo were overcome 3–2 in Spain, but Arsenal's defending – and the sloppy display mustered by their German goalkeeper Jens Lehmann in particular – left much to be desired. After the game, with the team waiting on the coach outside the ground, Wenger waited impatiently for Edu to complete the routine post-match drug test. Henry Winter, the football correspondent for the *Daily Telegraph*, was down by the dressing rooms at the time and witnessed the Arsenal manager losing his cool in his desire to leave for the airport. 'Edu was still taking the Uefa drugs test, but suddenly Arsène exploded at Arsenal's press officer, calling her all the names under the sun,' said Winter. 'It was quite spectacular. I felt really bad for her and even sent her a text later that night to check she was OK. A few days later she told me that she was used to this sort of behaviour, but also that Arsène had taken her to one side later that night to apologise at the way he had behaved that evening.'

The outburst was most likely an indication of the frustration Europe too frequently inspired in Wenger, even if Celta were seen off relatively comfortably in the return leg to set up a quarter-final against Chelsea. For Arsenal, unbeaten in the Premiership at the time, with the league title edging ever closer, this was a match that would surely play straight into their hands: it looked as if the 1–1 draw achieved at Stamford Bridge in the first leg courtesy of Pires's equaliser must pave the way for progress. Yet, with Claudio Ranieri's position in the Blues' dugout under intense scrutiny, Chelsea achieved the impossible at Highbury, with Wayne Bridge plucking the goal which catapulted the hosts from the competition.

That night, just as in Galicia, Arsenal's defensive frailties had been ruthlessly exposed as one of the season's principal objectives was snatched away. 'Of all the dreams that Arsène had that year, the first was probably to have gone the entire season unbeaten in the Premiership,' said Comolli. 'Given that he is always seeking perfection, he will have taken huge satisfaction in achieving that. His other dream was the Champions League. That is the trophy he desired more than any other. To have been eliminated, particularly to London rivals in Chelsea, hurt him.'

Occasionally, his inability as yet to earn Arsenal their first European Cup has been levelled against Wenger as a sign of failure. 'But he has been fighting against clubs who boast double his budget,' argued Comolli, glossing over the reality perhaps that the likes of Porto have won the competition in recent years, while Liverpool, a club comparable in terms of gate receipts, carried off the trophy in 2005. 'Arsenal rank seventh or eighth in the Premiership in terms of the gates they attracted at Highbury, and they would be even further down the scale when it came to Continental opposition. The club benefits from an overexposure in terms of the media coverage it generates largely because Arsène has such an extraordinary aura. People are also attracted to the type of football his team play. If you looked at clubs across Europe who attracted around 38,000 people to their home games – as Arsenal did at Highbury – you wouldn't constantly be haranguing them for not winning the European Cup. Atlético Madrid, Inter Milan, AS Roma, Borussia Dortmund or Schalke . . . people don't say the same things about them. It was inevitable that while Arsenal waited to move to the Emirates, they would effectively remain a club in the second tier of European clubs.'

Yet, according to Wenger, they should be part of a European Super League should it be set up. 'A structure like that would see the best of the best competing against each other,' said the Frenchman. 'I think it will happen sooner or later – we're edging closer to it all the time – and I would welcome the creation of a European league championship. I would even go as far as to say that it's a shame it doesn't exist already. If it did, its outcome would be fairer than the European Cup is at present. In a league system, the best teams would naturally rise to the top. For me, my only concern is that the best team wins at the end of the day. The aim of the elite is not that the least strong team wins.

'What I would like most of all is a European league to run alongside domestic competition, perhaps with only 16 teams in the top flight. In my scheme, national competitions would therefore continue to exist. And I would go even further: I think it would be possible to have the same team, or even the same players, in both competitions. Unfortunately, I don't think Europe is ready quite yet. We have even gone backwards with the new formula for the Champions League [with the reintroduction of knockout phases instead of the second group stage]. What takes precedence is what the television companies want. In Europe today your fate depends on the drawing of lots and all sorts of other things over which you have no control. I am in favour of this great championship but I don't think that the idea will be taken up, in particular by the television companies.'

Arsenal's Premiership title ensured qualification for Europe's elite competition yet again in 2004–05. They had safely – if not necessarily convincingly – negotiated passage from a group which included PSV Eindhoven, Rosenberg and Panathinaikos, and Bayern Munich awaited in the knockout phase. The Germans, who had attempted to lure Wenger to Bavaria back in the 1995–96 season, would prevail 3–2 on aggregate and, with José Mourinho having taken over at Chelsea in the interim to muscle the west Londoners above Arsenal in the Premiership, Wenger was forced to rethink his strategy. The summer of 2005 would see Patrick Vieira sold to Juventus, a move long mooted but always rebuffed. Some doubted the wisdom of releasing the France midfielder. 'But my only criticism would be that, possibly, Patrick was sold too late,' said Alan Smith. 'Yet the real mistake was not replacing him immediately.'

Wenger had initially earmarked the Brazilian Julio Baptista, then of Sevilla, as a potential replacement, but 'the Beast' chose to join Real Madrid instead. Yet when he did eventually move to the Emirates at the beginning of the following season as part of the loan deal that saw Reyes move to the Bernabéu, Baptista would mainly be used as a striker. Instead, Arsenal would have to rely upon the youngsters coming through the ranks – and Cesc Fabregas in particular – in their effort to reach the Champions League final at the Stade de France in May 2006.

The road to Paris was occasionally tortuous. The Swiss semi-professionals of FC Thun proved stubborn opponents, having the temerity to equalise before Dennis Bergkamp finally ensured the Gunners began their latest Continental campaign with victory. The victories at Ajax and Sparta Prague provided a springboard for the months ahead. 'They gave us the self-confidence for the matches ahead,' said Mathieu

Flamini. 'The manager just kept telling us to play in exactly the same way we did in the Premiership, to give everything, and it worked. We were particularly dangerous on the break and some of the sides we were up against couldn't cope.'

Top of the group, the draw was supposed to be kind for the second phase, though Real Madrid's inability to edge out Olympique Lyonnais in their qualification section thrust them into the second pot of seeds. A trip to the Bernabéu awaited yet. For all that Real's recent policy of purchasing *Galácticos* had not reaped rewards in recent years, still their side included Zinédine Zidane, David Beckham, Roberto Carlos and Ronaldo, a glittering selection up against a team who had just failed to defeat Bolton at Highbury and lost at Liverpool in their previous two Premiership games. Yet what unfurled in the Spanish capital that night must rank alongside events in the San Siro two years earlier as one of Wenger's finest hours in European competition.

The visitors set their stall out early, waltzing through Madrid's dithering defence after a mere 82 seconds, Thierry Henry and José Antonio Reyes slicing through at will. Iker Casillas blocked the first effort, but Arsenal's confidence – at such a low ebb in the weeks building up to this tie – was flooding back with every touch. Reyes tormented Cicinho down the left, Emmanuel Eboué and Cesc Fabregas growing visibly as they sauntered in between flustered opponents, upstart youngsters impudently terrorising a team who have grown used to pummelling the opposition from the first whistle. When the home side did threaten, there was Jens Lehmann, revitalised from the disenchanted figure of previous years, to thwart Robinho and Ronaldo.

At the interval, the only frustration was that – not for the first time – Arsenal's slick dominance had not earned them an advantage, though that was redressed two minutes after the restart. Fabregas slipped the ball to Henry in the centre circle with the striker carrying the ball forward at pace, beating Ronaldo's half-hearted challenge and Thomas Gravesen's lunge. The Frenchman glided unchallenged into Real's final third, veering away from Guti and Sergio Ramos before finishing superbly beyond the exposed Casillas. Real, deflated in arrears, could only muster hints at a revival and the visitors, marshalled by the experienced players in their midst, strolled to victory.

It was arguably the likes of Gilberto Silva, Henry and Freddie Ljungberg whose contributions were key at the Bernabéu in unseating the nine-times winners. There was a backbone to Arsenal's team that they had not boasted in domestic competition that season, the Premiership title race already a distant 20 points away. This was only the fourth time in the club's history that they had reached the last eight of Europe's elite competition, and, to put this in proper context, was also Real's first home defeat in 18 Champions League matches stretching back to October 2002. 'We needed our experienced players to do well and, through the team, Jens Lehmann, Kolo Touré, Gilberto, Thierry and Freddie needed big nights,' said Wenger in the aftermath. 'Seeing a performance like that, I believe we will be at the Stade de France for the final in May.'

Real, for all their busy intent, could not salvage the tie at Highbury (0–0), though Juventus in the quarter-finals remained an imposing fixture. Yet Wenger's side had found their Continental rhythm. The football conjured against the Italians in north London at the end of March took the breath, the quick steps of Fabregas and Henry leaving experienced defenders – Gianluigi Buffon, Fabio Cannavaro, Lilian Thuram and Gianluca Zambrotta would all feature in the World Cup final later that summer – perplexed as the hosts purred. Both scored, the 2–0 advantage retained after a goalless draw in Turin a week later. A passage to Paris was opening up.

Up against Arsenal in the semi-finals were Villarreal, the Yellow Submarines who had reached the Uefa Cup quarter-finals a year earlier but were venturing into new territory in the bigger competition. The Spaniards had long lived in the shadow of nearby Valencia. Villarreal, a small town known for its ceramics factory and little else, boasted a team which included Diego Forlan and Juan Riquelme in their number, both exquisite talents, and the abrasive Marco Senna at its heart. Kolo Touré's rare goal earned a first-leg lead at Highbury, but the return, so cagey and angst-ridden, was to go to the wire. It was time for Lehmann to prove his pedigree.

Some 88 minutes had ticked by at El Madrigal with the game goalless when José Mari tumbled under Gaël Clichy's challenge and the referee, Valentin Ivanov, dismayed the visitors by awarding a penalty. The Argentinean Riquelme stepped up, confronted by Lehmann's boldness on his line, and it was the Villarreal man who choked. The German dived to his left to parry away, and Arsenal had unearthed a 36-year-old hero. Lehmann's route to favour had been agonising. Back on 4 December 2004, Wenger had dropped his No. 1 for a Premiership game against Birmingham City (won 3–0), and the Germany international started an 11-match run on the bench, encompassing domestic and Champions League games, while Manuel Almunia performed in his stead. If Almunia's performance in a 4–2 home defeat to Manchester United had proved the final straw after an unimpressive run, it was arguably only the Uruguayan Sebastián Viera's inability to pass a medical in the summer of 2005 that allowed Lehmann a chance for redemption.

The manager had asked him whether he intended to leave following his original dropping; Lehmann chose to stay and work harder. As he prepared to face Riquelme's penalty, Thierry Henry had ambled up and suggested to his goalkeeper that he should remain static, as he believed the Villarreal player would strike his spot kick centrally. Lehmann ignored him and Arsenal reached their first European Cup final. 'It completes a work of nine and a half years and a lot of effort,' said Wenger of the landmark in his tenure to date.

It was as if fate had lured the Frenchman back to Paris for the final, where Barcelona – a side who had seared their way to the Primera Liga title, harnessing the glorious talents of Ronaldinho, Deco and Samuel Eto'o – awaited. Critically, despite their rather slapdash domestic form, Arsenal arrived in France having secured Champions League football for the 2006–07 campaign. Entering their final Premiership game, the last at Highbury before the move to Ashburton Grove and the Emirates, Wenger's side had needed to defeat Wigan Athletic and hope that West Ham took points from fourth-place Tottenham Hotspur if they were to break into the top four. This would also be the final home game for Dennis

Bergkamp, Robert Pires (en route to Villarreal), Sol Campbell and Ashley Cole at the club. But while the heroes of Highbury's past caught the imagination, the drama on show centred on the club's immediate future.

As a warm-up for Paris, this was scintillating. Pires may have grabbed a farewell goal, but Wigan stormed back to lead through Paul Scharner and David Thompson before Thierry Henry took over. The Frenchman had apparently grown unsettled at the club, perturbed by the reality that Chelsea, Manchester United and now Liverpool were out of sight above the Gunners at the top of the Premiership. At the time, those present as he ripped through the Latics must have wondered whether this was a goodbye hat-trick. Meanwhile, across the capital, West Ham were beating a Tottenham side decimated by food poisoning, and for Wenger all was well in the world. The manager, unusually hyperactive particularly when Arsenal had been losing, joined his players on the slow lap of honour post-match, signing autographs and touching hands with some of those in the stands chanting his name. 'For the history of this club and this building, I am personally very happy,' said Wenger after the 4–2 success, 'because I would have felt guilty walking out on a low. This helps us go on a high to the Champions League final.'

This had become something of a personal crusade as Wenger sought the first European trophy he craved. 'My career will never be good enough for me because it is the way I am,' he said. 'You always think about what you could have won and didn't win, and what you win you think: "That is normal." I will have to accept that people judge whether [my career] was good or not good but I am not too much worried about that. I want to win this competition for the club, for the players and of course for me, but it's not at the moment what worries me. I always think in every job consistency is quality. We can all be successful for five minutes but when you do it over five, ten or fifteen years that takes a special dedication, a special stamina in your motivation. But we want to win the trophy and I believe we will.'

Arsenal might have been backed by vociferous support, hopping over the Channel, but they arrived in Paris as underdogs. The manager had argued this was actually to their advantage – 'I think this gives us more positive vibes' – though, in the end, the Gunners would depart the Stade de France crying foul in their intense disappointment. On Wednesday, 17 May 2006, the Londoners strode out in their first European Cup final, their fluorescent yellow strip contrasting with Barca's classic red and blue, with their manager living his dream on the touchline. Then, not for the first time for Wenger in Europe, luck appeared to drain from his charges at the critical moment.

The Premiership side had begun splendidly, Henry twice forcing Victor Valdés to save in the opening three minutes. Yet, only 18 minutes in, Ronaldinho slipped Eto'o in on goal with Lehmann crunching into the Cameroon international as the striker attempted to round him. Ludovic Giuly might have tapped the rebound into the empty net, but the referee Terje Hauge had already blown his whistle for the foul and sent the German off. Pires, sacrificed for Manuel Almunia, skulked from the turf with his final game for Arsenal wrecked.

That Sol Campbell went on to thump the Londoners ahead

with a trademark header offered hope, and Henry might have added a second late on, but Barcelona steadily stretched the play to wreck Wenger's night. Eto'o, with 14 minutes remaining, and Juliano Belletti ten minutes from time deflated the ten men. Arsenal, exhausted, were powerless to recover.

After the final whistle, disappointment gave way to resentment. 'I don't know if the referee had a Barcelona shirt on because they kicked me all over the place,' said Henry, who had seen one of the original linesmen for the game, Ole Hermann Borgan, replaced at the last minute following the publication of photographs of him wearing the Catalans' strip. 'Some of his calls were strange. Maybe next time I'll learn how to dive. I expect the referee to do his job but I don't think he did. In fact, I'd like to have seen a proper referee out there. So many times [Carles] Puyol should have got a yellow card and so many times [Rafael] Marquez came from behind to take my ankles. I have ended with bruises all over my body. I've also been told that their first goal [by Eto'o] was offside. They are already a good team. If you help them, it's going to be very difficult to beat them.'

'It's difficult to accept losing a game anyway but worse when you have to accept losing it on a wrong decision,' said Wenger, outspoken in defeat and livid that Eto'o had not been flagged when sprinting on to Henrik Larsson's fine flick. 'That goal was offside and it was proven on television. At this level, we shouldn't have to accept it in the future. We have to do something about it. That goal is my biggest regret. To play eleven against ten and be on top of that situation, but then to concede an offside goal is difficult to accept. I thought the whole story of changing the linesman because of the Barcelona shirt was not important. But, when we concede an offside goal, no one says anything.'

The Frenchman accepted – albeit reluctantly – Hauge's decision to dismiss Lehmann for tripping Eto'o. 'It was a red card,' he conceded, 'but I wouldn't blame my goalkeeper for that. I heard the whistle blow for the foul before the ball hit the net, and the referee couldn't assume Giuly would score, so I understand that decision.'

What the Frenchman may have struggled to comprehend was the manner in which this game had been snatched away from his side at the last. Henry offered the team some consolation on their return to London with confirmation that his future lay at the club, and not at Barcelona's Nou Camp, with hopes raised that the move to the £400 million Emirates would confirm the club as a major player, both in terms of European competition and in the transfer market. The financial shackles had theoretically been removed, the Gunners' annual gates to be almost doubled to more than £70 million with some £19.9 million having been generated by the run to the Champions League final. With those resources behind them, there was hope within the team and the hierarchy that appearances at such showpiece occasions would become more regular and would eventually yield reward.

Yet the jewel in the crown remained the man in charge. 'Without Arsène Wenger I would not be here talking to you,' said Thierry Henry, sitting in front of a packed media conference having confirmed he would remain. 'I wanted to carry on at Arsenal with this team, and with this manager.' For Wenger, the quest for European silverware goes on.

PROJECTIONS

BACK IN OCTOBER 2005, Arsène Wenger's image stared out from the double-page advertisements taken out in magazines and the matchday programme. His portrait, a study of concentration in black and white, was accompanied by the slogan: 'Great things can be achieved when you stick to a winning formula. Highbury could soon be your home, too.' The red strap across the foot of the page proclaimed that Arsenal's home since 1913 was on the verge of being re-developed into luxury apartments. A relatively modest deposit of £2,500 would reserve potential purchasers one of the flats, the cheapest of which would fetch some £320,000. This was, according to the blurb on the advert, 'The chance of a lifetime' for all Gunners fans.

A few streets away, a new home was steadily rising from the rubble. The Emirates would still be served by the Arsenal underground station, with supporters exiting the Tube merely turning towards Ashburton Grove where they would previously have made their way down to Avenell Road. Yet the move represented major upheaval for club and sup-porters alike, with Wenger's tenure – by this time nearing a decade in charge – offering some stability. Wenger had become an emissary for this club: a figure who has served to advise his board of directors as well as masterminding his side's progress on the pitch.

The official line offered by manager and club was that Wenger was both in favour of and hugely influential in Arsenal's move to the Emirates. 'I pushed the board of directors,' he said at the beginning of 2006. 'I think the stadium is the result partly of my encouragement and the enormous courage of the board, because I don't know many boards of directors in the world who would have been as courageous as to enter into such a challenge.' However, those in the know claim the manager was not in fact as fervent a supporter of the project as has been claimed. Rather, he determined that it would have been folly to question the club's decision to pursue the move.

The Frenchman's philosophy has always been to create a legacy for Arsenal. Thus, when it came to the bricks and mortar of building a new home, he was happy to appear alongside his chairman, Peter Hill-Wood, at a press conference announcing the partnership between Arsenal and the Dubai-based Emirates Airlines, whose name would be associated with the new arena and the club's kit for seven years at least from the summer of 2006. 'The new stadium was used as a media tool,' explained Alex Fynn, a specialist in the business of British football. 'But I don't think Arsène wanted all the money from this partnership with Emirates to go to this new home. I think he wanted a functional rather than luxurious stadium.'

At the beginning of the decision-making process, Wenger and the vice-chairman David Dein had wanted the board of directors to consider all possible options for a new stadium without spending to excess. These options would have been, for example, to share the new ground with the club's neighbours and bitter rivals, Tottenham Hotspur – an idea which, admittedly, would have been abhorrent to the fans of both clubs – or even to 'rent' the new Wembley Stadium, redesigned by Norman Foster and eventually, after much delay, rebuilt.

'But Daniel Fiszman, the majority shareholder, and Peter Hill-Wood from the outset had wanted to do things on a grand scale, along the same lines as the club had always done in the past,' added Fynn. 'The Fiszman and Hill-Wood alliance thus won over Dein–Wenger. The position of Arsène, Dein's principal ally, was therefore to a certain extent weakened. It was the alliance of the nouveau riche [Fiszman] and the old traditionalist [Hill-Wood] which won the day over the two pragmatists who were, perhaps, more concerned with the continued development of the team. Once the decision was made, things moved so quickly that Arsène wasn't really involved apart from matters directly affecting the playing side.'

Others within the club disagree with that interpretation of the politics in the lead-up to Arsenal's move to Ashburton Grove. 'If Arsène has constantly mentioned the need to build this new stadium ever since, it is because he was personally involved in its design, just as he was with the training centre in Colney,' said the source, who suggested instead that the Alsatian was always totally committed to the move, visiting the stadium during its construction whenever he could and supervising everything from the laying of the turf to choosing the carpets throughout spring of 2006.

'Wenger and Dein certainly stated that they wanted the

new stadium to be built,' said Fynn. 'But that they didn't want it to be at the expense of transfer monies. They therefore expressed some reservations, but in vain – in the end, they were overruled.' The sporting and economic implications of this struggle in the boardroom were enormous. Over the course of the 2004–05 season, Arsenal's debt increased from around £150 million to £180 million. On the other hand, cash reserves rose from around £18 million to £75 million in the same period, through increased television revenues from domestic and European competition, and commercial sponsorship deals. 'It could be that the stadium at Ashburton Grove was the right decision in the end,' stressed Fynn. 'But it will only be so if Arsène stays and continues to qualify the team for the Champions League, accruing all the television and marketing revenues associated with that competition. As long as he stays at Arsenal and ensures them their success to date, they will be OK. However, should they fail . . .'

Arsenal's board have insisted publicly that the club have prepared for the worst-case scenario – a finish outside the Premiership's top four – but they would rather that never came to pass. When asked about the Emirates, Wenger merely stresses the benefits of the move. 'The club should pay off all the costs associated with the ground move in the next ten years,' he said. 'But the stadium initially cost us a lot. Now, though, the financial situation will improve given the size of the arena we have moved to, and the off-field benefits it will bring. It is true that it has been a painful few years, though. We have steadily had to cut the wage bill and invest less in transfers.'

Some among the English press questioned the naming rites

associated with the stadium, with the 'English institution' that was Arsenal effectively appearing to sell out to a foreign airline. In December 2004 an issue of the cult football magazine *When Saturday Comes* (*WSC*) denounced the deal with Emirates as 'shameful'. The piece similarly found it ironic that Arsenal should associate themselves with the former sponsors of their rivals Chelsea. But the deal reflected a growing trend in modern-day football and the game's demands, whether the club concerned is Bolton Wanderers or Wigan Athletic. Even Liverpool, after all, are considering selling the naming rights for their new stadium to be constructed on Stanley Park which they hope to open by 2009.

The venture in north London had immediate economic benefits for the area. Some 1,800 jobs were created in Islington, and 2,000 homes were built in the borough. The club now benefits from 150 executive boxes, three times as many as at Highbury. Revenues increased accordingly, with some 2,000 meals served in the boxes on matchdays, and an exclusive 'Diamond Club' facility with catering directed by Raymond Blanc. Add to that the 1,000-square-metre megastore at the new ground and the potential leap in income is clear. The economics graduate in Wenger would appreciate the implications of such progress. 'There is one further resource to be exploited: the Internet,' he said. 'For me, being a great club means being long lasting, getting consistent results, being on top domestically. This is not easy because today, in all countries, you can see clubs with enormous financial potential which fall from first to 12th place in the blink of an eye. We faced this problem.'

Towards the end of 2005, when Arsenal's form was

riddled with inconsistencies and the team languished well outside the Premiership's top four, the club teetered on the brink of such ignominy. 'It is a great disappointment to be so low in the table,' said Wenger. 'That disappointment is born of the fact that the club has grown, and with that growth, higher targets have been set. They are more and more demanding. But, at the same time, at present there are ten or twelve clubs in the Premiership who are of the same specific financial potential as us. That is not reflected in our ambitions.'

Looking at the figures for the club, there is a temptation to present Wenger as a businessman. Alex Fynn rejects this theory vehemently: 'I don't think it is fair to present him as a businessman, because he is not involved in the economic affairs of the club as such. He is not linked to any of the purely commercial decisions, such as getting sponsors or choosing suppliers. The only economic aspects in which Arsène is concerned are those linked to the game, and here he has strong views. For example, he sees no economic sense in Chelsea's lavish spending. 'If the football authorities applied the rules of business, Chelsea may not have the right to operate in the way they do – piling up debt as a result of playing costs,' Wenger said. 'For me, Chelsea are a club who use a kind of economic doping because their resources are artificial, because Abramovich has not had to adjust his investment in line with the revenue from the club. This is the real problem: the financial situation in England is not dictated by the clubs' natural resources, but by artificial pressure from Chelsea.'

Evidently, Abramovich and his oil dollars have exasperated Wenger. During the 2004–05 season, Chelsea poured some £110 million into players' salaries, double that of Arsenal, making for an uneven competition. But it is a situation Wenger has endured before. At the end of the 1990s, when Manchester United's turnover was by some considerable distance the biggest in the Premiership with Arsenal ranked only sixth, Alex Fynn shared a conversation with Wenger. 'He told me he was going to make Arsenal the biggest club in the world,' recalled Fynn of the chat with his neighbour in Totteridge. 'I replied: "You can't. Manchester United have a much better infrastructure than Arsenal, and a bigger fan base as well. The United brand has been out there for years and is therefore infinitely stronger than that of Arsenal." He acknowledged my point.'

To that end, the takeover of the club by Malcolm Glazer, assuming huge debts upon completion, rather perplexed Wenger. 'How, and why, can someone who is not particularly interested in football fight so ferociously to take control of a club, when football is a business which is rarely profitable?' he asked. 'Could it be that he really loves the game? When you invest more than a billion dollars in a club, it isn't to destroy it. I suppose before the Glazers arrived on the scene, when United were a listed company, they had to accept that if the main shareholders sell their shares, others will take control of the company. That is what happened.' In 2006, Wenger said: 'I prefer working within the framework of a private company. I can only be happy if I have the support of my board of directors. This is why I have been here so long. I have my freedom. This profession is difficult enough as it is, and if you also had to confront the owners it would become impossible.'

Those comments were made before the American businessman Stan Kroenke bought Granada's 9.9 per cent stake in Arsenal in the spring of 2007, a move that was widely regarded as presaging a takeover bid for the London club. The resistance of Hill-Wood and Fiszman to that possibility forced David Dein to depart the board soon after Kroenke's investment, sparking rumours of Arsène's own departure with some 15 months to run on his contract at the time. Wenger had lost his closest ally within the Arsenal hierarchy, the man who had been so instrumental in appointing him a decade previously. But Wenger refused to be drawn on the subject at the time, saying only that Dein's departure was 'a sad day for Arsenal'.

It was not the first time that his future had come into question. While still Arsenal vice-chairman, David Dein had fought fiercely to deflect interest in the club's manager from outside. As an influential member of the Football Association board, he resisted the call for Wenger to be offered the England manager's job and instead was instrumental in the appointment of Sven-Göran Eriksson in 2000. 'The football federations in Germany and France have both expressed interest in taking Arsène over the years, as have Bayern Munich and Real Madrid,' admitted Dein. The Spanish press insist he might have moved to Barcelona at the turn of the century, with one journalist suggesting: 'Arsène met [the Barca president] Joan Gaspart in Paris back in 2001, way before Joan Laporta took control of the Catalan club. The meeting was held at the Lutétia on avenues Montaigne but, because Gaspart was replaced by Laporta in the subsequent round of elections, it came to nothing. Two years later, Wenger was given the opportunity to move to Real Madrid as well. The decision to turn the Spanish club down was a tough one.'

Indeed, Wenger had already attracted the board at the Bernabéu. In 2001, his was one of three names on a shortlist to manage the club, along with José Antonio Camacho and Sven-Göran Eriksson. Just as Arsenal had initially chosen an Englishman in Bruce Rioch to manage their club, so Real eventually opted for Camacho. But interest has been maintained ever since. '[The Real president] Florentino Pérez has wanted Wenger for some years now,' said another Spanish journalist. 'Arsène is perfectly cut out for the job. His profile would be similar to that of Vicente Del Bosque, whose achievements with Real are celebrated [he won La Liga in 2001 and 2003, and the Champions League in 2000 and 2002]. Wenger treats all players as mature adults, he talks to them. He gives them tactical pointers during pre-season work and sticks to fine-tuning those during the season. With the *Galácticos*, this is exactly what is required.'

Wenger would insist, as he has done throughout his career, that he 'never breaks a contract', but his passage to Madrid was effectively barred when Real signed David Beckham from Manchester United in the summer of 2003. The Spanish club's policy of buying *Galácticos*, and then finding a manager capable of forging them into a team, would not sit easily with Wenger. Pérez opted to recruit Carlos Queiroz, No. 2 to Sir Alex Ferguson at Manchester United, and well known to Beckham.

'Madrid haven't really had a strong manager since the end

of the 1990s when Fabio Capello was in charge,' said Ivan Moda, a Spanish journalist. Capello subsequently returned to the club but has found it near impossible to recreate the glories of his first spell, particularly in the Champions League. 'Wenger was approached, but he was never really that interested. He knows just how little freedom he would have to do his job. He also feels that the club has become some marketing machine where the president is there to pull strings for financial purposes. One of Pérez's advisers confessed that if Real didn't win the title in the short term, it didn't really matter as long as they kept selling shirts around the world.'

More appealing, perhaps, would have been Bayern Munich. The Bavarians had approached Wenger in the mid-1990s, and the Frenchman had never truly forgiven the Monégasque board for refusing permission for him to speak with Bayern, particularly given that they were willing to release him a few months later. Yet, according to Rafael Honigstein, a Munich-based journalist, it may have been a blessing in disguise that Wenger was not lured to Germany. 'At that point Bayern were similar to Real in terms of the personalities and egos working in and around the club,' he said. 'Every one of Wenger's decisions would have been under the microscope. The politics between the president Franz Beckenbauer and the others on the board was very, very delicate. It would have been impossible for Arsène to manage the business in the same manner he did with Arsenal, where he is the only genuine decision maker. He does however still have a lot of admirers at Bayern.'

But Arsenal have thus far managed to hold on to their

man. 'When you look at our results, Arsène is the greatest manager this club has ever had,' said Dein. 'Arsène is the first to arrive at the training centre in the morning and the last to leave at night. A lot of clubs have copied his techniques. His arrival was the best appointment Arsenal have ever made.'

Whilst at the club, Dein would reiterate regularly that Wenger had a job for as long as he wished. In October 2004 the manager renewed his contract, binding him to the club until the end of the 2007–08 campaign – and after Dein's departure he promised to honour that contract. There were even discussions, albeit low-key, suggesting that the Frenchman might adopt a director of football role at the club once he decided his time in the dugout was up. 'But I don't really see my future mapped out in one particular way,' said Wenger. 'In this job, you are constantly called into question. To make a parallel with politics, results affect our position with the public and the respect we enjoy, in the same way as inflation and unemployment affect the standing of politicians. Winning is the best way to earn respect.'

Between Dein and Wenger, the feeling was one of mutual respect. 'Arsène is the best coach in Europe, and the most reliable,' said the former vice-chairman. 'He has turned the club around with his training methods. He knows just how to make good players out of average ones, excellent ones out of the good ones and turn the excellent into the great.' It is those skills that have prompted speculation in France that one day Wenger could be convinced to take up the baton with the national team to emulate the successes of the likes of Aimé Jacquet and, more recently, Raymond Domenech. Indeed, he boasts strong support within the French Football Federation and has long been touted for a role within the national side's set-up, based at the plush Clairefontaine site on the outskirts of Paris. Yet whether he would be considered too high-profile a figure to become national coach remains to be seen – the FFF have generally appointed from within in recent years, and certainly never on the kind of salary enjoyed by managers in the Premiership. For the moment, however, it seems that the Alsatian's thoughts remain very much on reinventing his Arsenal team for the challenge ahead.

Even so, there are still concerns from some quarters that a takeover by the mysterious Kroenke might change the manager's mind, even if his comments on the subject in the past have suggested a philosophical approach. When asked in the early 2000s whether he anticipated more clubs, including Arsenal, seeking to float on the Stock Exchange, the economics graduate had stated: 'It is inevitable. Clubs have become too powerful financially. Football has entered a transitional phase. We have moved on from the club chairman being its number-one fan to having boards of directors concerned only by economic realities of the game. They don't necessarily need to have a special relationship with the club they own. I remember when I was with Monaco in 1987 to 1988. We bought Hoddle from Tottenham, largely because we could offer him a better salary than Spurs could. How things have changed in such a relatively short period of time. We are in a market now where there is artificial competition, pushing budgets and spending forever up.

'And, furthermore, things are different in each country across Europe. In Italy, so many of the bigger clubs appear to be teetering on the edge of financial oblivion. In England, most appear to be in a position of financial wellbeing, largely because of the money pumped into the game by television companies. For me, this is a consequence of globalisation: an individual who is especially rich in one place can invest in another without being linked to the local context, at his sole initiative.'

Given his appreciation of the finances of the English game, Wenger has attempted to remain relatively realistic in terms of his own club's wage structure. 'The average footballer is overpaid, but a really talented player deserves his salary as he is playing in a big foreign club with an obligation to win, so he must be mentally strong,' he explained. Even before the 1998 World Cup, a tournament which arguably sparked the escalation of salaries across the continent and in England most of all, Wenger had anticipated a leap in wages. He anticipated contracts doubling over the ensuing three-year period and, with that in mind, constructed a salary system at Highbury aimed at coping with the hike. The upper echelon of players comprised internationals; the next was made up of high-quality Premiership players; and the final stratum was reserved for up-and-coming young talents. Wenger said: 'We get the impression that players aren't staying with us just for the money. Of course they earn a good living, but some of them could have earned even more elsewhere. Maybe this creates a type of special attachment.' In that context, the renegotiation of Thierry Henry's contract in the summer of 2006 to reach a salary of around £100,000 a week must have shocked Wenger.

'Here we have a real societal problem,' he said. 'From what point can you say that a salary is indecent? Someone who earns the minimum wage could think his neighbour's salary, two or three times the minimum wage, is indecent. What is normal or abnormal? These are points which need to be looked at by society. But we should not forget that those who earn large salaries contribute to society as they pay significant taxes. A player who earns £100,000 a month pays, in England, £40,000 in tax every month. At the end of the year, he will therefore have paid £480,000 to the state. Yet the reality is that with the escalation of players' wages, our club earns less money now than when I arrived despite taking 50 per cent more on ticket sales, and despite the fact that our turnover has doubled. Players' salaries are very high. But we know exactly how far we can go. There is a cut-off point above which we will not pay.'

When the sports minister, Richard Caborn, proposed a salary cap for the game at the end of 2005, Wenger had expressed his reservations. 'If it was to apply for the whole of society, I wouldn't object to the idea,' he said. 'But it can't just apply to football. You can't say a footballer has a maximum salary when a financial wizard can get a £15 million bonus under the pretext that he creates wealth.' The fact remains that if Arsenal are to compete with the elite both in England and Europe, they must boast the financial clout to offer competitive contracts, and Wenger would concede that much. When Barcelona and Real Madrid expressed their interest in Henry during the 2005–06 season, the worry was that the forward could be enticed away by the potential salary on offer in La Liga. 'Frankly, in my heart, I don't think it was a problem with money, as the salary offered elsewhere would be almost identical,' insisted Wenger. 'If Barca or Real wanted Thierry, they could offer him the same or even more money than us. Money is therefore not a determinant factor. But we've had to become cleverer in the market. Our scouting trips now extend to Brazil and Africa, but we aren't the only ones.'

What has proved popular, masking the leap in salaries for top-level players, has been the implementation of performance-related contracts. 'The player, on top of match bonuses, gets a target bonus at the end of the season depending on the number of appearances he has made and the performances he has put in,' said Wenger. 'It is the best way of maintaining incentives. When I hear Sepp Blatter [the president of Fifa] criticising the level of pay in this country, it annoys me. It is true that if you compare players' salaries with those earned by poor people throughout the world, they might seem indecent. But poverty in the world won't be resolved by paying players less. Grand words mean nothing. The thing to do with football is not to get rid of what is profitable, but to crack down on clubs which have not been able to balance their budget.' That could be deemed a criticism both of Chelsea and, perhaps more pertinently, of Leeds United, who went from Champions League semi-finalists to the ignominy of relegation to League One in six short years.

For his part, David Dein had been a leading light in the foundation of the Premier League and had his own views on salaries and the future of the game. 'I felt English football was like a sleeping giant,' he said. 'We still had a long way to travel, especially compared with the way the Americans managed their sports – baseball, American football and basketball. We were light years behind.' According to Dein, the trend was steadily moving towards the foundation of a European Super League. 'You can't stop development and change. Where will it lead? That is another problem. I think we are living in a society with a very liberal idea of capitalism, and one which also has its limitations. We are currently seeing this in the NBA, in basketball. In the most liberal capitalist country, they have chosen to put a ceiling on salaries. This is highly symbolic in my opinion. And it makes us sensitive to how things are developing here.'

Modern football, whether at Arsenal or at Watford, is driven by the market. A place in the Premiership is worth in the region of £60 million to each club following the renegotiation of television rights packages for the 2007–08 season. Wenger's reign – just like Sir Alex Ferguson's at Manchester United – has spanned a huge hike in the wages and commercial aspects of the sport, and Arsenal have had to buy into the trend. Indeed, their manager has, perhaps inadvertently, helped spruce up the club's image with regards to certain commercial deals. With the team playing such attractive football, the club has become an equally attractive proposition for prospective sponsors. 'Arsenal were lucky to get Arsène as he has increased the value of the Arsenal brand,' said Fynn. The Alsatian fronted the press conference announcing the deal with Emirates Airlines in 2005, having been present at a similar media event following Sega's three-year deal with the club announced back in 1999. A photograph of that unveiling hung in one of the executive boxes at Highbury, Wenger proudly holding up the Arsenal home kit – emblazoned with the Sega motif – to the sponsors' commercial director.

Sponsors, existing or potential, and shareholders alike were impressed by Wenger's demeanour. There were only a handful of major shareholders, with Danny Fiszman holding the biggest stake. The Arsenal board of directors would meet six times every year with Wenger invited to each of these meetings, though he only offered his thoughts on matters which directly concerned the team. His presence was, however, required for the annual general meeting of the 200 shareholders. 'These AGMs are a complete waste of time, but are held every year,' said an Arsenal insider. 'Everything has already been put into place with regards to the running of the club, well before these meetings. Small shareholders turn up for two reasons: firstly to listen religiously to Wenger, who they love; second to have pictures taken with the cups won the previous year by the Gunners. They are all massive fans. Two or three of them would like to ask questions about economic matters or sporting strategy, but they don't get the chance: questions are selected in advance by the board.'

'What was achieved out on the pitch gave the club a kind of new life off it,' said Fynn. 'Wenger effectively acted as a figure to charm the small shareholders, a man who impressed the board of directors and who was trusted by those who owned the club. He previously played a similar role at Nagoya Grampus Eight, where he also worked closely with Toyota.'

The link between Wenger and Toyota remains strong even now. In the summer of 2005, the Japanese firm invited him to a conference in Prague where they asked him to present his thoughts on management techniques to those present. The coach used a short BBC film on 'the Invincibles', the Arsenal side who had gone through an entire season undefeated, to illustrate his ideas. Arsène was similarly invited by the Toyota team to Silverstone for the Formula One Grand Prix in July 2005, where, accompanied by his partner Annie, he sported a crash helmet whilst presenting Gunners kits to the drivers Jarno Trulli and Ralf Schumacher.

If Wenger had set out to change Arsenal's notoriously dour reputation, then he has succeeded spectacularly. 'The whole culture of the club changed after his arrival, as perhaps did the whole outlook of English football,' said Steve Bennett, a long-standing Arsenal fan. 'His players put on a show. With the manager's attacking philosophy flowing through the team, Arsenal have become one of the most attractive teams to watch in Europe. He and his French players gave the club more discipline, or rather changed the off-field image of the playing staff. I can't imagine Henry or Pires stumbling out of a nightclub and causing a fight. Their presence helped to calm the English players at Arsenal down, especially the younger players who followed the example of these more experienced professionals from abroad.'

'To be honest, for our supporters, the likes of Patrick Vieira and Thierry Henry were primarily Arsenal players, then Frenchmen,' said Wenger. 'That goes to show that we have created a cultural identity within the club where every-one can express himself. We are united in our intention to play beautiful, attacking football. People often perceive football as a purely financial world but Arsenal is a club which has held on to its human values.'

Even during the tricky 2005–06 season, when Chelsea were

marauding their way to a second successive title and the Gunners were slipping further and further behind – after the home defeat against Chelsea on 18 December, they languished 20 points from the league leaders – there was as much praise for Wenger as there was criticism. Even so, some did find reasons to grumble at the Frenchman. 'Arsène has failed to recruit good young English players, like Joe Cole, Michael Carrick or Paul Robinson,' said one. 'But I suppose you need to be prepared to pay top dollar to secure talents like that and Wenger will not pay over the odds.'

For many, however, Wenger remains something of a mystery. Arsenal supporters can be frustrated at times by their hero's apparent reluctance to express his emotions in public. 'It is hard to know what he is thinking,' said one fan, John Regniez. 'From time to time he reveals signs of frustration, but this is quite rare. When Arsenal wins, signs of joy are equally rare. I saw another Arsène only twice: when we won the title in 2004, and on the occasions when we have beaten Manchester United.'

Wenger himself has always welcomed the thoughts of the club's supporters. 'I place huge importance on the opinion of the fans,' he said. 'Supporters are the democratic voice of the club. Their opinion of the manager evolves in the same way as political opinion polls. Things fluctuate, but there is a consistent core.' Wenger has never passed up the opportunity to talk with the club's supporters. Jamie, an economics student and steward at Highbury on matchdays, met the manager during the end-of-season celebrations after the title win in 1998. 'I was a bit nervous to find myself sat opposite him, but straight away he put me at my ease,' he said. 'We talked about my studies, and after five minutes I was chatting to him like you would to any other guy in a pub. He has an ability to talk to people on their level.'

Wenger, for his part, has become something of an Arsenal supporter and, when he can, watches the club's women's team sweep all before them in their domestic league. 'One of my backroom staff, Vick Akers, is the team manager,' said the Frenchman. 'I keep up to date with their results and watch them when I can. Like us, they have won league and cup doubles, and in 1998 they paraded their trophies alongside us through the streets of London.

'But the real fans are the key. Arsenal have been around for 120 years. The English support their club in every sense of the word. Loyalty is the key word, here. When my team loses, I always think of the unhappiness we have caused to so many families, but their passion continues to amaze me. Such love is truly incredible. You have the feeling that here the public suffer with their team, but in silence. And they really support it with fervour.'

It is clear that Wenger is the perfect ambassador for Arsenal. He has become the heart and soul of the club. In the autumn of 2005, one of the Gunners' most loyal servants, Bill Graves, died. 'Bill had worked for Arsenal for more than 40 years, doing a bit of everything – from scouting to looking after the kit,' said the former England and Arsenal striker Alan Smith. 'I attended his funeral that autumn and among the guests were figures such as George Graham and other managers under whom Bill had worked. But I noticed Arsène there as well, keeping a low profile at the back, even though Bill had long left the club by the time Wenger arrived. But he felt he had to be there regardless. That sums up the role he feels he must play at the club, but people will always remember the Wenger era as a period when Arsenal played the most scintillating football in the club's history.'

'Arsène is nothing if not a true gentleman,' said Peggy Goulding, the president of Arsenal's supporters' club. 'When he came to the end-of-year function organised for the fans, and to which the team had been invited, he never danced but was always very polite. From his manager's bench he seems untouchable, but on these Christmas evenings he was very open. It was a real gift for the fans. He signed autographs, books, kits, agreed to have his photo taken with anyone present. He was always available. When Arsène speaks, you listen.'

'To say little, you need to think a lot,' said Jean-Marc Guillou when summing up his friend. However, Wenger takes his time to weigh up his words when confronted by the press pack every week. Friday is pre-match media day. 'It is a mass meeting of journalists,' explained Wenger. 'It is the chance to give the press something to write about because, the rest of the time, they don't have access to training, and I have to say that is quite nice. A trainer can stay focused on his work for the whole week without being interrupted by journalists. It happens, of course, but it is rare.'

The routine is regimented, with time allocated to broadcast, radio and newspaper journalists in turn. The press attaché, who follows Wenger around and studiously notes what is said, is quick to remind those present if they overstep the mark. Yet Wenger complies with good grace, humour and no little irony. 'Communicating well with the press is part of the job these days,' he conceded. 'But I avoid one-to-one interviews, otherwise each journalist would want to spend an hour one on one with me.'

At the stadium in Ashburton Grove, 215 workstations are reserved for journalists to use in the press suite. They come from far afield, with the Japanese press retaining an avid interest in the former Grampus Eight manager and devoting a large amount of space to English football. The local paper in Nagoya, *Chûnichi Shinbun*, is a regular visitor and the Chinese also follow Wenger closely.

José Touré, the former Monaco player now working for the French subscription television channel Canal+, has observed Wenger's demeanour during press briefings over the years. 'Arsène tries to defuse delicate subjects so he uses humour. But for those who really know Wenger, he is sincerity and honesty incarnate.'

'Wenger's strength is that he respects everyone, from the reporter who asks him a stupid question to his players, who he never fails to protect,' said the journalist Steve Stammers, who has covered Arsenal for both the *Evening Standard* and the *Sunday Mirror*. Journalists have learnt to accept the limits of what Wenger will divulge. This is a manager who prefers to keep the club's problems in-house. When Lauren returned to London several weeks after winning the African Cup of Nations with Cameroon in 2002, the management made no public comment at all, despite the clamour in the press suggesting the defender would be sanctioned and possibly even sold. Similarly, when a journalist asks Wenger if he is to spend £10 million on a certain player, the query invariably prompts a knowing smile and a feigned 'Sorry, I don't understand the question . . .' Some things are not for public consumption, and while Arsenal fans would surely love to know more about their hero, they accept and respect their manager's unique personality and desire for privacy.

'He never ducks a question,' said the *Mail on Sunday*'s Daniel King. 'Today there are press officers at all clubs and their job is less to facilitate communication between the manager and the press, but more to block awkward questions. At Arsenal, even if the press attaché seems troubled or concerned about a question asked by a journalist, Wenger will always try and answer it. I have almost never seen him fail to answer a question. When people are critical, Wenger prefers to be the one coming under attack rather than his players. If the team is criticised, he always tries to defend it. This is another quality of his, but it is also annoying because, from time to time, players commit unacceptable fouls. Yet he will never criticise them or call them into question. In fact, he normally responds: "Sorry, I really didn't see what happened." Yeah right! Selective blindness has become something of a trait of his.'

At times, that can be infuriating for the English press. Back in September 2005, Arsenal laboured to defeat the Swiss team FC Thun, unfancied and far from potent opposition, in a Champions League group match at Highbury. The home side's cause had not been helped by the dismissal of Robin van Persie for a horrible stamping offence on the stroke of half-time, the Dutchman becoming the 60th man to be sent off since Wenger took up the reins at the club. In his post-match television interview, however, the manager launched an astonishing defence of Van Persie, claiming the stamp had in fact been an 'accident' and that the red card was anything but justified.

Asked why the Londoners had struggled so pitifully to see off the Swiss 2–1, Wenger had retorted: 'I'd like to see you take on a team like that with only ten players. See if you can do better in the Champions League.'

'But don't you think you could have played better on the night?'

'You can always play better, even when your team plays at its best . . .'

Yet, in general, there is a 'respectful atmosphere' at press conferences according to one regular at Colney. The relationship between manager and press corps is generally that of a teacher and his pupils. 'In ten years, he has only sworn once at a press conference,' said a journalist. 'It was after a match in the spring of 2005 against Crystal Palace [Arsenal had won 5–1]. When he was asked why he had fielded a team comprised solely of foreign players, he exploded, saying he didn't give a shit about their passports and that he chose players according to their talent and not their nationality. He even said "fuck", something I'd never heard him say before. It made the back-page headlines the following day.'

'Not all journalists admire him, but they all appreciate him because Arsène respects them,' added Steve Stammers of the *Sunday Mirror*. 'He never dismisses them under the pretext that their question is embarrassing or uninteresting.' 'He is appreciated by the press because he is courteous, polite, intelligent and open,' said Daniel King. 'I really think he always tries to give us something new.'

'I'll systematically criticise something each time to give the tabloids something to write about,' admitted Wenger, yet he can also resort to diplomacy if matters threaten to get out of hand. King recalled, in particular, the manager's reaction to the flood of Japanese journalists who attended his briefings following Arsenal's signing of Junichi Inamoto. 'Arsène had to answer a lot of questions from Japanese reporters,' he said. 'Every week, they asked Wenger the same question: "Will Inamoto play in the next match?" Arsène, who always left him on the bench, always answered with great patience: "I don't think so, no. In fact he won't be playing."'

'You can go to a press conference at Arsenal and ask Arsène: "What do you think of Great Britain's financial contribution to the annual budget of the EU?"' laughed the BBC journalist Mark Pougatch. 'He will answer, and very thoughtfully as well! It is totally inconceivable that another manager in the Premier League would ever do the same.'

At the same time, as an experienced interviewee, Wenger carefully controls his image and protects his privacy, whether from the press or the fans. Over the years, Wenger has become almost untouchable among the club's supporters, inspiring complete respect whilst simultaneously remaining relatively distant. 'He usually raises a shy hand as a brief thanks for the encouragement from the stands behind the goal,' explained Bernard Azulay, a supporter who has attended well over 500 Arsenal matches. 'He remains almost unknown as far as we're concerned. You don't hear juicy stories about Arsène like you do with other established Premiership managers. In fact, the real story is that there is no story. He clearly prefers to hide behind his players so they can take the plaudits.'

It is therefore surprising to hear of the snippets that he has divulged such as his brief dalliance with politics. Back in the 1970s when he had combined his football development with his economics degree, Wenger had kept the door open to politics. These days, he smiles when looking back at his ideological struggles whilst on campus in Strasbourg. 'I was confronted with Communism and, frankly, it wasn't for me,' he admitted. Rather, he had different priorities. 'I was 22 or so and on a date with a girlfriend,' he said. 'She told me she had gone to see a fortune-teller who, having scrutinised my star sign, had told her: "I wouldn't spend too much time chasing this guy. He'll never earn any money." Maybe she meant to say that I wasn't really interested in money. If I've earned well over the years, it's really been incidental. It hasn't been my motivation at all. I am passionate about a job which, by chance, also happens to be lucrative.'

Quite what the future holds for Wenger, particularly following the departure of David Dein and with the months ticking down on his current contract, remains to be seen; but what is not open to doubt is the reality that he has left an indelible mark on English football. In early 2007, the Queen admitted to being something of a closet Gooner. Back in the summer of 2003, her honours list had conferred on Wenger an honorary OBE, presented to him by the Foreign Minister at the time, Jack Straw, for 'services rendered to British football'. 'I am extremely proud and pleasantly surprised,' Wenger had said, accepting an award equivalent to the French *Légion d'honneur*, which he received the year before.

He was flanked accepting the award by his friend and compatriot Gérard Houllier, who picked up a similar honour for his work at Liverpool.

'It is a great honour for me to be on the receiving end of such a huge reward, and being able to receive this tribute alongside my good friend Arsène Wenger makes this event all the more special to me,' said Houllier at the time. 'It also gives Arsène and myself the opportunity to say how grateful we are to be working in this country, doing a job we love with people we value and hold in the highest regard.'

Whether it is on the training pitch at Colney or the playing surface at Highbury, Wenger's reputation has grown steadily in England. To many, the ambassador is as close as football comes to an academic. In November 1999 he was awarded an honorary PhD by the University of Hertfordshire. London Metropolitan University followed suit by awarding him an honorary degree. Roderick Floud, vice-president of the university, explained the gesture by emphasising the 'enormous contribution of the club and its coach to the community in which we work'.

Back in Duttlenheim, Claude Wenger – no relation – manages the local football team these days where Arsène first kicked a ball. The clubhouse still sports a photograph of the Arsenal manager in reverence to what he has achieved since leaving his sleepy home town. Claude, along with other members of the team, had been a guest of Arsène's at a game back in 1998. 'Arsène had saved us seats for the Manchester City match – he paid for the tickets out of his own pocket. Arsène paid for everything. His hospitality was outstanding.'

As mentioned earlier, in February 2005, that generosity extended to a talk delivered to an audience of around 400 at London's plush Savoy hotel. Tickets set guests back some £125, with all proceeds going to charity. 'We could have filled Highbury, we had so many requests for tickets,' recalled one of the organisers. Wenger had been awarded the coveted Silver Heart by the Variety Club in recognition of his contribution to English football, with all the money raised at the event to go towards the purchase of equipment for disabled children.

'We seldom honour sportsmen, but everyone leapt at the chance of inviting Mr Wenger,' said the organiser. In order to attend, the Arsenal manager had to bend one of his own rules by going out on the eve of a game – the following day, his side were due in Sheffield for an FA Cup match. 'He may hate the limelight, but he clearly enjoyed the night,' added one of the guests.

'I would say that this man is generous, and he clearly has great human values,' said Didier Roustan, a journalist and founder of the Foot Citoyen association back in France of which Wenger is honorary president. 'He lends us his image, gives us his time and even his money when we need it. Foot Citoyen is a social project which aims to help young people and teach them values through football, which is their passion. The project combines pros and amateurs, as kids tend to identify with those they see at the top, hence the importance to find representatives who are also good role models like Arsène. I wanted an honorary president who would be a true professional in the field and who would be ethical as well as flawless in his sportsmanship in order to serve as an example to the kids. Arsène fits the profile perfectly.

'A lot of people give beautiful speeches but, when you scratch below the surface a little, you realise it's little more than a front. Arsène is different. He is one of the only men truly worthy of trust amongst the masses of hypocrites you will find in the world of football.'

The warmth felt towards Wenger is shared by many who have worked with him. With that in mind, it is remarkable to consider the suspicion which surrounded Wenger's arrival in England back in the autumn of 1996. 'When I started my first full season there, I remember reading that a foreign manager would never win the championship,' he recalled. 'At the time, I said: "You're wrong. There's a chance that, one day, all 20 English top-flight clubs will be coached by non-British people. So one of them is sure to end up winning the title." ' Despite his failure to claim a European Cup for the north London club, and Arsenal's rather patchy form of recent seasons, Wenger's success at Arsenal remains staggering and extends well beyond three Premiership titles and four FA Cups. These days, with the Alsatian having reinvented one of English football's long-established institutions, Arsenal are unrecognisable from the rather muddling club of the mid-1990s, wheezing in Manchester United's slipstream. They boast a glittering new arena, one of the most promising young sides in the world game, and a man in charge who retains the hunger to maintain the revival. The turnaround ultimately reflects gloriously on their manager. 'Arsène is the greatest coach this club has ever had,' offered Tony Adams. 'Accolades do not come much bigger than that.'

ACKNOWLEDGEMENTS

My biggest thank you goes to the ever-reliable Dominic Fifield, whose translation from French to English is more of an adaptation which makes for I believe, a great read in English. I had had the pleasure of working with him on *Robert Pires: Footballeur*, and it was again a great experience to work alongside him this time.

A huge thank you, also, to my friend Alex Fynn, who has always encouraged me, giving his time and support, and contributing, through his own books and comments, to this work.

I'd also like to thank my editor, Natasha Martin, for all her work and patience, knowledge and kindness, and everyone at Aurum who made this project possible.

The seventy-odd people I approached for this book all, without any exception, agreed to talk to me. Every one of them said that they hoped, by opening up in these pages, to be able to convey the regard, respect and friendship they felt for Wenger. Close friends and acquaintances of the man, observers of his methods or witnesses of his, each and every person has in their own right, by giving these no-holds-barred accounts, helped shape this book. All these discerning eyes shed light on what happens behind the scenes, providing a better understanding of the stage Wenger the coach's life unfolds upon.

A huge thank you to the players, past and present, who agreed to open up the changing rooms of their memories and to reveal some of 'coach Wenger's tricks and secrets': Tony Adams and Robert Pires in particular, but also Emmanuel Petit, Freddie Ljungberg, Alan Smith, Mathieu Flamini, Cesc Fabregas, Gaël Clichy, Dennis Bergkamp, all interviewed in London; Rémi Garde, Gilles Grimandi, Claude Puel, Manu Amoros, Jean-Luc Ettori and José Touré, as well as Jean-Luc Arribart and Jean-Marc Guillou, interviewed in France; Masaru Hirayama questioned in Japan; and George Weah, interviewed in the US.

I am forever grateful to his first-line confidants and high-flying friends like Richard Conte, Yann Rougier and Philippe Boixel, but also Damien Comolli, Paul Frantz and Max Hild, who were all so accurate and patient; Daniel Jeandupeux who made himself (and his very valuable personal notes) so available; Claude Wenger (and his personal picture collection!), Jean Petit, Gilbert Gress, Jean-Claude Cloet, Tiburce Darrou, Fabrice Dubois, Robert Zaigue, Christophe Capron, Raymond Blanc, Jean-François Cécillon and Marcel Legros who, each in his own way, shed a new and often exclusive light on Wenger. By telling their anecdotes, by confirming facts and remarks, they backed up and honed this portrait of the coach. Four of the best and most privileged French observers now take their spot on this list: Christian Damiano, Aimé Jacquet, Gérard Houllier and Guy Roux.

In addition, I would like to thank the journalists Jasper Rees (whose writings and contacts were extremely useful), Daniel

King, Steve Stammers, Gabriele Marcotti, Henry Winter, Richard Clark, Stéphane Floricien, Mark Pougatch, Mark Irwin and Matt Tench in England; Takashi Kawahara in Tokyo; Yi Jiang in Beijing; Guillem Balague, Graham Hunter and Ivan Moda in Spain; Rafael Honigstein in Munich; Jean-Pierre Rivais and Jean-Marc Butterlin (*L'Équipe*) in the South and East of France, Karine Gélébart in Strasbourg, as well as Didier Roustan, Lionel Vella and Daniel Ortelli, in Paris. Thanks to all these collegial points of assistance.

And let us not forget those Arsenal fans who were so keen to share their passion for the team: Bernard Azulay, Bill Davis, Peggy Goulding, Josie Newman, Stewart Joseph, Jamie and John Regniez and the biggest 'Gooners' of all of them: Nicolas Thiriot and Benjamin Lambert. A very, very big thank you to Philippe Auclair, the London-based *France Football* correspondent whose documentation on Wenger, accumulated and referenced for the past ten years, made for a genuine treasure cave. My book would not have been completed if Philippe hadn't opened up his riches.

And, most of all, thank you from the bottom of my heart to Arsène Wenger who, by answering all of our questions, whether serious or silly, on a regular basis ever since his arrival in 1996, from the Highbury tunnel to Colney's cafeteria and his stadium offices and training centre, greatly assisted us in giving these tales their definitive shape and marrow. Moreover, two British books came highly recommended: *Wenger, the Making of a Legend* by Jasper Rees and *The Glorious Game: Arsène Wenger and the Quest for Success* by Alex Fynn and Kevin Whitcher. Last but not least, the www.noblesauvage.com forum provides a continuation of the story and carries on the debate . . .!

INDEX